Second Wife, Second Best?

Second Wife, Second Best?

Managing your marriage as a second wife
GLYNNIS WALKER

1984
Doubleday Canada Limited, Toronto, Ontario
Doubleday & Company, Inc., Garden City, New York

Library of Congress Catalog Card Number 84-1560
ISBN 0-385-18464-6

Typeset by ART-U Graphics Ltd.
Printed and bound in Canada by T. H. Best Printing Company Ltd.
Jacket design by David Wyman

Canadian Cataloguing in Publication Data

Walker, Glynnis, 1951-
    Second wife, second best?

Bibliography: p. 271
ISBN 0-385-18464-6

1. Wives   2. Remarriage.   I. Title.

HQ1018.W34 1984   306.8'4   C84-098188-0

Library of Congress Cataloging in Publication Data

Walker, Glynnis, 1951-
    Second wife, second best?

1. Remarried people—Psychology.   2. Wives—Psychology.
I. Title.

HQ734.W18678 1984   306.8'4   84-1560

ISBN 0-385-18464-6

*To Stanley, my first and only husband,
from your second and only wife*

Acknowledgments

This book would not have been possible without the support and concern of all the second wives who took the time to talk to me about their lives and who expressed a sincere wish that their efforts may help other second wives and women who may become second wives.

Contents

Second Wife, Second Best?

1   *All Wives Are Not Created Equal*

"A Second Marriage: The triumph of hope over experience."
Samuel Johnson, 1770.

Introduction

THIS BOOK HAS BEEN written because all wives are not created equal. This inequality has nothing to do with economic status or religion. It transcends the boundaries of race and culture. It is merely a question of timing.

In spite of the advances achieved by the women's movement in recent years supposedly on behalf of *all* women, there are still *some* women who have yet to taste the benefits that were touted as being universal. What has happened is that those who have enjoyed the bulk of the social and legal advantages so newly obtained are often doing so only at the expense of other women. These other woman are second wives.

For the purposes of this book, a second wife is any woman, regardless of her own previous marital status, who marries a man who has had another wife. A second wife, therefore, prior to her current marriage, can have been single, as were 61 percent of the women in the survey conducted to research this book, or she can have been previously married, as were the remaining 39 percent.

A woman's previous marital status has little bearing on what she will experience as a second wife because many of the problems she is likely to face are related specifically to her status as a *second* wife and not to how much experience she may or may not have had in the marital arena. Even women who have been married before are often not prepared for the realities of being a second wife.

The first-time wife has had her expectations shaped by observing the marriages of friends, or parents, or from her own experiences with previous long-term relationships. The second-time wife tends to expect her position as wife to be basically the same in the mistaken belief that "a wife is a wife is a wife." In either case she is not ready for what awaits her as a second wife. It is only after she has taken this step that she begins to realize the inherent implications in being second.

Given the widespread lack of comprehension concerning the innate differences between first and second wives, it is little wonder that, while I was conducting the research for this book, one question was invariably asked of me: "What's so different about second wives?" Suffice it to say this question was never posed by a second wife. *We* are already too well aware of what the differences are. Hence I was never at a loss for words when this question came my way. As far back as you care to remember, and at whichever culture you are prepared to look, women who have become second wives have appeared in the eyes of their society, under their laws, sometimes to their own husbands, and worse, even to themselves, as second best. Our own culture is particularly tough on the whole issue of being second—at anything; witness the third and fourth definitions of the word "second" in *The Concise Oxford Dictionary of Current English*, fifth edition: "of a secondary kind, subordinate, derived, unoriginal, imitative, of inferior position or quality, not the principal, of less importance than what is first...."

In such a competitive society as ours, with everyone intently striving to be first as often as possible, coming second is often the same as not placing at all. A second wife, then, often just does not place in the game of marriage. In spite of what may be the actual circumstances, our society tends to focus on the first marriage, and consequently on the first wife, as the "real" thing, and anything that comes after is often considered to be ancilliary.

Second Wives: The Myths

This attitude promotes offensive and ubiquitous stereotyping of second wives. Who can say that they have not encountered the mythical archetype of the second wife? She comes in two basic styles: "the full-chested floozy," who sets out to lure another woman's husband away from hearth and home, dangling her physical charms like a carrot in front of a donkey, or "the scheming, conniving, golddigger," who seeks not so much a healthy man in her bed as a man with a healthy checking account in the bank. Hardly complimentary. Yet both these types are found frequently in our popular mythology and both have very little bearing on reality.

In spite of these common misconceptions about second wives, it is rare to find a woman who actually set out to become a second wife. Unlike being a first wife, it is not really something to which most women aspire. The problems are significant and the rewards sometimes elusive. The days when a woman would take a man, any man, just so she could have an *M-R-S* in front of her name are long gone. These days, there are lots of men out there who would make better husband material than the worn-out, battle-scarred hero of someone else's failing marriage. It's not as if women were restricted to their own age, social, or even racial groups anymore. They are more or less free to marry men older, younger, richer, or poorer than themselves. So, if there are no men in their immediate group who suit with respect to marriageability, they can always look elsewhere for the mates of their choice. As for the chances of anyone's staging a financial coup by becoming a second wife—well, let's just say, if you *are* planning on becoming a second wife, don't give up your day job!

These stereotypes are not the only cultural myths about second wives that need to be debunked. Frequently branded as homewreckers, husbandstealers, and, not to forget, wicked stepmothers, second wives are, more often than not, the victims of a set of circumstances they did not create. Without setting out to do so they may find themselves labelled as "the other woman" even after they are married. What first wife has ever been "the other woman" in her own marriage?

As part and parcel of these negative views, second wives are often ignored by in-laws who would have welcomed them if they had been number one; harassed by ex-wives, the lawyers of ex-wives, and the families of ex-wives; and challenged by the children of ex-wives in their own homes. In addition they are in love with men whose egos are already bruised from failed marriages, so they tend to spend a lot of time in their own marriages treading very softly and trying to avoid getting caught up in the fog of guilt that often enshrouds their mates. Should any of this get to be too much for them, they will be advised to seek some sort of professional help to aid them in solving their problems. Can you honestly imagine anyone seeking out a situation like this on purpose?

Second Wives and the Media

The erroneous stereotyping of second wives is evidenced by the unflattering portrayals of these women in books, television, and film. The error is compounded by the fact that when not focusing on the traditional stereotypes of the second wife, the media often ignores her completely. It is difficult to believe that although marital status remains one of the most common means of categorizing women in our society (as witnesses the ongoing debate about the use of Miss, Mrs., and Ms.), the media fails to attach any significance to the status of being a second wife, even when it may have a direct bearing on the particular situation. As James Reston said in his address to the 1963 graduating class at Columbia University, "Change is the biggest story in the world today and we are not covering it adequately." Now, twenty years later, rather than being the harbinger of change in our constantly changing world, the media is, in many cases, merely echoing the attitudes of yesteryear. Rarely does it demonstrate much awareness of the growth in numbers of second wives and their corresponding rise in importance in our social structure.

This is not to say that the issues which concern second wives do not find their way into the media; they do, but they are almost invariably written from the point of view of someone other than the second wife. There is a particular case in California (the Sullivan case) concerning an ex-wife who is suing her husband for a percentage of his income because she says she helped put him through medical school. The precedent-setting case will have far-reaching ramifications when a decision is finally handed down. In the process of investigating the case, the media has interviewed the husband, his ex-wife, their respective lawyers, and other interested parties, but it seems no one has approached the doctor's second wife and reported on what she thinks and on how the decision will affect her life and her marriage. Can it be that she has no opinion, or is it that the media has simply fallen prey to the common but old-fashioned view that goes on between the husband and his ex-wife is none of the second wife's business?

Treatment such as this has brought us to the point where the second wife is most conspicuous in the media by her absence, even though she is as much a part of the changing shape of our society as divorced fathers and single mothers. It is this pervasive and unfortunate attitude whereby the second wife is treated as only a peripheral personage, often even in her own marriage, that reinforces the idea she is not only not newsworthy and therefore unimportant, but really is, after all, only second best. As such, her opinions are not sought and her feelings not recorded, in yet another perpetuation of the classic vicious circle.

There is much to be found in the media about the problems and experiences of ex-wives, and even though these portrayals

are not always sympathetic, at least ex-wives are getting coverage, as these examples illustrate.

> *HUNDREDS OF EX-WIVES SEEK MORE ALIMONY*
>
> *Hundreds of men are being hauled into court by their ex-wives
> looking for more money as inflation erodes the value of alimony
> awards made in the late 1970s. The women have to wait three or
> four months for a court date because there are so many applications
> for increased alimony.*
>
> *A Supreme Court decision released yesterday ordered a remarried
> Ottawa doctor to pay his former wife a lump sum of $15,000 plus
> $350 more a month in alimony and $250 more in support for their
> two children and family law specialists say there is nothing unusual
> about this.*

There may well be "nothing unusual about this," but why not
point out that the value of everyone's income is being eroded
by inflation, not just the value of alimony awards made to
ex-wives? Why is it so easy to state *de facto* the case of the first
wife and to exclude mention of the possible ramifications for
others concerned, such as the ex-husband and his second wife?

Another considerably more sensationalist story, headlined
HUSBAND SUES EX-WIFE IN BOWLING BALL ATTACK, commits a
similar sin of omission. The article describes the case of a man
who is suing his ex-wife for a physical attack that occurred
while he was sleeping. The ex-wife apparently entered the
husband's home armed with a .22 caliber pistol and a hammer
while the man and his second wife were away bowling. She
waited until they fell asleep and then attacked him with his
own bowling ball. Amazingly, the comments of the man's
second wife were not recorded in the article. (It seems highly
unlikely that she would have had nothing to say.)

The next example appeared under the headline *MAN'S
WIDOW MUST SUPPORT HIS FIRST WIFE*.

> *The wealthy second wife of a dead insurance executive has been
> ordered to pay $1,300-a-month support to his first wife of 26 years*

because he made no provision for her in his will....
    His first wife, a nurse in poor health, was forced to go on welfare.

There is no doubt that the first wife in this case deserves sympathy, but the writer failed to print the entire story. The story implies that the second wife was an opportunistic gold-digger by calling her "wealthy," and by citing a laundry list of what her husband left her in his will and what she collected from his insurance. Also deemed worthy of mention is the fact that the second wife was able to pay $195,000 in case for a house after her husband's estate was settled and that in that house she is currently raising a child from her first marriage. The writer of this piece did interview the first wife and quotes her as saying the court case was a "harrowing experience," and further, "I wouldn't say I'm comfortable, but the judge's award keeps the wolf from the door." It is quite clear that the writer doesn't think much of the second wife, although he never attempted to make contact with her and hear her side of the story (which, it was later discovered, she felt very strongly about and would have been willing to relate). Instead he states that the alimony the husband had been paying his first wife "was cut off by his second wife" upon his death. (By this, are we to assume that the writer thinks every second wife is morally and should be legally obligated to continue alimony payments to a first wife if the husband dies? It would seem so.) What this article does in implying that the second wife came along just before the end of her husband's life and inherited everything, is reinforce a discriminatory stereotype on the basis of an insubstantial investigation.

Ex-wives, it seems, make much more interesting copy than second wives or ex-husbands. They are often set up so as to be the recipients of a good portion of reader sympathy, even when they are the perpetrators, not the victims. In another article headed *THREATENING PHONE CALLS BRING 15-MONTH JAIL TERM*, the court case of a first wife who was prone to making threatening phone calls to her husband and his second wife, is described. What is interesting about this case is that the first wife, despite her repeated violent threats, still manages to elicit considerable sympathy not only from the writer of the article, but from the judge presiding over the case.

> *"This woman's life has not been a happy one," the Supreme Court judge has said.*
>
> *But, although he felt sorry for her, he sentenced her to 15 months in a reformatory for making phone calls threatening death or injury to her husband and his new wife.*

It seems that what tipped the scales against the first wife was the indesputable fact that she had five convictions on her record, all involving charges of harassing her ex-husband. The judge is quoted as saying "he was sceptical that she ever intended to carry out the threats." The first wife is quoted as saying "It's been a very difficult time for me." The husband and his second wife, it seems, were either not approached for comments, or it was deemed that their viewpoints did not merit mention. As it is likely that their comments would have been pertinent, it does seem that the interests of objective reporting, if nothing else, were not best served by this article.

The next example was headed with this attention grabber: *EX-BUNNY-COP GETS LIFE.* Although this case is really too tragic to be funny, there is an underlying note of ridicule in the reporting particularly at the outset of the article, as well as an overt lapse into discriminatory stereotyping of the second wife involved.

> *MILKAUKEE (UPI)—A former Playboy bunny and police officer has been sentenced to life in prison for the shooting death of her husband's ex-wife, apparently because she wanted to end his financial burden.*
>
> *A jury took 3½ days to reach its decision that Lawrencia Bembenek, 23, dressed in a green jogging suit and a wig and entered the home of her husband's former wife and shot the woman to death.*
>
> *The prosecution contended Bembenek killed Christine Schultz*

last May because she resented the fact her husband had to make child support payments.

"It was the most circumstantial case I've ever seen, with lots of individual pieces that would not have convicted her," said Judge Michael Skwierawski. "But taken as a whole, the jury could reach only one conclusion."

"The evidence was horrible," said defence lawyer Donald Eisenberg.

He said police "did a sloppy job" in gathering evidence and "I'm really suspicious she was set up." He had suggested during the trial one of the witnesses might have actually committed the crime.

It is incredible, given the severity of these circumstances, that the press saw fit to so readily revert to stereotyping of the second wife involved. She is depicted as something between a comic character and a sex symbol (as witnesses the use of "Ex-Bunny-Cop"). How is her having been a playboy bunny germane to the case, let alone worthy of being headline material? Further, what rationally thinking person would see killing an ex-wife as a viable means of eradicating child support payments? Might not a more accurate and logical representation of her possible motive have been that she resented more the *size* of the payments, and less the payments themselves? After all, between the lines of even this article is the implication that the second wife and her husband were shouldering a considerable, possibly unworkable burden as a result of the size of these payments. Once again, the press does not seem to have relayed sufficient information about the proceedings and has allowed a certain prejudicial slant to color what does appear.

In a recent article in *Cosmopolitan* on this trial, James Horowitz said, "The media covered the trial as if it were a cross between a soap opera and a fashion show.... Who cried on the stand? What was Laurie [the accused] wearing? He also quotes the accused herself as saying, "Are you supposed to cry for two weeks? And the press always writing about how I was dressed.

The press tore me to shreds. It was so unfair." And further, "My biggest anger is I think against the press. What did I ever do to them? They just brought up sensational things. It was done with viciousness."

As the "Ex-Bunny-Cop" case illustrates, second wives are not always ignored by the media. When they do make news, the media does seem very quick to pigeonhole them into the old stereotypes, regardless of individual circumstances; one has to wonder which is the better scenario—to be portrayed as such, or to be ignored completely. Ideally, in time, the media will at least make more of an attempt to be objective.

Most women who become second wives are blissfully unaware of what can await them on the other side of the altar. If you think that none of this applies to you, remember that approximately one-third of the marriages in any given year involve a man and his second wife. It is important that you know what to expect if it happens to you. You will probably have to go out to work, not to make ends meet for your family, but to help your husband make ends meet for his. Among the wives who participated in the survey, there were some who worked virtually just to pay their husbands' alimony and child support from their previous marriages. Others saw a large chunk of their salaries go to support ex-wives who did not work. Seventy-four percent of the second wives in the survey worked, while 60 percent of their husbands' ex-wives did not. There is even a legal catch-22 in some places that you should check out before you dash out and become a working second wife. In California, for example, the court can consider the income of a second wife in determining the husband's ability to pay alimony to his former spouse. In other words, as a second wife, the more you earn, the more she can ask the court to award her.

Should you want to have a family of your own some day, you may find that you have to postpone having children until your husband's from his previous marriage are no longer dependents. Of course, there is a good chance that by then you will be too old to start a family of your own so you may just decide to forego having children. There is a possibility that by the time he gets to you, the novelty of the 2:00 A.M. feeding has already worn thin for your husband, who may decide he's already done his bit as a progenitor. Only 20 percent of the wives in the study had children from their current marriages. Thirty-six percent more wanted children but had postponed having them either for economic reasons or because their husbands really did not want more children.

If you are concerned about finances as a second wife, you can be reasonably sure that unless the man you marry is very wealthy or had a very good lawyer at the time of his divorce, yours will be a lower standard of living than his first wife's. After all, a man can only set aside so much of his income for mortgage payments and chances are you won't be the one living in the house he's paying the mortgage on. Things won't necessarily get any better as you grow old together. Some courts incorporate pension plans into divorce actions and have been known to order distributions between an employee and his former spouse.

As a second wife, you would be more than wise to consider what will happen to you (and your children) with respect to the distribution of your mate's estate should he predecease you. This is a particularly touchy issue, but a very necessary one, especially if your husband is much older than you are. Consider this instance. If your husband had a will contract with his previous spouse (a contract that pledges that the surviving spouse will not alter the terms of his will or otherwise enter into an agreement that can disinherit the children or other loved ones from his previous marriage), you may find yourself (and your children) out on your ear if he dies, even though you are his current wife.

In *The Legality of Love* (Jove Books, 1981) J. Sonenblick exemplifies the type of thinking that may be encountered:

"This type of contract (will contract) is good protection for the first wife against the possibility of a later marriage, when the surviving parent, consumed with love for his new wife (and children) may become disenchanted with the children of his previous marriage." Thus he may be tempted to make some alterations in his will to include his current family, but these will be impossible. While no one would argue that the first family should be disinherited, the reverse is commonly accepted. Don't the second wife and her family have a right to equal protection under the law? Under many circumstances, at present, no.

Even without a will contract, there is still the possibility that an ex-wife and/or her children may attempt to attach some or all of your husband's assets should he die. At best, this can tie things up in the courts for years, and at worst, it may see you lose everything to his former family.

It is more than evident from this type of thinking that while the second wife is expected to share the debt load her husband brings to the marriage, she is not equally entitled to a share of his assets. A second wife is potentially a financial victim twice, once when she marries and again if she is widowed or divorced.

Finally the law also makes provisions for the good care of the husband's children from his first marriage, since a parent's waiver of support rights for a child in a divorce action is not binding on the child. Even if a mother decides she doesn't want support for her children, they can go to court on their own and legally demand it.

If all this does little to cheer you up, you are not alone. As a second wife, your chances of getting divorced are rising. In the late 1970s the divorce rate for second marriages in North America stood at 35 percent; it will rise to a projected 57 percent in 1984. Is it any wonder? If you do get divorced, don't expect a settlement comparable to what his first wife received.

In spite of these difficulties, most second wives work hard at keeping their marriages together partly because, if they have been married before, they cannot afford the emotional trauma of another marriage breakdown and, partly because, from the perspective of increased maturity, they realize that the value of their relationships exceed the problems that accompany them. There are other advantages to being a second wife, which can often make the way a lot smoother, and the following chapters will expand on these.

It is hoped that this book will be of interest to many people, but it was written particularly for second wives themselves because so many of them individually expressed the feeling that they were alone. They felt decidedly guilty about what was happening to them and their marriages. Worse still, many believed that their problems were a result of something wrong with them and not a product of legal and social attitudes working against them.

Through speaking to these women, assuring them that they were not alone, that their problems were something with which second wives in general appeared to contend, I was able to alleviate some of the needless and destructive feelings of guilt. It is time more women found out they are not alone and that there should be no stigma attached to being a second wife.

Perhaps my primary reason for writing this book is that I am a second wife. For three years now I have grappled with all the problems that generally arise from a situation where a previously married man marries a single woman. I know what it is like to feel that you are alone with a particular set of problems and to look inward for the cause.

In the beginning of my marriage I could not get rid of the feeling that something, somewhere, was not as it should be. I had a lot of trouble adjusting to a set of aggravations and prejudices which I had theretofore never expected from any marriage—particularly not mine.

Because so many of us are unsure of just what to expect as second wives we are frequently caught in situations that, were we first wives, would not arise. Many second wives become so involved in trying to maintain the status quo or to win over the people who are already in their husbands' lives that they put their own feelings and needs aside. It is almost as if they start by subscribing to the idea that because they are second they have to try harder. This sets up an unfortunate series of chain reactions within the new marriage and really does not serve to achieve the desired assimilation of the second wife into her new husband's world. It can also cause the second wife to question herself and her relationship after the initial attempts to please everyone wear off. She may realize that without doing anything more than saying "I do," she has gone from having a wonderful love affair with a terrific man to being treated as an outcast by people who don't even know her well. Suddenly she has gone from having him all to herself to sharing him with a whole host of people who can be hostile and who are a significant part of her marriage. There may be children, grandchildren, ex-spouses and possibly their mates, as well as curious friends and cool associates who do not look upon her as the person she knows herself to be, but only as *his* second wife.

It is not so much the criticism of her *per se* (most second wives realize fairly early in their marriages that such negative feelings would be directed at anyone their husbands had chosen to marry and are not reserved specifically for them), it is, above all, having to share the man she loves so early in their marriage. It is not just his time she has to share but his affections and their joint finances as well. Indeed many second wives cannot help but wonder just where they fit in in the hierarchy of those who make regular demands upon their husbands. It is a sad fact that many ultimately decide they are not number one—or even number two—but are much farther down the list. It is a peculiar reality that many men leave their families and focus their attention on finding new wives, but once they have them, their attention reverts to their established responsibilities. Second wives know that they cannot be first chronologically, but most of them still cannot appreciate why they cannot be number one emotionally.

All of this contributed to the idea of a book about and for second wives, one that would finally tell their side of the story.

Once I began to talk to women who were second wives there was a lot of positive reaction, but acceptance of the idea did not occur across the board. I met women, even second wives, who would verbally pat me on the head and tell me that it would be best if I "came to terms" with my situation. Perhaps if I had been younger, or if I had not known that there were so many others going through all the things I was going through, I might have acquiesced. But to me, coming to terms meant agreeing that the many negative stereotypes people accepted about second wives were true. I knew that they were not true of me nor of thousands of other women, either. It also meant taking for granted laws that are simply unjust and based upon a perception of marriage and family that has no connection to the present reality. Why should we accept second best?

It is not enough just to say that our society needs to be educated to the problems of second wives without mentioning how many women are involved. Each year for the past five years, approximately one-third of all the marriages in the United States and one-tenth of those in Canada have involved women who became second wives. In round numbers this translates to an average of 750,000 women a year, in North America alone, who find themselves saying "I do" to a man who has been married before.

With so many women involved, it is unfortunate that, to date, there is a disturbing lack of available information on the subject of second wives. The issues concerning life as a second wife have yet to capture popular attention. While you may be able to go down to your local bookstore and find a surfeit of information on unwed motherhood, divorced fathers, living with your lover, and children of divorce, you will be hard-pressed to find out much about being a second wife.

The explanation is quite simple. The situation is so new as to be relatively unexplored by the media. While it is true that there have always been second wives (depending on which version of creation you like to believe, Eve was Adam's second wife; she only got the job because Lillith wouldn't toe the line), it is also true that second wives have never existed in such large numbers before. Only since the recent liberalization of the divorce laws have enough men been changing partners in mid-dance, to allow for a rash of suddenly-single-but-formerly-married males seeking new mates. With current divorce rates in the United States running at 50 percent and in Canada at 30 percent, the chances are very good that one day you, or your mother, sister, or best friend, will become a second wife. The steady increase in the number of second wives will see this group become a force of its own within society, and the prevailing attitudes and laws will have to change to reflect the magnitude of this group.

As evidence that the change is already underway there is a growing awareness among younger second wives that they really do not intend to take a back seat to anyone, including their husbands' first wives and their stepchildren. Today's second wife wants and expects to be treated with the same rights and privileges as a first wife. It's that simple.

The Survey

There are many scientifically sound ways to conduct a survey but, in order to achieve the most reliable information, it is best if a random sample is used. This means that the people who respond and upon whose responses you base your findings are selected from the population (in this case the second-wife population) on a random basis. For this study, the respondents were not randomly selected by me; rather they randomly volunteered. Because of the nature of the population to be studied, it was necessary for me to put out a general appeal for second wives to contact me and then use that group as my random sample. It was necessary to gather the bulk of the information by using a questionnaire; because my sample was so geographically diffuse, I could not possibly visit all the women who contacted me and the survey would have been too long to conduct over the telephone.

Normally it is a good idea, when making up a questionnaire, to use a pre-test. This will allow you to get any kinks out of the wording and add any additional questions that may have made themselves apparent in the meantime. The initial questionnaire consisted of eighty-five questions about life as a second wife. These were derived initially from my own experiences and from interviews with other second wives.

When the original pre-test questionnaire was reviewed, it was decided to add some questions to allow the wives a greater range of response. Even so, it was necessary to cut the questionnaire off after one hundred and ten questions because length (this one was getting very long) will often be a discouraging factor with respondents. The final edition of the questionnaire consisted of questions in six basic areas: marriage, finances, children, ex-wives, feelings, and sex. The wives were asked to be as subjective as possible in their answers in order to gather an emotional profile as well as statistics.

Since it was nearly impossible to locate women who were second wives through any of the ordinary research channels, I spent several weeks doing on-air interviews at local and national radio and television stations in the United States and Canada. I talked about the project, the problems of second wives, and my own experiences, and I asked second wives who were interested in taking part in the study to contact me. There followed short telephone discussions and then the questionnaires were mailed out. The turnaround time for the questionnaires was about five to six weeks, which was good, considering the length. A 7 to 10 percent return rate is considered good for a mail-out survey. My return rate was nearly 30 percent—an overwhelming figure, considering that most people who show interest in a study of this type, in which many of the questions are of a very personal nature, are not, in the long run, highly motivated to return the questionnaire. The return rate alone was proof enough to me that there was a substantial, if undocumented interest in the subject of second wives. Reproduced on the next six pages is the text of the questionnaire.

SECOND WIFE?!
QUESTIONNAIRE

OCCUPATION OF RESPONDENT: _____   AGE: _____

HUSBAND'S OCCUPATION: _____   AGE: _____

Please answer the following questions. Remember, the purpose of this questionnaire is to ascertain your feelings about being a second wife, as well as to obtain the facts. Be as subjective as you like with your answers and give as much detail as you can. Try to avoid simple yes or no responses where possible. Not everyone will be able to answer every question. Your ability to answer specific questions depends entirely on your personal circumstances. Therefore, answer the questions which are directly applicable to your situation.

1) How did you and your husband meet?

2) How long did you know your husband before you were married?

3) Why do you think your husband asked you to marry him?

4) Why did you decide to marry your husband?

5) What was your wedding like? (i.e. large, traditional, small, city hall)

6) Who was invited to your wedding? (i.e. your family and friends, his family and friends, children etc.)

7) Did you have a honeymoon? Where?

8) What was your husband's first wedding like?

9) Did he honeymoon with his first wife? Where?

10) Did you live together before you were married?

11) If so, where did you live? (i.e. his place, your place, somewhere new for the two of you?)

12) Where did you live after you were married? (i.e. apartment, house, condominium etc.)

13) Where did your husband and his first wife live when they first got married?

14) Have you ever lived in the place he shared with his first wife?

15) If so, how did you feel about this arrangement?

16) How long have you and your husband been married?

17) Do you generally use your husband's last name or did you keep your own name when you got married? Why?

18) How does your husband introduce you? (i.e. "This is Jane," "This is my wife, Jane," "This is my wife," etc.)

19) Have you ever been married before? How long?

20) Is your husband divorced or widowed from his first wife?

21) Did your husband leave his first wife for you or did he meet you later?

22) Was your husband married more than once before he married you?

23) How many brothers and sisters do you have?

24) Does your husband have any children from his previous marriage?

25) What were their ages when he married you?

26) Did his children live with you when you first got married? Now?

27) If his children do not live with you does he see them frequently?

28) Do you have any contact with his children? If so, what are the circumstances? (i.e. business, social etc.)

29) Do you feel that his children have directly or indirectly been responsible for any problems in your relationship with your husband? Explain.

30) Do you and your husband have any children of your own?

31) If not, do you want to have children?

32) Does your husband want to have children with you?

33) If you wanted to have children and your husband did not, what do you think you would do?

34) How did you feel about your husband's children when you first got married? (i.e. like, dislike, indifferent etc.)

35) How do you think they felt about you?

36) Has your relationship with his children changed since you have been married?

37) If you and your husband had children of your own, how do you think his children would react?

38) If you do have children with your husband, how do you think he feels about them compared to the children of his first marriage? (i.e. loves them the same, more than, less than)

39) Did you work before you got married?

40) Do you work now?

41) How would you say that your marriage has affected your career?

42) Did your husband's first wife work before or during their marriage?

43) Do you and your husband share living expenses or does he support you?

44) Do you contribute to the support of his children from a previous marriage?

45) Does your husband's contribution (if any) to the support of his previous family affect the standard of living which the two of you enjoy?

46) If so, do you feel any resentment?

47) If your husband were to make out a will, would he leave everything to you (and any children from your marriage) or would he divide his assets between you and members of his previous family?

48) If you were to make out a will, would you leave everything to your husband, knowing that if he died after you, it might go to members of his previous family?

49) Did your husband put assets acquired during their marriage in his first wife's name?

50) Has your husband put any assets acquired during your marriage in your name?

51) How long did your husband's previous marriage last?

52) Is his first wife still living?

53) If so, does your husband still maintain contact with her? Explain.

54) Why did your husband and his first wife get divorced?

55) Have you ever felt responsible for breaking up your husband's first marriage? Explain.

56) If his first wife is deceased, does she still seem to figure prominently in his thoughts? (i.e. does he talk of her often to you or others, remember their anniversaries etc.)

57) If so, how do you feel about this?

58) Do you have any contact with his first wife? Explain.

59) Is his first wife anything like you in appearance, personality, background etc.?

60) Does your husband's first wife still expect him to do some of the things he did while they were married (i.e. take care of her finances, fix things around the house, etc.)

61) How do you feel about this?

62) Does he ever confuse you with his first wife? (i.e. calling you by her name, remembering things he did with her as though he had done them with you)

63) With what you know about his first wife, what do you think about her as a person?

64) Have you ever felt sympathetic to his first wife?

65) Would you say that your sex life is satisfying?

66) Do you think that previously married men generally make better lovers?

67) Does your husband try to please you sexually?

68) Do you think that your husband's first marriage contributed significantly to the shaping of his sexual habits?

69) Does your husband ever refer to his sex life with his first wife? Explain.

70) To your knowledge was your husband sexually satisfied in his first marriage?

71) Do you think that your husband enjoys sex more with you than with his first wife? Why?

72) To your knowledge has your husband ever had sex with his first wife since he has been with you?

73) Do you ever find yourself feeling jealous of the intimate moments he shared with his first wife?

74) Since your marriage have you ever considered having an affair? Why?

75) To the best of your knowledge, has your husband ever had or considered having an affair since he has been married to you?

76) To the best of your knowledge was your husband faithful to his first wife?

77) Do you ever feel that your husband is comparing you to his first wife?

78) Has he ever tried to change you in any way to make you more or less like his first wife?

79) If so, have you complied with his wishes?

80) Have you ever felt that in some way your husband still feels married to his first wife?

81) Have you ever considered divorcing your husband? Why?

82) If you did decide to divorce your husband, do you think that the divorce settlement would be comparable to that of his first wife? Explain.

83) Which of you tries harder to make your marriage work?

84) Are you basically happy in your marriage?

85) Are there any things about your marriage you would really like to change?

86) Do you think these changes are possible?

87) When you and your husband argue, what would you say you argue about most often? (i.e. sex, money, children etc.) Why?

88) On vacations, has your husband ever taken you to places he went with his first wife?

89) How did you feel about this?

90) Do you have any contact with friends your husband shared with his first wife? Explain.

91) Are you comfortable with these people?

92) Do you feel comfortable with your husband's family (other than his children)?

93) Does your husband still associate with his first wife's family? Explain?

94) How do you feel about this?

95) How did your family feel about you becoming a second wife?

96) How would you say your husband's friends from his previous marriage feel about you?

97) Do you ever feel that your husband loves you more or less than his first wife?

98) Would you say that your husband is more satisfied generally with his second marriage than his first?

99) What would you say were the basic problems that a second wife should be prepared to face?

100) Were you prepared to face these problems or did they come as something of a surprise?

101) What would you say are the advantages of being a second wife?

102) Do you ever wish you had been your husband's first wife or that he had not been married before he met you?

103) Have you ever felt second best or in second place because you were your husband's second wife?

104) Do you feel that there is anything you have missed in your relationship with your husband because you are his second wife?

105) With what you know about being a second wife, would you marry a man who had been married before if you had the chance to do it over again?

106) If you have been both a first wife and a second wife, what would you say were the differences between the two situations?

107) Do you think that your husband ever feels guilty about leaving his first wife?

108) Have you ever had any guilt feelings that relate to your being a second wife? Explain.

109) Would you say that in some ways your husband still feels possessive about his first wife? Explain.

110) How did you feel about filling out this questionnaire and what were your reasons for doing so?

The Wives Surveyed

Two hundred second wives took part in the final phase of the survey. They ranged in age from twenty-two to seventy-one, but their average age when they became second wives was thirty-two (thirty-seven at the time they answered the questionnaire). The majority (61 percent) had been single prior to their marriage, although several had had live-in relationships with men other than their current husbands. Thirty-five percent of the wives had been previously married and were divorced; 4 percent had been widowed. Slightly more than 75 percent had lived with their current husbands before marrying them.

Seventy-four percent of the wives worked before and after their marriages at careers as diverse as psychologist, accountant, model, police officer, and ballerina. This list gives a complete breakdown of the occupations of the wives involved, as they were noted on the questionnaires.

Teacher 20	Consultant 3
Psychologist 2	Retired 1
Cook 2	Word Processor Operator 4
Dental Assistant 2	Model 1
Homemaker 52	Actress 1
Accountant 1	Finisher 1
Broadcaster 2	Writer/Editor 2
Receptionist 3	Lawyer 1
Vice-President 1	Secretary 18
Dancer 1	Executive Assistant 11
Research Technician 2	Service Representative 1
Police Officer 1	Ballerina 1
Sales Clerk 7	Administrative Assistant 6
Girl Friday 10	Personnel Consultant 5

Student 5   Retail Manager 3
Physiotherapist 3   Child Care Worker 4
Nurse 4   Waitress/Bartender 6
Flight Attendant 3   Real Estate Agent 4
Payroll Clerk 5

(One second wife listed her occupation as slave, a status which many women, marital status notwithstanding, ascribe to the one who does the housework.)

The Husbands

The average age for the husbands was thirty-eight when they got married the second time (forty-two at the time of the survey). They ranged in age from twenty-nine to eighty-five years old. The age differences between the husbands and wives ranged from no difference to thirty years; the average was seven years. Eighty percent of the husbands were older than their wives.

The wives surveyed recorded these as their husbands' current occupations or fields of pursuit.

Manager 22   Manufacturer 4
Self-employed 31   Sales Engineer 1
Airline Pilot 2   Hairdresser 1
Teacher 16   Engineer 3
Tool and Die Maker 1   Salesman 15
Foreman 2   Truck Driver 5
Steel Worker 1   Police Officer 1
Writer 1   Professor 1
Editor 1   Photographer 1
Computer Technician 4   Retired 2
Decorator 1   Courier 1
Receiver 1   Psychologist 1
Marketing 2   Mechanic 2
Sales Manager 6   Administrator 10
Restauranteur 3   Lecturer 4
Accountant 2   Farmer 1
Bond Salesman 2   Lawyer 2

Businessman 18	Stockbroker 3
Producer 2	Advertising 4
Personnel 3	Merchant 1
Interior Designer 1	Firefighter 1
Consultant 4	Security Officer 1
Civil Servant 2	Doctor 2
Developer 2	Real Estate 3

Eighty-four percent of the husbands had children from their previous marriages and 20 percent of these had custody of those children. Some of the husbands had as many as five or six children by their previous wives. Most, however, stuck to the national average and had only one or two. The children themselves tended to fall into two separate categories with respect to age. Minors (those under fifteen) were eight years old on the average, and adult children, twenty years old. Seventy-four percent of the husbands had at least one child under age fifteen.

The husbands and wives had known each other for an average of two and one-half years before they married. The average length of their current marriages was six years. The husbands' first marriages lasted twelve and one-half years on average, and the wives' twelve years. This is convergent with U.S. demographic statistics which show that the largest number of divorces for men and women occur between ten and fourteen years for a first marriage.

From this information we can draw a typical profile of a second wife. She will likely be in her early to mid-thirties and has probably never been married before. She may have lived with a man other than her husband and will probably have cohabited with her husband for a time before they got married. She worked both before and after her marriage, and as a result, she has postponed having any children from that marriage. Her husband will be in his late thirties to early forties. Most probably he was divorced from his first wife. In all likelihood he will have children, some of whom will be minors requiring financial support for several years before they reach adulthood.

In Summary

Second Wife, Second Best? must not be regarded merely as a chronicle of the woes of second wives. While it is hoped that the book will have a major appeal to second wives and to those who are about to join the ranks, there is a much broader scope for this subject. If you are the husband of a second wife, if you are the child or parent of a second wife, if you are the employer, best friend, or counsellor of a second wife, this book may be worthwhile for you to read because it should help you to understand what is going on in the life of a person who is close to you. If you are a single or divorced woman who anticipates one day getting married, you may benefit from reading this book because there is a strong possibility that you will become someone's second wife. Finally, if you are a first wife you may wish to read this book because, as one first wife recently said to me, "I'll read your book. Maybe I can find out a few more ways to stick it to my ex-husband." What she may or may not realize is that in "sticking it" to her ex-husband, she will also be "sticking it" to his second wife.

2 Life as a Second Wife

"Marriage is a wonderful institution, but who wants to live in an institution."   Groucho Marx

ALMOST EVERYONE HAS some idea of what it means to be a first wife. They have preconceived notions of how first wives meet their husbands, where they live, how they live, and what they can expect from married life. But, how do second wives live: Is it any different? What can second wives expect their married lives to be?

Married life is different for second wives in many ways and this difference is directly related to the fact that they are number two. For instance: Second wives can look forward, generally speaking, to lower standards of living than first wives; four out of five second wives will marry men who have children from previous marriages, and in three out of four cases these children will be minors; 74 percent of second wives will go out to work because they have to; only 33 percent of second wives will say they married for love.

Second wives in large numbers are a relatively new phenomenon. As such they tend to lack a collective identity. Since no one is really sure exactly where the second wife fits into current family and social patterns, many second wives spend a lot of time and effort trying to squeeze themselves into the role of first wives as they have learned to see that role, only to find out that they are often square pegs in round holes. The second wife's role is a different one because it is irrevocably altered by the husband's past life.

Unfortunately there still prevails in men, women, and the law in general, that subcurrent of feeling that the first wife is the real wife and anyone who comes after her is only an addendum to the husband's life. Societies often fail to reflect current trends and ours still tends to treat the second marriage as an unwanted deviation from the desired norm instead of an increasingly prevalent phenomenon, a reality.

Nothing in life is static, including the makeup of the family unit. Today we have one-parent families, binuclear families, blended families, and second wives. It is inevitable that as we live longer we will be forced to live differently. A large number of men and women alive today will live well into their eighties and, therefore, the possibility of a second or even a third spouse is not unrealistic. With increased longevity, the rate of marriage breakdown will also increase because marriages are exposed to more disruptive influences as the life span of the respective spouses increases. The tradition of marriage being an institution dedicated largely to the raising of children is changing. According to George Masnick, Professor of Behavioral Sciences at Harvard, an increasingly large proportion of American households have no children at all. Those that do are choosing to have fewer of them and to have them later in life. In addition the prospect of spending another twenty or thirty years with the same spouse after the children have left home is no longer the only alternative in modern marriages. The desire for personal satisfaction in life often conflicts with the values that held marriage to be an institution lasting a lifetime. The concept of marriage as a duty is being replaced by that of marriage as a pleasure.

In the last ten years the divorce rate doubled. Divorce most frequently occurs in homes where there are children either under the age of ten or over the age of twenty. The rate of remarriage is also rising phenomenally. Eighty-four percent of divorced men remarry as do 75 percent of divorced women (the men sooner than the women). The rate is even higher for widowers, with three remarrying for every widow. It is out of this changing topography of married life that the second wife emerges and will continue to emerge in ever-increasing numbers.

Meeting and Reaching the Decision to Marry

Where do most second wives find their husbands? Statistics show that the majority meet through work or are introduced by close friends. In the survey for *Second Wife, Second Best?* 54 percent of the wives met their husbands this way. A few met through each other's children or through a relative (usually a sister or brother) and some had even dated as teenagers and then drifted apart, only to come back together after one of them was divorced. Unlike previously unmarried couples, second wives tended not to meet their husbands at parties, bars, dances, or through school or sporting events.

> *I met my husband when I was eleven and he was sixteen. We were girl and boyfriend in a casual way for several years. He came looking for me after he got divorced.*

> *We met through a correspondence club. Though it sounds a bit "lonely hearts" it wasn't. It was a group run by our church to try and get divorced people together.*

> *My husband and I were both working for the same company but in different departments. We met when our union went on strike and we were walking the picket line together.*

> *I introduced my husband to his first wife (she was my best friend). The marriage didn't work out and after they got divorced we started dating.*

The decision to marry is usually less impulsive and more carefully considered for second wives. They do not tend to marry in haste. Thirty-eight percent of them knew their future husbands for five years or longer before saying "I do," while 46 percent knew them for one to five years. The median age for marrying for a second wife was thirty-four years old as compared to twenty-two for a first wife. This casts a new light on the old stereotype of the second wife as a young husband-stealing seductress (one of the images that so rankles second wives). In spite of the prevalence of this popular misconception, 67 percent of second wives do not meet their husbands until *after* they are divorced or separated from their first wives. Another 8 percent marry men who were either deserted by their first wives or widowed.

Unlike most first wives, second wives are much less likely to marry for what they call love. Only 33 percent of the women surveyed listed "love" as the main reason they married. Eight percent said they married because they were pressured by their future husbands to do so. The other 67 percent listed a variety of other reasons, including: liking/caring (12 percent), security for themselves or their children (11 percent), giving in to societal or familial pressures (10 percent), loneliness (6 percent), the desire for a commitment (6 percent), convenience (5 percent), love of the husband's children (4 percent), and to consolidate their status because of the presence of an ex-wife (5 percent).

I think my husband was really lonely. He loved me, I'm sure, but more than that I think he needed someone to mother him.

I married him because I was in love and at that time of my life when I wanted marriage and children, or thought I did.

I married my husband because he had young children and I wanted to mother them. Also I needed the security and friendship of a married relationship.

I married my husband for several reasons. First, I loved him madly and I wanted the security of marriage. My family was concerned that he was just using me (you know, the older man, younger woman thing) and I felt that if he really loved me he would marry me. Also, he had a ex-wife around who wanted him back.

Ten years ago we would have been disregarded socially and by our church if we did not marry. I thought it would make me feel more secure in our relationship especially with his ex-wife living in the same small town.

I wanted the recognition of being his wife.

Second wives felt that their husbands also married them for a variety of reasons other than love, although 30 percent said they thought love was the main reason for their husbands' marrying the second time. Fifteen percent of the second wives thought their husbands married them because of a strong feeling of liking/caring rather than romantic love, and another 15 percent took a more practical approach and said they thought their husbands married again because of the need to have mothers for minor children in the home and to have someone to keep house for them. Other wives said that their husbands married for convenience, out of loneliness, because of familial or societal pressures, for stability or happiness, because their second wives refused to live with them otherwise, because they liked the general idea of being married, and, finally, 7 percent of the second wives said that their husbands married them because they wanted a younger woman.

My husband married me because it suited his male ego to have a woman twenty years younger than he was who he thought he could satisfy sexually and who he could boast about to his friends.

I pressured him into asking me to get married because I felt insecure and didn't know where I fit into his life.

I think it was because he loved me but also I know that it takes the pressures off of him of being a housewife.

He felt left out. At age forty-five he felt life was passing him by and that society was still really geared to couples so he panicked and asked me to marry him.

I was pregnant, so he asked his kids if he could marry me and they said yes.

He wanted me to live with him but I felt that unless we were married his first wife would constantly interfere with our life so I made him make the choice, marriage or nothing.

Most of the second wives in the survey married men who had only been married once before (84 percent). The length of the husband's previous marriage was ten years or less in 46 percent of the cases. Twenty-nine percent of the wives married men who had been previously married either less than five years or between ten and fifteen years. The actual length of the husbands' first marriages seemed to make little difference to the problems encountered by the second wives except in the cases where the men had been married twenty years or longer and the psychological bonds between the husbands and their first wives were understandably much stronger.

The Wedding and Honeymoon

Once the decision has been made to marry, what can the second wife expect in the way of a wedding and a honeymoon compared to the first wife's?

Fifty-one percent of the second wives preferred to follow the accepted route and had a traditional wedding ceremony, although generally on a smaller and less elaborate scale. Thirty-eight percent of the first wives also chose a small traditional wedding. Only 17 percent of the second wives held large formal weddings with all the trimmings, although this was the favorite choice for the first wives. City hall weddings were about the same for both groups with 15 percent of the second wives and 17 percent of the first wives selecting this type of ceremony. Other alternatives, which differed between first and second wives, were that 5 percent of the first wives eloped and 11 percent of the second wives were married in their own homes.

> *We had a small wedding in the garden of my house. His little girl was the bridesmaid and his ex-wife came to the reception.*

> *My husband's first wedding was large and traditional, about 200 people. He had the reception at the Plaza and I was a bridesmaid. When we got married we had a small wedding and the reception in our apartment.*

> *Our wedding was only average size, about 100 friends and family. Although it took place in a church it was non-traditional. We went out of our way to create a ceremony that was very special and just for us. I didn't want to repeat the same vows he had said with his first wife. Somehow "'til death do us part" seems a bit unrealistic when you're marrying a man who has already been divorced once.*

Many second wives stuck with the idea of a traditional ceremony, but few had a "traditional" honeymoon. For most second wives the honeymoon consisted of one or two nights in the local hotel or a week at the family cottage. Several used their honeymoon time to travel home and meet new relatives or get better acquainted with their husbands' children. Many cited financial reasons for their decision not to take a honeymoon. Others said they would take one later when they could afford it better or when they did not have to worry about what to do with the children.

> *We were arguing so much about money and his children etc., that we ended up going on separate honeymoons just to get away from each other for a few days and cool off.*

> *We spent one day in Ottawa where we got married but we couldn't stay any longer because we had to get back and look after his baby from his first marriage.*

We spent two weeks in the Caribbean but we took my husband's two children from his previous marriage because they were off school for the holidays and it was part of his agreement to look after them then. They spent the entire two weeks reporting to their father everything I did. For instance, their mother didn't drink so every time I had a drink they would run to their father and say "Jenny's drinking again." It was very nerve-wracking and in spite of the locale it was very hard to be romantic with the two little spies following me everywhere. I was glad to get home and send them back to their mother.

Needless to say, this sort of situation does not arise for the first wife. There may not be too much difference in the approach to the wedding itself (except for the size) but first wives fare much better when it comes to the honeymoon.

I wanted to go to Niagara Falls for our honeymoon but he had already been there on his first honeymoon so we decided to go somewhere else where there would be no memories.

When his first wife found out that we were going to Acapulco for our honeymoon she phoned up to tell me all the best places and most romantic spots to go to because she had enjoyed them so much on "their" honeymoon. I wouldn't go to any of the places she suggested and all the time we were there he kept saying "We went here and we did that." It was awful.

Perhaps one of the reasons that second wives miss out on the honeymoon (aside from children, ex-wives, and money) is that 73 percent lived with their husbands before marrying as compared to only 22 percent of the first wives. Therefore the need for that "getting-to-know-you" period was not as essential. Many of the second wives confessed, however, that they secretly missed the chance to get away from it all to some romantic spot even if it were just for a few days. This was particularly difficult for the second wives who had not been married before and, therefore, felt they were missing their only chance at a honeymoon.

What's in a Name?

When it came to deciding what to do about changing their names, most second wives decided to take the traditional approach and use their husbands' last names instead of their own, even though, in many cases, there was already another "wife" still calling herself by that name. Sixty-five percent of the second wives changed their names to their husbands' when they married. Only 25 percent kept their own names, either for professional reasons, or because they had no desire to be an also-ran in the name department. Four percent hyphenated both last names, and another 8 percent tried a different compromise—using their own names for some people and their husbands' for others. Most second wives agreed that, if they had children, the children also would use the husbands' last names.

I prefer to keep my own name for business reasons. It does have its drawbacks though whenever we run into people who don't know my husband and I are married (i.e. friends from his first marriage). They usually think I am just his girlfriend.

I took my husband's last name because I respect him and want to be known as his wife.

I hyphenated our name because I thought it would be fair to me and to him. Also I don't want to get mixed up with his first wife.

I use my own name because I don't want to be the second Mrs. anybody.

I use his name and it is a bit difficult sometimes because his first wife still uses it and I get phone calls and mail for her etc. I don't understand why she doesn't go back to her maiden name like they do in Europe. After all, she's not his wife anymore, I am.

I kept my own name (i.e. from my first husband) because it is the name my children bear.

I use his name socially among his friends. On official documents I use both our last names and among my friends and business associates I use my name.

When I was working I used my own name but now we have a child I use his.

Still on the subject of names, it was decided to look at how husbands introduce their second wives, specifically what percentage of them qualify the introduction by explaining that they are "second" wives. As it turned out, few husbands found it necessary to qualify their introductions with the word "second," although most preferred to tack on the word "wife" as part of their formal introduction. A few husbands were reportedly not introducing their wives at all, letting them fend for themselves whenever the occasion arose. Some of these wives credit their husbands' behavior to embarrassment and most just found it annoying.

Living Day to Day

Once the wedding and the honeymoon are over how does day-to-day life differ for the second wife?

In 1981 the median family income was $23,220 U.S. Out of this amount more than one-third went for food and shelter. Another third was spent on household operation, medical care, and clothing. That left one-third for other things such as transportation, recreation, and personal care. How, then, does a woman married to a divorced man manage, when that man is supporting not one household but two. She usually goes out to work. Seventy-four percent of second wives go out to work compared to 52 percent of women in general. This is not necessarily because they are career oriented or because they are looking for personal satisfaction, but rather, it is because they have to help their husbands stretch their earning power to cover the expenses of two households. Out of the combined salaries of the husband and his second wife, at least one-third will disappear in child support, alimony, and additional costs like college tuition for members of his previous family. The standard of living for the second wife and her husband often does not reflect their earnings and effort. Their real income is far less.

Where do second wives live? For those who lived with their husbands before marriage, 67 percent lived in apartments and 31 percent lived in houses (often his or hers from a previous marriage). After they married this changed a little, with 40 percent reportedly living in apartments and 60 percent in houses. This again points to the desire on the part of second wives for a traditional married relationship. In comparison to first wives, second wives appear to do a little better in terms of abode in the early years of their marriage considering that 67 percent of first wives lived in apartments when they married, 19 percent in houses, and 14 percent with in-laws.

One must also take into account, however, the age and economic status of the two groups. First wives are, on the average, thirteen years younger when they marry, and they are living with husbands who have usually just set foot on the bottom rung of the career ladder. Second wives, at thirty-four years old, are married to men who have already moved several rungs up the ladder, and yet they are still not able to live at the level their age and economic status would indicate. Second wives are not as economically well off as first wives of the same age and economic status. Also second wives are married to men who often are one-third to one-half of their way through their career lifecycles when they marry, so their chances of attaining the economic security that could be theirs are diminished in comparison to those of women who have been with their husbands since their early twenties.

It should be noted here that of the 40 percent of second wives who have been married before, many kept their original family homes and were, therefore, in better economic circumstances than second wives who had not been married previously. Sixteen percent of second wives shared the houses that their husbands had lived in with their first wives usually as a result of death or desertion; they, too, were economically more stable.

> *My husband and I bought a house (I paid for it) otherwise we would have had to live in an apartment because he couldn't afford to buy another house when he was already paying the mortgage on the house his first wife was living in.*

> *We lived in his apartment which he originally shared with his first wife. Ironically he couldn't and still can't see why I wasn't thrilled at the prospect of living in the same place and sleeping in their old bedroom.*

Children and Ex-Wives

How do children fit into the scheme of things for a second wife and how much contact can she expect to have with her husband's first wife?

Twenty percent of the second wives in the survey had children from their current marriage, and 30 percent more wanted children but felt they could not afford them while their husbands were still paying for children from their previous marriages. This is not surprising when you consider that it takes about $135,000 to raise one child to the age of eighteen and this does not include any preparation for funds for college.

> *I wanted to have children but we could not afford it. It would mean I had to stop work and we would have to exist on his salary alone. It was impossible, so he got a vasectomy. I have accepted it now though I would have liked to have children of my own. I dote on my niece and nephew instead.*

If you become a second wife there is a good chance that you will marry a man with children. Eighty-four percent of second wives find themselves faced with the prospect of being step-mothers. Because of the presence of children from a first marriage, 44 percent of second wives say that their husbands continue to maintain contact with their first wives. Children, however, were not the only reason that husbands kept in touch. Twenty-seven percent said that it was guilt that kept their husbands talking to their first wives. Eight percent of second wives said that their husbands still saw their first wives for sexual reasons, another 8 percent listed legal or financial reasons, and 4 percent said it was because of geographical proximity. Thirty-seven percent said that their husbands had absolutely no personal contact with their former spouses.

My husband still has lunch with his first wife once in a while and she calls frequently. She still wants him to make decisions for her. I can't help it but I find her constant intrusion in our life very irritating.

My husband has very little contact with his ex-wife, only when it comes to signing legal documents or when he calls to speak to his daughter and she answers the phone.

My husband and I have no contact with her and neither do the children. After she left her second husband and two children she became involved in the gay community. Any contact we have now is strictly through our lawyer.

She phones to complain all the time that she's not getting enough money. She really upsets my husband with these calls because he already feels guilty enough for leaving her. Afterward we often have fights because of this.

Since the first wife is still a presence in the husband's life in so many cases, it is not surprising that 38 percent of the second wives said, yes, their husbands did, at times, confuse them with their first wives. This confusion commonly manifested itself in husbands' calling the second wives by the first wives' names (80 percent), recalling incorrectly what they did with whom, confusing the dates of anniversaries, weddings, birthdays, etc., or vital statistics, sizes, favorite colors, or perfumes. In some cases the second wives said that it was not their husbands but their husbands' families who did the confusing, and some thought that this was done purposely to make them feel uncomfortable.

For the first two years of our marriage my husband brought me flowers on "their" wedding anniversary. It seems funny now but at the time it hurt a bit.

We were watching the news when Prince Charles got married and my husband asked me if I remembered the time we went to the coronation together. I reminded him that I had not been born at the time.

While some husbands may get confused, others are quite certain who is who. That is why 15 percent of the second wives said their husbands tried to change them to be more like their first wives, and another 20 percent said that they were physically similar, or had similar personalities or backgrounds, to the first wives. The majority of husbands, however, preferred to marry women who were different from their first wives.

My husband constantly brings up his ex, calls me by her name and talks about her as though she was in the next room. I hate it. It's unnerving and makes me feel competitive (which is why he does it). We are almost identical to look at, the same middle name, same taste, and same astrological sign. Sometimes I think he married me because he wanted to marry her all over again.

I am completely opposite to her. She was short and dark and I am tall and fair. She wanted to be nothing more than a wife and mother and all I ever wanted was a career. We are completely different personalities. I think that's why he married me, because I am not one bit like her.

I am very outgoing and have a good sense of humour. She was very stern and quiet. I think that's why he got bored with their marriage and why he looked for something completely different in his next wife.

His first wife had red hair. In the beginning he was always after me to dye my hair red. I told him if he liked the color so much he should go back to her.

It is difficult to shrug off the bonds of an old relationship even when a new one is at hand. Twenty-five percent of the second wives said they felt that their husbands, at times, still felt married to their first wives. This was not necessarily an expression of ongoing affection for the first wife, but an indica- . tion that the psychological ties of a marriage are often harder to break than the emotional ones.

Even after we were married there was still the feeling that I was his mistress and she was his real wife. Only after she came to stay with us once did he say that it was with considerable relief that he realized that he was married to me.

Not only does my husband not still feel married to his first wife he says sometimes it is hard to believe that he ever was.

My husband still feels married to his first wife "financially" because he is still supporting her and their two children.

My husband is a Roman Catholic and I believe that in his heart he feels they are still married because his church will not accept divorce.

In spite of the many pressures placed on a second wife, 80 percent of the wives in the survey said that they considered their marriages to be happy, although 35 percent said that there were things they would like to change, many of which related to their husbands' having been married before.

We are very happy together. The only thing I would really like to change is that I would like us to be able to afford a house and to have a child of our own. But that is not possible at the moment because we need both our incomes just to meet our current expenses including his alimony and child support.

I am happy though I do wish at times that I had been his first wife. I know he would not be the same person if he had not gone through that experience with her but still, I wish he had only lived with her or something so that there were no legal ties and hopefully no children. It would make our marriage a lot easier.

I am happy some of the time with him but when his children come over our whole relationship changes. He completely ignores me in favor of them. I feel like I am just his housekeeper.

We are very happy together. I wish I had met him years ago and that the two of us were just starting out in life together, without all the complications we have now.

Life as a second wife *is* different. There are often problems to cope with which may be difficult to handle and situations which arise that are often totally unexpected. There will be many times as a second wife when it is not always clear what is expected and many times when too much is expected.

Second wives must get used to the fact that their married lives will, of necessity, be different. This does not mean that second wives should accept their lot without question, or that they face situations qualitatively any better or any worse than those first wives have to face. But with the rising number of second wives, society in general needs to recognize that married life for a second wife comes with a unique set of circumstances. That married life, however, can be happy and rewarding once we learn how to deal with the differences instead of ignoring them.

3 There's No Such Thing as an Ex-Wife

"I'm a marvelous housekeeper. Every time I leave a man, I keep his house."   *Zsa Zsa Gabor*

THIS QUOTE DEFINES the subject of this chapter. It is indicative of our society's current attitude toward divorce and explains why, as far as many second wives are concerned, there is no such thing as an ex-wife. Our social mores, the law, guilt, children, and financial responsibilities all contribute to making a couple's divorced relationship last longer than their married one in many cases. All of these things, not to mention the volatile emotions, which are exacerbated by the divorce situation in our culture, make sure that supposedly divorced couples continue their contact even after it would be better for both of them to move on to new lives, apart.

Researchers at the University of Wisconsin who have been studying the new phenomenon of binuclear families (family groups that include former spouses, children, and new partners) have found that 65 percent of the spouses in the study maintained regular contact with their former partners. For those with children the contact was more in-depth and the divorced parents also communicated regularly on matters not relating to their children. Over 65 percent of joint-custody parents spent time together as a family unit. Approximately 35 percent of the couples in this study fit the stereotype of the disagreeable

43

and conflicting divorced partners, but they still maintained contact.

An Income for Life

The quote from Zsa Zsa Gabor, who is perhaps the quintessential idea of what the modern divorced woman is like, first may bring on a smile because it is an amusing play on words. It is not funny, however, in the sense that it promotes the idea of women obtaining their economic security only through their husbands, and that their husbands somehow deserve to be financial victims. The fact that our laws encourage this by placing women in the position of chattels (totally dependent economically on their husbands) at the time of divorce does nothing to further the cause of equality. It is, in fact, a way of acknowledging that women cannot take care of themselves. Although the marriage may be defunct, the husband is still the responsible one, responsible for a wife's welfare, often for the rest of her life. When, on occasion, the situation is reversed and a husband is granted alimony from his wife, it is usually until he finishes school, gets a job, or is retrained to be economically independent. Women are not encouraged to seek this same economic independence. Our laws, attitudes, and traditions tie the divorced woman to her husband for the rest of his life in many cases, or at least until she remarries. The tacit understanding here is that with another man to look after her she will no longer require the support of her ex-husband. In some societies the women are handed from father to husband like a possession and never exist without the support and protection of a male. So-called liberated women of the 1980s may find this idea offensive and insulting, but these are very often the same women who, with divorce looming on the horizon and the help of their lawyers, suddenly require huge support payments.

Many women are convinced that they cannot work because they have no skills or because they are bringing up small children. In cases of necessity, where there are no ex-husbands to lean on, that is, for widows or deserted wives, these women do often make an economically viable existence for themselves, albeit not at the level at which they would like to live. It is not, then, a question of economic survival, but of the level economic survival. Many ex-wives are convinced that when they stayed home and took care of the house and the children they contributed to their husbands' career opportunities and, hence, deserved their financial support. This is true, and it is a realistic assessment of their contribution to the marriage. When that marriage is no longer in existence, however, their contribution has to be re-examined in light of the changed circumstances and so does their reimbursement.

Research for this book showed that among the sample interviewed, 60 percent of first wives did not work, although many had worked prior to their marriages, and 74 percent of the second wives did. Why?

The Wife Who Won't Let Go

The ex-wife who won't let go is motivated by a variety of emotions. High on the list is revenge: "If I can't have him then no one else can." This feeling is quite independent of whether her husband left her or she left him and is particularly acute if the husband shows signs of remarrying, because by doing so he is evincing the ultimate rejection of his ex-wife and their marriage. What he is saying is, I will be happier living without you and marrying someone else. A divorced woman's thoughts of revenge may serve to bind her even more closely to the ex-husband and hence to his new wife. Money is one of the most effective and convenient methods of revenge. By being an economic drain on her ex-husband and his new wife, the first wife is at the same time ensuring, through the monthly checks, that she is a constant presence in their marriage, and punishing him by receiving support without contributing.

Jane, a thirty-six-year-old secretary, has been married to Alex for six years and confesses that she still gets mad when his first wife calls and is more than just a little bitter about her constant interference in their marriage, not to mention her frequent demands for more money.

I am not above hanging up on her if he's not home. She's always trying to blackmail Al into giving her more money or something extra for the kids. She got practically everything in the divorce and now that we've managed to build up some financial security for ourselves, she's after that too! It's as though she still thinks of him as her husband. I can't stand it. The last time she called, it was to cajole him into buying her a townhouse so that the kids could live closer to us. I wish she would find someone else and get married again. But why should she? Most men don't earn what Al pays her in alimony. She's set for life the way things are.

Many first wives will go to any length to make their presence felt in their husbands' new marriages. This is particularly easy to do if there are children involved, because they can go back and forth between the two homes and are a constant source of information.

My husband's children visit every other weekend.... When we bought a new couch a few months ago, she was on the phone to him the minute they got home demanding that he get a new couch for her too.

Besides being a source of information and a reason for continued contact, children can also be a weapon in the divorce war.

My husband's ex-wife uses his son as a way of getting at him. It's revenge. She wants to cause him pain and she doesn't seem to care if the child gets hurt in the process. Mark used to love to come and visit us. His mother didn't like that. I suppose she didn't want her child liking me too much and besides she wanted to punish Jeff. Now, every time we go to pick him up he screams that he doesn't want to see his daddy anymore. She says things to Mark like "Your daddy doesn't love you anymore and that's why he won't give us more money." The boy is only three and he doesn't understand yet what's happened. It hurts my husband a great deal. But then, that's what she wants and there's not much we can do about it.

Not all mothers are willing to use their children so cruelly just as a means of retaliation. Some prefer to simply exaggerate their children's problems in an effort to get more attention from their ex-husbands, to give them aggravation, or to make sure that the ties of parenthood will bind them to the family even when the ties of marriage are broken.

My husband's ex uses their children whenever she can't get his attention any other way. When one of them was hurt in football practice (he wasn't even admitted to hospital, just a couple of stitches over one eye), she phoned my husband at work and made him come down to the emergency room by telling him that the boy had a severe concussion. And once she called him over to her house to have a serious talk about their daughter's failing grades (they were B's and C's) and suggested that the girl needed the stability of the home life they had while married. . . .

This last example indicates the way many second wives feel first wives think, especially if the divorce is still fairly fresh.

We are going through a very stormy period which seems to be centered around my feeling 'threatened' by his ex-wife. By threatened I mean that I think she may still want him back, and he still feels guilty and responsible and concerned about her well-being. It's all so difficult for me because I never expected to have to 'share' my husband in any way with anyone.

When my husband went to pick up his children one Friday night, she met him at the door in some filmy lingerie. There were candles and his favorite dinner and champagne. She tried to seduce him back into their relationship. The funny part was that she was never like that when they were married.

Why would a first wife want her husband back after the unpleasant experience of divorce? There are, of course, many ex-wives who have no interest in the husbands they've rejected or who have rejected them. There are also those who, when faced with the realization that the relationship has ended because of deliberate rejection by their partners, will go far to prove that this is not the case. Rejection is one of the most difficult situations we have to handle in life because it threatens to nullify much of what we have done as people. It makes us question our self-esteem. The rejected wife who gets her husband back proves to herself, and everyone else, that she is indeed worthwhile and that her efforts as a wife were not in vain.

Some women, particularly those born in the first third of the century, rely on their marriages to define themselves as individuals. To join the ranks of the divorced deprives them of the major portion of their identity. Marriage was their career as well as a relationship. They still see themselves as "wives," but are robbed of their *raison d'être*.

A first wife may try to regain her husband because marriage with him was safe (although it may have been unfulfilling) and therefore a preferable alternative to having to broach the unfamiliar modern singles scene. But the first wife who can't let go perpetuates a destructive cycle for herself. She spends so much time and effort trying to regain her ex-husband and pretending that their marriage is still a viable relationship that she has no time for creating a new life for herself.

The husband may succumb because it is hard to resist the familiarity, the memories, the promise of sex as he remembered it in the beginning, the possibility of being reunited with the children, and the good feeling that he has put something right which should never have gone wrong in the first place. The second wife does have an advantage in situations like this. She is there, living with her husband every day and making a new life with him. With time and tenacity, the benefits of their daily life together can overcome the fond memories and safe harbors

of the past. Here is how two second wives handle their husbands' involvements with their ex-wives and the ex-wives'
attempts to get them back.

*I thought if I was understanding about their relationship and even
a little sympathetic to her side of things, it would wear off between
the two of them and they would naturally drift apart. That was ten
years ago and he still sees her regularly. In a way its like he's
married to both of us only he sleeps with me.*

*My husband has nothing to do with his ex-wife any more. She was
getting too close for comfort and I had to put a stop to it. He is my
husband now not hers. I told him if he still wanted to be involved
with her in any way, shape or form then I would put an end to our
relationship immediately.*

Two extremes of the spectrum. The second, although it may
seem harsh, is probably the more effective because it gives the
second wife and her husband a chance at a life of their own,
free from the pressures and demands of the former spouse. At
the same time it frees the first wife to make a life of her own.

Not all ex-wives want to live with their husbands again, but
many want to carry on a relationship because they see themselves as the real wife, and the second wife as nothing more
than a glorified mistress (as perhaps do his friends and family).
Why else would so many first wives continue to call themselves
after their ex-husbands' last names when there are now other
women who lay claim to that title? To suddenly find themselves
among the divorced strips them of their identity, like the man
who finds himself unemployed. They are wives, but they may
now be deprived of a major portion of their identities.

Second wives can be the only women in the world who do
not garner the usual respect from married status but face the
attitude that they are the other women in their husbands' lives.
From a practical point of view, the first wives are the other
women in their marriages.

The Husband Who Won't Let Go

The first wife is not always responsible for the tie that binds. Many first wives find that whether they want it or not, they are the recipients of husbandly attentions from men who are no longer their husbands. This type of behavior exhibited by ex-husbands may be called the harem syndrome. Many husbands suffer from this for a period after their divorces and often into their new marriages. Essentially it is typified by the husband keeping in close contact with his ex at his own instigation and fulfilling many of the roles (protector, provider, father) he did when they were married. Harem-syndrome husbands try to keep both their ex-wives and their current wives happy at the same time, a nearly impossible situation. These men run themselves ragged putting up two Christmas trees, mowing two lawns, fixing two sets of plumbing, and generally being husbands to two women at once.

Chris is thirty-three years old and a sales manager. Her husband of four years "more or less" drifted away from his first wife, or so he told her, due to lack of common interests and mutual goals. Chris's problem was that she found out after they were married that he hadn't drifted quite far enough.

John was always going over to their old house to fix things or to see the kids, or help her out in one way or the other. It really used to bother me that he hadn't cut his ties with her but I was afraid to nag him too much about it in case it gave him even more reasons for going over there. The last thing I wanted was for him to seek sympathy from her. So, I kept pretty quiet about how I felt and tried to keep him so busy in our home that he didn't have time to go over to hers. Then, on our first Christmas together I asked him what time he wanted to have Christmas dinner and he said that he generally preferred to have it in the afternoon but for me not to cook until the evening because he was going to have dinner over there first. I couldn't believe it. He was going over there on our first Christmas together. That was when I finally let him know how I felt about his continuing his relationship with his ex-wife. He told me that I was being selfish and unreasonable and that if he didn't go over there she would be all alone. It didn't seem to occur to him that I would be all alone if he did.

Two things motivate a husband who is suffering from the harem syndrome: guilt and ego. Many husbands feel responsible, correctly or not, for leaving their first wives and so will bend over backwards to make amends.

When John left his first wife he felt so guilty that he left her with everything but the clothes on his back. That's why now, after ten years, he is still paying alimony to her even though she doesn't need it. She earns thirty-five thousand dollars a year.

When Marianne, a thirty-four-year-old homemaker, married Fred, he had been wallowing in his private guilt about the breakup of his first marriage for three years. Marianne confesses that for a while she felt Fred and his ex had handled their divorce in a very civilized fashion, and in fact, they even saw each other socially and were on generally good terms. She was totally unaware of Fred's guilt.

I never realized that Fred felt so bad about the breakup of his first marriage. I suppose if I had looked for the signs I would have seen them but I really thought he had gotten it all out of his system. Then one day I met his ex-wife in a department store and we stopped to say hello. As we were talking I noticed a ring she was wearing. It was identical to the one that I had. Of course I asked her where she got it and without a blush she told me that Fred had given it to her. After comparing notes a little further I realized that Fred had been giving his ex-wife presents all the time we were married. In fact, every time he gave something to me he gave something to her. I was shocked. I had to tell him that I didn't think it was right for him to be buying gifts for his ex-wife, not when he was married to me. I hated the idea that some of the things were identical. It meant I wasn't special to him or at least no more special than her. It was then he told me how guilty he felt about leaving her. Somehow, buying things for the two of us eased his guilt a bit, I suppose. I would like to think that if I had been her I wouldn't have accepted gifts from another woman's husband, though.

Ego is the other reason that many husbands like to keep more than one wife around at the same time. This brings to mind the days when the more wives and children a man had, the more important he was. A husband who is suffering from a bruised ego as a result of being party to a failed marriage is easy prey for this type of thinking because, at the back of his mind, he can say to himself, I didn't fail at marriage and the fact that two women want me is proof. Of course not all first wives want their husbands back or even around. But some men just can't bear the idea that a woman can get along fine without them especially if she is his ex-wife. This can be just as annoying to a first wife as to a second wife, and often both women wish he would just get his priorities in order and behave as the situation dictates and not as his ego would have it.

The idea of possession is closely related to ego satisfaction, but it is not always immediately apparent to the second wife that the husband still feels possessive about his first wife. Sometimes it takes something like a wedding to bring it all to the surface.

Isabelle is an editor aged forty-two. Her husband, David, was on good terms with his first wife and children and so was she. In the five years they had been married Isabelle had experienced few of the problems that can plague a second wife with an ex-wife in the background—until David's first wife got married again.

I saw a side of David that I had never expected. After all those years of marriage to me I had no idea he still felt that way about Francine. When she announced that she was going to get married again, David started acting like the jealous lover even though we hardly ever saw her. He wanted to know "who this guy was" and "have him checked out." You'd have thought they were still married the way he carried on. At the wedding he spent the entire time looking daggers at her new husband. I don't know who was more embarrassed, Francine or me. It hurt me that David still felt possessive about his first wife. I wonder even now if he doesn't feel just a little bit that they are still married.

Friendly First Wives

Not all relationships between ex-husbands and ex-wives are antagonistic. Many divorced couples continue to be good friends or at least not enemies. What does this mean for the second wife? While many second wives may be prepared for the time when they will come up against some issue involving the first wife, few are prepared for the opposite to happen. What do you do if his first wife wants to be buddies? Friendly first wives have been known to go as far as indoctrinating their replacements in the ritual of the caring for and feeding of the husband.

When we first got married, his first wife came over and gave me a list of his favorite foods and how he liked his shirts done and when he preferred to make love. I couldn't believe it at first and he thought it was very nice of her to be so concerned. I resented the interference. In effect she was saying "Look I really know this man better than you because I had him first." I tried to avoid her after that because I didn't want her running around comparing notes on her marriage versus mine.

The motive behind all this can be to let the second wife have firsthand knowledge of her husband's previous marriage and thereby establish it as the original, suggesting that anything else could only be a carbon copy. Another reason that first wives don't mind imparting a little personal information, if they are predisposed to do so, is that it gives them a certain satisfaction to know that all his little idiosyncrasies that once

drove them to distraction will now be doing the same to someone else.

It can be said, though, that détente between the two wives,
whether frosty or friendly, can have its advantages. The first
wife can go a long way to preserving everyone's peace of mind
if she makes it perfectly clear to the children that there is no
overt animosity between the two households. There is nothing
like a vituperative first wife who spends the entire week malign-
ing her ex-husband and/or his new wife so as to make those
"daddy weekends" pure hell for everyone. In fact, many second
wives admit that, at least for a period of time, they do feel
sympathetic toward their husbands' first wives.

> *When Ron asked her for a divorce, it came as a complete surprise to
> her. I can sympathize with her feelings then. I know how I would
> have felt.*

> *Sometimes I felt sorry for her because I knew that he had not made
> life easy for her. They were young and broke when they got married
> and he fooled around a lot. But then, he told me that every time he
> told her he was leaving, she told him she was pregnant and he
> stayed. I'm sure she knew that he wanted to leave her and she used
> the children to hang on to him. I really feel sorry for both of them
> because they just kept getting in deeper and deeper into their trap.*

> *His first wife and I are friends, not exactly drinking buddies but
> she will come over from time to time and we seem to have worked
> out a nice balance in our relationship. I see her as the mother of his
> children not as his wife.*

In spite of the sympathetic feelings that some second wives
have for their husbands' first wives (feelings seldom recipro-
cated), there are still many second wives who openly admit
that their husbands' ex-wives create unnecessary pressures on
their marriages. Sad to say, some women, whether first wives
or second wives, have even resorted to murder in an effort to
get rid of the persons they see as disturbing forces in their lives.

There are many documented cases of first or second wives resorting to violent acts to rid themselves of the competition.

The Dead but not Departed

Although we have been discussing what can happen when there is an ex-wife in the background of a new marriage, we have so far limited our examples to the living ex-wife, because this is what the majority of second wives will be required to face. A much smaller percentage will face a different set of problems in marrying a man whose first wife is deceased. Although she is no longer a physical presence who can influence what goes on in the marriage, the deceased former wife is not without her own degree of authority. Sometimes this authority is generated by the former wife before her death, and in other cases it is something that is bestowed on her by others after her death. In either case, it can make life unpleasant for the second wife.

As many men do, my husband put a large portion of his assets in his first wife's name. When she died unexpectedly he was shocked to find that her will bequeathed everything that he thought of as "his" to other people including his children. A clause in the will indicated that if he were to contest the will everything would go to charity and his children would receive nothing. He did not contest the will but this final slap in the face from beyond the grave is something which he still has not come to terms with. I suppose he will always wonder what made her do it. Even though it has been years since she died and we got married, this subject and of course she still figure frequently in conversation.

My husband's first wife died tragically when their children were still quite young. I know he loved her very much and would never have considered divorcing her (or she him for that matter) if she had lived. When we met I fell deeply in love with him but I know that even though we are married now and have our own child she is still the love of his life. It hurts sometimes to know that he loves her the way I love him and that this is never really going to change.

My husband was divorced from his first wife and we were already married when she died. Before she died he had very little good to say about her but afterward she became a saint. I couldn't believe it. And of course in comparison I became a normal fallible human being who makes mistakes and has bad moods etc. I certainly don't benefit from this comparison.

My husband's first wife was killed in a car accident. She was an alcoholic. After we were married we got custody of his three children which was fine with me except that they blame me for their mother's death. You know, "If daddy hadn't married you then maybe mother would still be alive." It is very difficult for me to deal with this especially as I know she was an alcoholic before he left her but the children still see me as the villain.

My husband refuses to get rid of reminders of his first wife. We live in the same house he shared with her and all her things are still there waiting for her to come back. For the first two years he wouldn't even let me clear off the dresser and put her make-up things away. It's as though he thinks she's going to walk through the door any minute. He even talks to her picture.

As you can see, the problems for women married to widowers are somewhat different. Marrying a man who has been widowed is not the same as marrying one who has been divorced. The reason is simple. Divorce is an elective step taken by one or both parties to end a marriage. Even if the husband wasn't the one who wanted to terminate the relationship, he knows that the wife was, and that at least gives him a different perspective about their relationship. When she dies suddenly, however, he has to contend with the grief of losing a woman he still loves and wants, not a woman who has fallen out of love with him, or he her. It is for this reason that many men find it so difficult to get over their first marriages even while they are in the midst of their second. For the second wife who finds herself in this circumstance, the realization that a woman she thought was permanently gone from her husband's life is still an entity to be concerned with, even if only in his imagination, can be quite a blow. In many cases it is a no-win situation for the second wife because, after all, most of us only remember the good things about people when they die and so an aura of saintliness, unreasonable though it may be, often colors a man's memories of his deceased first wife. No second wife can contend adequately with this because anything she says about the situation may be held against her. When there are children involved, the second wife must contend with their grief and their possible antagonism toward her, particularly if they are under the impression that she somehow "caused" their mother's death by marrying their father. Men also sometimes view themselves the "cause" of their first wives' deaths. One second wife, whose husband's first wife died of cancer, found out that her husband felt he was responsible for his first wife's death. He apparently had read an article about cancer being caused by stress and assumed that his relationship with his second wife had been the "stress" factor behind his first wife's cancer.

Sometimes time will help in cases like this; the younger the husband, the greater the chances he will forget and readjust to his new wife. In many cases, however, the deceased former wife is someone whose presence never completely fades. Women who have living ex-wives to contend with can, therefore, consider themselves somewhat luckier than the women who marry widowers, because at least living ex-wives may remarry or move out of their lives at some point. Deceased wives seldom do. Much of this *angst* could be avoided if we were to recognize the reality of some marriages as serial arrangements rather than permanent or concurrent ones. Once a marriage is finished, the two parties involved should be encouraged by everyone, friends, family, society, the law, to build new lives, apart. Current attitudes are responsible for much unnecessary anguish in the modern marriage, a great deal of which is suffered by the second wife who often inherits a lot of unnecessary and unexpected baggage when she marries a previously married man. It would be kinder and more realistic for both the first wife and the second wife (not to mention the husband, who is often in the middle of a tug-of-war between them), if we could all accept that today marriage is not necessarily forever. It is a fact of life that relationships often break down. No one should be punished for the death of a marriage. While it may be perfectly all right to mourn the passing of a relationship with someone we once loved, to continue to do so for years and to try to hang on to that person, however tenuously, is unhealthy.

Life is full of change and today's woman does not have to define herself in terms of marriage. Consequently it should be easier for a woman to accept divorce and move on to a new life instead of trying to recapture and hang on to a past life. It is time society accepted the idea that there should be such a thing as an *ex*-wife.

4 Cinderella Exposed

"Children begin by loving their parents; after a time they judge them; rarely if ever do they forgive them."

Oscar Wilde

IF CHILDREN DO not forgive their parents, they are harder still on their stepparents. In particular they are hard on their stepmothers because in our culture where the mother is often the nucleus of the family—the essential core that holds it all together—the very existence of the stepmother is symbolic of the breakdown of the family group. In addition, the tacit suggestion that Mother can be replaced rocks the foundation of the family.

The negative feelings we have about second wives in general and stepmothers in particular are nurtured very early and are epitomized by the fairytales *Cinderella* and *Snow White*. These ageless tales, which mothers have told their children for generations, are responsible for instilling not one but two unfortunate stereotypes in young minds. The first, which has been attacked recently by those interested in erasing erroneous sexual stereotyping from children's literature, is that of the helpless young girl who waits passively for the prince to remove her from her unhappy situation. The second is the equally erroneous stereotype of the wicked stepmother. Unfortunately this characterization has *not* been challenged; it is, for now, accepted. Stepmothers are wicked.

In *Cinderella*, more stress is placed on the greed and avarice of the stepmother and her daughters than is attached to the relationship and eventual marriage of Cinderella and her prince. One can imagine the affect this has on young readers with stepmothers, particularly on those living in blended families (families where each spouse has offspring from a previous marriage). Even though today we pride ourselves on being less biased against minorities, this erroneous and warped presentation of family life is still allowed to flourish. *Snow White* is a similar case in point. Snow White's stepmother, the villain in the story, is not particularly greedy or lazy like Cinderella's stepparent, but she is so vain that she attempts murder four times on her stepdaughter after her mirror pronounces Snow White to be more beautiful than she is. This second wife is not only a wicked stepmother figure, but because of her excessive vanity, she enters into a warped life-and-death "competition" with her stepdaughter. Adults obviously can see the degree of exaggeration in the comic-strip representations of the stepmothers in these tales, but young minds do not have sufficient experience to be so discerning. Very often, many second wives discover the deck is stacked against them by prejudices first engendered by such fairy-tale propaganda.

Cinderella and *Snow White* may be old tales, but they nevertheless still accurately represent today's attitude toward stepmothers. There is something inherently disconcerting to us about a woman raising another woman's children. Why? In many cultures the raising of children is a community effort. In such cultures what is important is that there are children to be nurtured and adults willing to do the job. As far as child rearing is concerned, blood relation is not a significant issue.

In our society, however, which draws its strength from its commerce, the high significance of possession and ownership cannot be served by the communal attitude toward children typical of many less economically complex cultures. Inheritance based on birthright, sex, and age is still a highly important aspect of our family life. It is, therefore, extremely important in our culture for a man to know which are *his* children and who their mother is in order to act accordingly—to do the right thing—when it comes to their support and the carrying on of his line. A man who has amassed many possessions in a lifetime wants to make sure that he passes them on to *his* children and not to anyone else's. This is still very much a prevalent male point of view in our culture.

Its corollary on the women's side is that a woman is only as valuable as the children she bears, and if she wants to ensure her continued economic survival, she had best look after those children. There is obviously no room for a stepmother here, and in the old days, if not now, stepmothers were more or less expected to do vile things to their charges in the hopes of supplanting these charges with their own natural children in the husbands' economic futures, thereby ensuring their own futures as well.

Nothing typifies this outlook better than the story of Cinderella. In all the years that have elapsed since mothers began to warn their children about Cinderella's wicked stepmother (Perhaps their own someday?) not much has changed. The first wife still fears for her own and her children's economic livelihood when the second wife appears, and stepmothers continue to have a very bad reputation.

This reputation was very much a matter of convenience. We simply couldn't accept that the evils endured by Cinderella would have been perpetrated by her real mother. The stepmother is a handy substitute, and her reputation is sacrificed to maintain the sterling character of the biological mother. She becomes the person who often bears all the blame for the ugliness of a disrupted family life, thus allowing the biological parents to remain untainted in the minds of family members at large.

Eighty-four percent of the wives in the survey were step-mothers. Some of them enjoyed the experience, and some hated it. Suffice it to say that, for most, it was not what they expected.

Facing Instant Motherhood

One of the great differences between first wives and second wives is that first wives marry men. Second wives usually marry families. Nearly two-thirds of second wives were previously single women unencumbered by the responsibilities of parenthood. For a woman who has been pursuing her own career and lifestyle, the shock of instant motherhood can be overwhelming. Suddenly the spontaneity and go-where-you-please life is irrevocably curtailed. Perhaps you'll now need a babysitter before planning to go out, and those lazy romantic weekends you had before you were married will be replaced by weekly custody visits.

> *Before I got married I used to spend my weekends shopping, going to movies etc., just to relax after a hectic week at the office. Once we were married, the weekends became more hectic than the week days. From Friday at six until Sunday at six I had to feed and entertain his two children. We never had any time to ourselves anymore and I really began to resent this intrusion in our lives.*

> *I travel in my job and it was very difficult for me to cope with his two children and do that at the same time. We had them for two weeks every month and so I had to try and arrange to make my out of town traveling during the other two weeks which wasn't always possible. My husband and I often had heated discussions about my being away when the children were at our place because then he would have to look after them himself.*

Whether your husband has custody or just periodic contact with his children, your marriage will be different. Instant motherhood can be very disorienting. After all, you don't have nine months to plan for the big event. You also have to cope with your husband's attitude toward your position in his children's lives. He may very well expect you to stay home and be a full-time mother if his first wife did, when you want to or have to continue working. Some men do marry again to ease the burden of child rearing. This is something that should definitely be straightened out before you marry. If you are not child oriented or at least not ready to be a mother even on a part-time basis, make this perfectly clear up front. Explain that while you are happy to have the children over, you do have a life/career of your own and are not about to become a mother substitute. Make sure that you know the details of his custody arrangement before you get married so that you will know just what to expect. Remember, custody arrangements are subject to change under new court decisions. Is this likely to happen?

Statistics show that with first marriages the introduction of a child in the early stage of the marriage had a direct correlation to the chance of that marriage ending in divorce. A newly married couple need time to establish their relationship before they open themselves to the pressures of rearing children. Obviously, then, a ready-made family right at the beginning of a marriage will add an extra burden to the second marriage.

I'm sure my husband felt that once we were married I would assume most of the parenting duties for his three children when they came to visit because "that was the woman's job." I made it very clear right from the beginning that they were his children too and that he should shoulder at least half the responsibility for them.

We never had the carefree early months of marriage because his children were with us much of the time. Even though I love them and enjoy their company there are still times when I wish we could be just a couple again.

Yours, Mine, and Ours: The Making of the Blended Family

Since nearly 40 percent of the second wives had been married before, many of them had children of their own, and custody laws being what they are, most of them had custody of these children. This situation leads to an entirely different set of problems. Now there are the wants and needs of you, your spouse, and his children and your children to be considered. All of these must somehow be co-ordinated so that everyone is satisfied. This arrangement, called the blended family, is perhaps the most difficult set of relationships to manage because there are so many people involved, not to mention that hostility may pervade because of the disruption of divorce and the aftermath of adjustment.

You must be prepared for the armed-camp approach in the beginning as your children will be very covetous of you and everything they consider their territory. So will his. Invariably his children will see you as a threat in the relationship between their father and themselves and may blame you for their parents' break-up. They will be jealous of his love for you and torn between their affection for you and their love for their own mother. There may be a vast age difference between your children and his, which has the effect of creating two separate families under one roof, each with their respective needs. You will likely have two ex-spouses involved in your lives because of custody and visitation arrangements. There will be additional mouths to feed, beds to make, and money to spend. All of this would be very taxing in a solid marriage of long standing, let alone your budding relationship with your husband. It will not be The Brady Bunch.

> *Every third weekend we had six kids in the house. It was chaos. First of all his are all in their teens and mine are between five and eight so we had two different sets of rules, two different bedtimes, different demands for food and television programs and it was very very cramped in our three bedroom home. I was always glad on Sunday nights when at least some of the children would be leaving.*

> *Sometimes when my ex-husband was picking up the kids or she was dropping off my husband's kids for their weekly visit we would all end up in the living room at the same time. It was so tense. I'm sure*

the children must regard their lives as somewhat of a circus with all this coming and going and different adults around who tell them what to do.

My children and his children would not get along. We were constantly breaking up fights between them whenever they were all together in the same house. I didn't really expect them to love each other right from the start but I had sort of hoped they would tolerate each other at least. No such luck.

Some blended families do very well, but others never seem to jell. There are so many factors involved in making the successful blended family that it is almost impossible to predict which ones will make it. Those that seem to do best are the ones where both parents are committed to the idea of trying, neither parent favors his or her child over the others, and ex-spouses on both sides do not interfere—an ideal world. Those with the most problems are ones where either one or both of the parents does not really want the other's children, where the father (or mother) fails to make it clear that the new spouse is going to be around for a long time and cannot be ousted by any efforts on the children's part, and where the ex-spouses use the children as a means of driving a wedge into the marriage by making them as hostile as possible toward their stepparents.

If you are in the position of orchestrating the contented blended family there are two very important elements to consider: communication and time. The children should be kept informed about what is happening if a parent remarries. Springing it on them after the fact or at the last minute will not help you to get their co-operation. They should have time to get to know the "new" parent and stepchildren before any arrangements are made to move in together. You can, of course, expect sides to be taken and lines to be drawn up by the children themselves, but if you make an effort to show your impartiality and give them a feeling of love and security, they will likely work out their own compromises. Children are much more adaptable than adults to changes like this. You will need to instill in them a sense of permanence though. After all, divorce has disrupted their lives too, and they may be feeling that if their home (which they took to be a constant) can be broken up then nothing is ever going to last again.

The next thing you have to be prepared for is that this is all going to take some time; it will not happen overnight and cannot be forced. Children are very territorial when it comes to their toys, their rooms, or their parents. They will not be instantly ready to share any of what they consider theirs. Time and familiarity, however, should help them to realize that maybe this isn't such a bad thing after all.

Once you have figured out the intricacies of raising his and/or your children from previous marriages harmoniously, there is yet another possibility to be considered. What if the two of you decide to have a child of your own? In some cases children from a previous marriage relate very well to a new baby in their world. It can be a way of reassuring them that although their family is changing it is still going to continue. Others feel nothing but resentment and jealousy for the new child because, rightly or not, they feel that it will replace them in their father's eyes or, worse, in his bank account and will.

When Christin was born Alex's children were just thrilled. They wanted to come over all the time just to see the baby. I think too that after the baby they began to see me as a real mother and not just someone that daddy was living with so our relationship improved.

My husband's daughter was extremely jealous of our new baby (a girl). She wouldn't look at her or touch her and she started to revert to doing baby things herself like sucking her thumb. After she realized that we loved both our babies the same she became more interested in her little sister.

My husband's grown children thought it was disgusting that a man of his age (45) should become a father again and they let him know it. Both he and I knew though they were more concerned about the possible change in his will than about whether we had a baby or not.

My husband's teenage son thought it was terrible when his father and I told him I was pregnant. The first thing he said was to do with how were we going to pay for his college education now. How selfish.

Wife or Stepmother?

Many second wives ask themselves this question: "Did he marry me because he wanted me or did he just want someone to help raise his children?" The answer may be yes to both, and some women are quite happy to be married just to help a man raise children. Others want to be married for themselves alone. It depends on your own priorities and on what you want out of marriage. The worst thing that can happen is to find out that you thought he loved you as a person when all he really loved was the idea of you as a stepmother.

> *My husband's wife died when she was thirty-four and left him with two small children. I had known him for years through our office and always rather liked him. I was so thrilled when he started to ask me out. Things escalated very quickly and I was so much in love with him. When he asked me to marry him I was so happy. It wasn't long after the wedding that I realized he had given me the rush because he needed someone to look after the children. I was so hurt and yet I still loved him. I think he likes to have me as his wife but I know that the real reason he married me was to have a stepmother for his children.*

Mommy's Little Messengers

Another problem that second wives have to face when it comes to learning to live as wives and mothers simultaneously is the fact that children who reside in two households, however infrequently, open up lines of communication that most second wives would rather not have exist. Children going back and forth between two parents are prone to act as reporters. They tell each parent everything that goes on in the other parent's household. Sometimes they are encouraged to do this, of course, as a means of keeping tabs on the ex-spouse, and sometimes they just naturally repeat what they have seen and heard. Most second wives resent this intrusion into their private lives, and yet it is difficult to curtail, particularly if the children are being encouraged by the absent parent.

> *My husband's children reported everything to their mother after every visit. If I bought something or cooked something they didn't like or let them stay up a little later for a special occasion they would tell her when they went home. She would be on the phone right away reiterating her lists of do's and don'ts for the children. As she said, they were her children and she wanted them to be brought up a certain way. She made me feel like an incompetent babysitter not an adult capable of making decisions about the children's welfare. I think now though that she was just doing it to try to throw her weight around a little with me and let me know where I stood.*

> *Every time we had a fight in front of his children they would tell their mother and she would phone up to give him a shoulder to cry on and incidentally let him know she would always be there if he wanted her back. I tried to bite my tongue, of course, but sometimes you just have to speak your mind and there she would be hovering around him afterwards.*

Children like to pit one parent against the other as a means of getting their own way. This works especially well if there are two households between which the children know there is hostility. It is very important, therefore, to make clear to the children from the beginning that this is your home, what goes on there is your business, and that they should respect it. Naturally if you are asking them not to relate your business to their mother, you and your husband must evince, in turn, no interest when they start to tell you about mother's new boy-friend.It is a two-way street.

A Child of your Own

One of the saddest pieces of information to come out of the research for this book was the number of second wives who wanted to have children of their own, but who had to postpone them or give up the idea entirely because they were too involved either emotionally or financially with raising the hus-bands' children from a previous marriage.

I would very much have liked to have had a child with Doug but with his three children being so young I knew that there would not be enough time for another one, especially since I had to continue working. If I had a child I wanted to give it all my love and attention but I felt that that would not be possible under the circumstances.

His children won't be on their own for another ten years and then there will be college. We simply cannot afford to have a child of our own though I would have liked one. It's just something I have to get used to I suppose.

This letter appeared in an advice column in the Fort Lauder-dale *Sun-Sentinel*. It typifies the attitude of many people to the idea of a second wife having children of her own.

Dear Dr. Berek and Ms. Grant:
I want to take exception to your statement that a man should make sure he can support his children from his first marriage before starting a second family. I am the new wife and we have not, nor do we plan to start a second family—but my husband still cannot afford to pay his child support. Financial situations which affect one's obligations do change. Are you saying that an ex-husband should wait until his child is self-supporting before he remarries?

(Answer) Situations do change.... And yes, we are saying that a divorced man with children should carefully evaluate his financial circumstances before accepting additional obligations.

In addition to the financial pressures there are also situational pressures that often encourage a second wife *not* to have a child of her own. Many second wives find that by the time they get married their husbands have already gone through their child-rearing years with their first wives. While they may have enjoyed the experience at the time, they are not ready to go back to the diapers again, and their interest in having young children around is considerably diminished. These men often discourage their second wives from having a family because they know the sacrifices to be made and they are not willing to repeat the experience.

Not all husbands overtly discourage their second wives from having babies. Many will simply say that if she really wants one they will go ahead with it. This implies that while they are willing to accept the physical circumstance, they are somewhat lacking in emotional commitment. For a second wife in this position, the joy of sharing a pregnancy and then a child with the man she loves is muted because it is something she is embarking on more or less of her own volition. She becomes almost a single parent.

> *My husband said that if I wanted to have a baby he wouldn't mind but I knew he was trying to do it just to please me and because he felt he shouldn't deny me the experience but his heart wasn't in it. I kept thinking about having a child whose father was really not that interested and I decided against it.*

> *I really think that it takes two people who are committed to the idea of raising a child to do the job right. I didn't want to be a married single parent so I decided not to have a baby with my husband.*

It is not always the husband who causes the second wife to

change her mind about becoming a mother; sometimes it is his children.

> *I wanted to have a baby with Joe but when I got to know his children from his first marriage I thought, do I really want to be responsible for bringing people like that into the world?*

Competition and Comparison

For the second wives who did decide to have children with their husbands, there surfaced other difficulties with which to deal besides the financial repercussions. The second wife often harbors an unspoken fear that her husband will not love their child as much as he loves "her" child. First children, like first wives, have always been regarded as more important (look at our inheritance customs), and many second wives are concerned that their children will be treated with the same sort of quiet disregard as themselves.

> *I know it sounds strange but I didn't want children of mine growing up and being known as "Brad's other children."*

> *I was hoping we would have a little girl because my husband's other children are all boys and I knew that she would be more special to him than another boy.*

Although these fears are quite often groundless, for those women who do have their husbands' second families, there are frequently feelings of competition about the children as much as there are about the first wives in other areas of the marriages. Many second wives hope that their children are as smart, as good at sports, and as healthy as "hers." They do not want their children to compare unfavorably with those of their husbands' first marriages. This deep-seated and often unspoken competitiveness is based on the false logic that if the husband's first lot of children turned out better than hers, then the fault lies not with him (because he has already proved himself, so to speak), but with her. Pursuant to this is that she is not as good as the first wife.

> *When my baby was born he was small and sickly. My husband's other child had been big and robust, a very lovely baby. I couldn't help it but I felt somehow that I had failed him.*

> *My husband's first wife was practically dropping them in the field as they say. Joy worked right up until a week before both her children were born. She had easy, uncomplicated deliveries. In my case I was as sick as a dog the whole time and had to spend the last three months in bed in order not to lose the baby. Then, on top of all that I had to have a caesarean. My husband just couldn't figure it out. His previous experience with pregnancy had been that it was an easy, simple experience. They say a little knowledge is a dangerous thing. He just couldn't understand why I was having such problems and he kept on telling me that "Joy did this or ate that and she was fine." He couldn't or wouldn't accept that this was just the way things were with me. He made me feel terribly inadequate.*

The problems of competition do not always begin and end with the second wife. When there is a second family, often children will vie for daddy's attention, or even daddy's money, depending on their ages.

> *My husband's children from his first marriage became much more clamorous for his attention after our baby was born. It was as if they felt that because of the new child they would be displaced in his affections. We made a great effort to assure them that their father loved all his children equally.*

Whatever the circumstance, competitive feelings, whether between first and second wives or their children, are part of what a second wife must expect to face, and something with which a first wife is not usually confronted—unless her husband marries again.

Discipline Problems

If you are part of a blended family or a some-time stepmother you will eventually run up against the problem of discipline with your stepchildren. The issue of who disciplines whose children and how much is a thorny one for most second wives. Discipline is a difficult matter for natural parents because we all have different views on what to discipline children for and how to do it. For stepmothers, however, the problem is exacerbated for several reasons.

Unlike the natural mother the stepmother has not had the children since birth and, therefore, has not been able to lay the ground rules for what she considers appropriate behavior. With the many different options in parenting today, it is entirely feasible that a woman with conservative views on child raising can marry a man whose first wife prefers a very liberal approach. The stage is set for confrontations between the two women, between the stepmother and the children, and between her husband and herself.

Monica still subscribes to that sixties mentality that says children are natural beings and should be allowed to develop any way they please and that they will ultimately do what is right. Her children come over every weekend and act like savages. They eat with their hands, don't wash, stay up all night and leave the place looking a disaster. Finally I couldn't take it any more. My philosophy of raising children is totally opposite to hers. I think that children need rules in order to guide them as they grow up. I think they need someone to tell them no. I had to tell my husband that I wouldn't have his children in my home while they were acting like that. Now when he wants to see them he takes them out for the day or sees them in their own home. It was the only solution.

Often in the tense early years of marriage, second wives will find that the discipline of the children is the focus of arguments between themselves and their husbands, either because the children are directly responsible for the problem at hand, or because they represent to the second wives a lingering reminder of their husbands' marriages. Second wives often feel shut out when it comes to their husbands' children if they have no say over the children's behavior. They can overcompensate by being too harsh or too soft with the children, which confuses a husband who has developed a system of discipline with his first wife that may be quite different. This leads to husbands who say, "They're my children and I'll deal with them," which, of course, only adds to the problem.

> *My husband and I could not agree on how to discipline his son who was a sulky, rebellious thirteen-year-old when we got married. One time I sent him to bed early because he was acting up and when my husband came home he yelled at me for treating the boy that way. He said he was Scott's real parent and he knew best how to handle him. So I said fine then you handle him.*

Many second wives, who have had children of their own or had many dealings with children on a daily basis, are often nonplussed when it comes to disciplining their stepchildren. There are few things more difficult to handle than a willful eight-year-old or teenager who regards you merely as an intruder and not an authority figure. Stepmothers often run up against situations where children refuse to listen to them on the grounds that, "You're not my mother." What should you do about discipline?

The first thing is to get it straight before you marry that you have to discipline the children while they are in your care as does your husband or his ex-wife. Deciding who is going to discipline the children, and how much, is essential for smooth co-existence between you and your husband, as well as between you and your stepchildren.

The best solution is for both parents (and ex-spouses) to present a united front on the issue of discipline. This will provide a uniform environment for the child that will supply the continuity between households the child needs in order to feel secure. A unanimous attitude toward discipline will also make life easier for all of the parents.

> *Jo (my husband's ex) and I made an effort right from the beginning to agree on how to handle the children. We felt that it was important to be consistent with our discipline efforts otherwise the children would be confused and try to play one of us against the other. Fortunately we both hold similar opinions on how to raise children so it was easier than it might have been.*

If a united front is not possible due to ex-spouse antagonism, the second-best alternative is to establish clearly with the children and the ex the fact that it is your home, and that anybody who comes into it—even your husband's children—is expected to conform to a certain standard of behavior and nothing less is acceptable. This is sometimes a hard line to take, particularly if you do not have the full support of your mate on the issue of discipline. Don't forget, though, that most men leave the discipline problems to their wives, unless the problems are related to severe behavioral disorders. The question of discipline will primarily involve you and his ex-wife in most cases. Do not acquiesce. You have a right to discipline the children while they are in your care and you are responsible for their well-being.

When He Gives Up His Children

Many husbands have little or no contact, either voluntarily or enforced, with the children from a previous marriage except for financial reasons. This is often something that is decided at the time of the divorce, and it may have nothing to do with the second wife. Sometimes, however, it occurs only after the second wife has come onto the scene, especially if the first wife tries to restrict custody as a means of punishing her husband for marrying again. This happens too often to be ignored. In some cases it may occur after the ex-wife sees that her children are getting too affectionate with their stepmother. She may restrict custody because she feels threatened about her own relationship with her children.

There are some husbands who voluntarily give up seeing their children because either they find it too painful or they find it too difficult to deal with the constant wrangling with their ex-wives every time they go to pick up the children. And again some husbands are so adamant about having nothing to do with "her" that they sacrifice the children in the process because it is the only way to make a complete break.

My husband had regular access to his children on weekends and holidays until I came along. When she heard he was going to marry me she went to court and got an order from the judge saying that my husband could only see his children at her house and if he took them out I could not be there.

After we were married my husband's ex made it so hard for him to see the children. She wouldn't let him come in the house and would keep him standing outside in the rain for half an hour at a time when he went to pick them up, or he would go over there and she'd say she'd changed her mind, he couldn't see them that day. Once she even took the children away without telling him and he was frantic for days because he thought he'd never see them again. Finally with all the emotional strain we decided it would be best if he just didn't see them any more. It was a very hard decision to make and I wish it could have been different but really he is much more content now that he doesn't see them.

The following letter illustrates it is sometimes the attitudes and actions of the children themselves that drive husbands to give up visitation and maintaining contact.

Dear Abby:
I am a 17-year-old girl. My parents are divorced and when he left, Dad signed everything over to Mom—the house, the car and all his

properties, plus he agreed to pay support for me and her. Mom had her own career so we could probably get by without his money, but why should we?

Dad has remarried and has a family, but I don't think that should entitle him to pay us any less.

Last year I tried to help Mom get an increase in support. I went to court and gave evidence as to what I knew from visiting Dad— what he owned, how nice his apartment was, etc. Well, the judge didn't think that Dad could afford to pay us more, but Dad got stuck with the legal fees.

Dad hasn't written or asked to see me since that day in court and I don't think that's fair. I am his child too, and I figure he owes me something.

In all custody and access cases, the deciding factor with the courts is, theoretically, the welfare of the children. The custodial parent can refuse to allow access on the grounds that it is not in the child's best interest. In a recent case, wherein the mother (and custodial parent) was a staunch Roman Catholic who refused to allow the children to see their father in his home because he was living with another woman (an act she considered to be a sin and against the children's religious best interests), the judge agreed. Unfortunately, however, many other motives can be cloaked in the idea of "what is best for the children."

The right of access is generally indicated as part of the divorce agreement, and many judges prefer to allow the non-custodial parent "reasonable access." This is a way of letting the parents work it out between themselves. What frequently happens, however, is that one or both of the parents is not inclined to be reasonable, and in this case "defined access" may be indicated. Specific times and even locations for access may be determined by a court order for the noncustodial parent. It is the custodial parent in either case, however, who still holds most of the cards. That parent may be forced to allow visitation, but then there is always the possibility that the child is ill or off on a school trip at those times. This can be very frustrating for the noncustodial parent. Although it may be improper to withhold legal access to the children, the only recourse left to a noncustodial parent is to cite his or her ex-spouse for contempt of court. Since the penalty for contempt is usually a jail sentence, the courts are obviously reluctant to prosecute and convict a custodial parent. It is also improper to stop maintenance payments, if access is being denied. There really isn't much the noncustodial parent can do. Some parents with custody will go so far as to move the children geographically out of reach, making access so difficult that, while they are not breaking the law, they are making the probability of visitation highly unlikely. Whatever the case, when it comes down to it, the right of access never prevails over the right of custody.

Not all fathers are forced to give up seeing their children after a divorce, but according to University of Pennsylvania sociologist Frank Furstenberg, active paternal involvement with children by the noncustodial parent is not as prevalent as we like to think. There is no doubt that a divorce or permanent separation often leads to a complete break in the parent-child relationship. In fact Furstenberg's study of children aged eleven to sixteen showed that only 17 percent had contact with the noncustodial parent on a once-a-week basis. The longer it has been since the divorce, the less the chances of contact. Of noncustodial parents divorced ten years or longer, 64 percent had no contact with their children for at least a year. Some of this can be explained by the fact that the children do grow up and leave home to begin their own lives, but this study supports the fact that, once the father is out of the home, his contacts with his children are severely and permanently impaired.

Whatever the reasons for giving up their children, some husbands take it harder than others. It can even lead to extremes of behavior such as kidnapping. In this case the second wife often gets lost in the shuffle because the husband's desire to regain his children (or show his ex that she is not going to have the final say) is so intense that it supercedes all his other concerns.

Many second wives (and friends or family) quietly blame themselves for taking their husbands away from their children. It is important to remember that this is not true. In spite of what anyone says, you did not come between your husband and his children. That decision was made by his ex-wife and/or by him; they are responsible, not you. So, no self-recriminations.

Throwing in the Towel

While you may have approached the business of being a step-mother a little apprehensively but with the best of intentions, there may come a time when the only reasonable thing to do is to throw in the towel. In spite of all your efforts, your love, and your understanding, and no matter how hard you may have tried to find a place in his children's lives, it may very well be impossible to get them to like you, let alone love you. Their own mother may be sabotaging your efforts by demeaning you every chance she gets. You may have a natural personality conflict. After all, just because you love their father doesn't unequivocally mean that you will love his offspring, or they you. They may be so upset with their father for "leaving their mother" and breaking up their home that they will take their hate out on anything and anyone, including you. (Especially you, because by making you upset, they know that they are making their father unhappy.)

Whatever the reason, there may come a time when you just have to stop beating your head against the wall. If you've done your best and they still do not respond, then perhaps you had better turn your attentions elsewhere and get on with your life and your marriage. It may be best if you can simply stay out of the picture. Remember, however, that legally and financially the children may still be partly your responsibility.

I tried with my husband's children for years. I bit my lip many times when I should have said something only so that I wouldn't rock the boat. Finally one day I had had enough. They had been treating me like a slave and because they were my husband's

children I had put up with it for his sake. I wouldn't have put up
with that from my own children. Anyway, I just let it all out and I
told them exactly what I thought of them. Now, they don't talk to
me at all. But I feel much better about myself. So what if they
think I am the proverbial stepmother. Why should I let them push
me around more than they did their own mother just because I was
their father's second wife?

It is important to remember that "children" is an umbrella
term; it is not restricted to minors. It also refers to adult offspring who may have their own marriages and their own lives
to lead. When it is suggested that the second wife might consider "throwing in the towel," it is *not* being advocated that she
abnegate her parental responsibilities to minor children. When
a situation is being made untenable for a second wife because
of "children" who may be her own age or close to it, for her to
bow out and minimize her contact with them is not only a
valid course of action to consider, but sometimes the best one
to take for all concerned.

The second wives in the survey listed children as the thing
they argued about most with their husbands. It is not surprising. Children are a financial drain on their marriage. The
presence of children from a former marriage often prevents the
second wife from having a family of her own. They are a
constant reminder of, and constant link with, the former spouse.
They can cause considerable emotional turbulence between a
second wife and her husband.

Avoid burdening yourself with guilt. Sometimes it may be
necessary to re-arrange the amount of time the children spend
with their father or where they spend time with their father.
Some stepparent-stepchild relationships are strong and rewarding; others are just not meant to be. Remember, if your
relationship with your husband is being jeopardized by his
children, or vice versa, both spouses do not necessarily need to
be involved in parenting. When you married, likely your first
priority was to be his wife. It is not always necessary, and
sometimes impossible, to also be mother to his children.

5 Friends, Foes & Families

"My family was shocked and surprised to say the least when I told them I was going to marry a divorced man. They do not believe in divorce and cannot see how I could marry 'another woman's husband.'"   Second Wife

"Complex family groups are characteristic of tribal societies. They are the basic focal units for ritual and other social activities. In short, they provide the primary social ambience within which people live and are the chief reference points for social identity."   Frank Robert Vivelo
            Department of Social Sciences,
            University of Missouri

IN A SENSE our society could still be described as tribal. Not, perhaps, on an everyday basis, but definitely when it comes to important occasions like births and marriages, the influence and attention of family members, no matter how geographically diffuse, is still felt and sought after. These occasions are among the last vestiges of connective tissue among family groups that are now sometimes spread across continents. They provide an often needed excuse for contact with distant family members. Whether family members are across the country or just down the street, they still provide, along with friends, "the chief reference points for our social identity," as Vivelo says. When we marry or make any major life decision, the thoughts and feelings of those people who make up our primary social group will have an affect on us.

Most families and friends view marriage as a positive step. They often try to make the prospective partner feel at ease and will be loath to voice any negative opinions about the couple or their relationship, at least to those directly involved. Somehow the promise of a wedding (and babies) tends to lend a wholeness to the relationship, which satisfies the desire for stability. The fact that they may not like a particular partner or think that the couple is not well-suited does not dissuade them from issuing congratulations and best wishes at the appropriate time. Most people would admit that weddings *per se* are joyful occasions, and the institution of marriage is something that the majority of the population should seek out as a way of obtaining the most complete level of personal satisfaction in life. As such, few people think of actively interfering with a couple's desire to marry—the first time. Frequently when a man or woman marries for the second time, however, those people that comprise his or her immediate social network may exhibit behavior contrary to these patterns. The friends and families of the bride- and groom-to-be often feel that their opinions about the prospective spouses or the idea of the marriage itself should be heard even if these opinions are very negative. They may go so far as to withdraw familial contact or friendship if their thoughts on the matter are not taken in sufficient regard. The second wife, then, is walking into a potentially volatile social situation. Her family and his family will have lots to say, not to mention their respective friends, and even his ex-wife's family, who may or may not still be in the picture.

Friends

For those second wives who do not associate with the friends their husbands had with their first wives, the attitude or opinions of these people toward the second marriage is irrelevant.

But for the 76 percent of second wives who said they maintained contact with their husbands' friends from their previous marriages their feelings may prove significant.

We live in a very close-knit area. All my husband's friends from his first marriage are our friends, in fact some of them are dating his first wife.

We see a few of his friends from before but only on rare visits. I've always found they receive me very warmly and seem to understand that he got divorced and remarried. Once I got used to them and thinking about them being "her" friends I felt quite comfortable but we don't overdo visits as it puts pressure on them to take sides.

We don't see his friends from his first marriage anymore because most of them were friends because of their ethnic origin (she didn't want him to have any friends of his own). On occasion we have bumped into them and I feel a bit uncomfortable because no matter what, they still see me as "the other and much younger woman who stole him from his family."

We see his friends a lot. In fact his friends became our friends while my friends who did not approve of the marriage sort of drifted away.

The majority of second wives, 84 percent, report that they do feel comfortable with at least some of their husbands' friends from their first marriages, although their initial reaction was discomfort, awkwardness, and fear of being compared with the first wives. Many were afraid that their husbands' friends would not view them favorably. Most said they were willing to try to get along with these people if it was important to their husbands. None of the wives maintained contact with friends from the husbands' first marriages if the husbands did not express a desire to do so. When it comes to how the friends felt, or how the second wives thought they felt, 67 percent said they thought their husbands' friends liked them, 21 percent said they didn't know how their husbands' friends felt, and 8 percent said they were actively disliked by them.

It is no surprise that when a couple splits up, friends are often included as part of the spoils of the divorce. It is rare to find friends who can go on being friendly with both marital partners after a divorce. It seems that divorce creates allies and enemies; even attempting to remain neutral can be interpreted as a sign of betrayal, and no one can cross the field periodically to fight on the other side. For those friends who chose the side of the husband, accepting his new wife is a true test of their friendship. As we have seen, some will go out of their way to make her comfortable and welcome, while others take delight in bringing up the past and constantly reminding her of his former life. But friends often change as life's circumstances change; new situations, new friends is often the rule. Those people who find they cannot accept the second wife can, and most likely will, soon be succeeded by others who can accept her. Unfortunately families are another matter entirely. Families cannot be divorced. For the second wife who becomes a stepmother, there will be the feelings and opinions of relatives with which to contend, including the additional mothers- and fathers-in-law left over from the husband's previous marriage, who have more than a passing interest in the husband's children and hence in his choice of a second wife.

The Second Wife's Family

When it comes to confronting family members with the news that they are getting married, second wives generally have more with which to cope than first wives. Starting with her own family, and then his family, and finally his first wife's family, the second wife encounters many people who feel that they are entitled to an opinion about her, her wedding, her financial situation, his children, his financial situation, and on and on.

In answer to the question about how their own families felt about them becoming second wives, 52 percent of the wives said that they had a positive reaction from their families, while 37 percent said the reaction was negative. Eleven percent said it was none of their families' business.

My family felt terrible. It was a total shock for them that I would marry a divorced man with children.

My mother told me he was just using me to fool around with. She couldn't understand how I could love a divorced man with children. When we got married she refused to come to the wedding and has refused to see her grandchild since he was born.

My parents were happy that my husband loved me and wanted me as his wife and to help me raise my children. They see his children and mine as just one big family for them to love.

My family were happy for me. They believed the myth that the second wife always fares better than the first wife and that she gets everything. How wrong they were.

There were no problems really although there were several warnings to go slow and to be sure. I suppose they figured once divorced maybe twice divorced.

My family was just so thrilled that I finally got married!

They were not too happy. They wanted the best for me and I suppose that meant a first-time husband too.

My mother and my sisters, all of whom are second wives, sat me down first and filled me in on the whole situation. Then they said if you still want to go ahead at least you know what you're getting into.

I know that my mother was very disappointed because he had been married before. I think she wanted me to have a new husband not someone else's old one although I don't feel that way at all.

They worried that he would not be able to support me and that I would have to spend my hard-earned money to support him while he financed his first family. They were right.

They were concerned with my relationship with his children. They told me to stay out of "family" arguments and decisions to avoid causing disruption in my marriage. I realize now that they were right.

It seems that most families, while willing to respect that their daughters have a right to marry whom they please, would still rather that they marry men who had not been married before. There is a feeling that previously married men have too many problems and responsibilities, and that they are, in a sense, "used goods." Apparently previously married men are not what most parents think of when they say they want the best for their daughters. Even in the face of initial family disapproval, however, the second wives, more often than not, gave their relationships with their husbands precedence over the feelings of their family members even to the point of giving up their association with their families, if necessary. Mothers, more often than fathers, tended to play the most important role, either by advising their daughters what to look out for or by being the ones truly opposed to the marriage. Fathers, on the other hand, were more willing to accept previously married men as sons-in-law probably because, as men, they were more able to see themselves being in a similar position.

The Husband's Family

The majority of second wives, 82 percent, said that they felt comfortable with their husbands' families.

One of my husband's sisters has been through it all and so she understands but the rest of the family will not accept me and refuse to have anything to do with either one of us.

I get along really well with his family and his dad is especially good to me even though he is a bit of a male chauvinist. He says he's happier his son got a "better looking one, this time round."

We get along alright but I'm not bosom pals with any of them because his first wife and sister still are and I don't think they can handle two of us.

His family never did like his first wife. They treat me as though I am number one.

His family were quick to accept me and make me feel part of the family and I am very grateful for their support, especially since I met with so much resistance from his children.

His parents will not accept me but his four sisters do and they came to our wedding even when his parents would not.

I like his family very much. In fact, I am the main contact for him with them. I write all the letters and arrange all the get-togethers etc.

It seems that it is easier for the husband's family to accept the idea of his having a second wife in most cases than it is for the second wife's family to accept her being one. Perhaps it is because they have seen him suffer through an unhappy marriage and a devastating divorce and hope that this time he has found the right woman, one with whom he will be happy. There will still be those relatives, most often parents, who insist that his first wife is his only wife and refuse to accept anyone else. In most cases it is they who will be shut out of the loving relationship between the husband and his second wife by their behavior; they will be the ones missing out, not the husband and his second wife.

The First Wife's Family

There is no doubt that when a man has been married to another woman for a period of years, particularly if there are children from that marriage, there are familial bonds that have been built up between him and his first wife's family. Such relationships may not necessarily end just because the focal relationship between a husband and wife ends in divorce. Friendships and business relationships have sometimes formed, and grandparents cannot be divorced from their grandchildren, at least not emotionally. How does the second wife fit in with her husband's previous in-laws, and how many husbands continue to maintain contact with these people?

Seventy-four percent of the wives in the survey said that their husbands did not maintain contact with the families of their first wives. Of those who said, no, there was no contact, 83 percent said that personally they were indifferent to the idea of their husbands, seeing or not seeing members of the first wives' families. Of the remainder, 11 percent said they thought it was a good idea, and only 6 percent felt it was a bad idea for their husbands to break off previous relationships with the ex-wives' families. Note that the 83 percent who said they didn't care if the husbands saw their ex-in-laws may have been influenced by the fact that the husband doesn't see his ex-in-laws anyway, and, therefore, the parties involved have never had to confront the possible related problems.

Of those wives who said that their husbands did maintain contact with the first wives' families, only 55 percent thought it was a good idea, 22 percent thought it was definitely a bad idea, and another 22 percent said they were more or less indifferent.

There was never much contact between them before but even if there was I don't think I would feel that it could be a problem now.

No, we do not see them at all. He was working for his father-in-law at the time of the divorce and stayed on in the business afterwards but his father-in-law turned on him and tried to ruin his reputation with the clients and blame all the company's misfortune on him. Finally, he had to leave. I think that his father-in-law's behavior is indicative of the whole family.

His wife's uncle is his business partner so they still keep on as before. It doesn't bother me so much now, but it did in the beginning because I thought a clean break would be better for everyone, but it just wasn't possible.

Yes, he sees his mother-in-law and sister-in-law regularly as she (the mother-in-law) is a widow and depends on his advice. I agree with this completely. It isn't their fault he isn't married to their daughter anymore.

He says hello to them. Her stepfather gave us the family cottage so she won't talk to him now. We speak to her mother and brother. I know them all and I feel good about it because I know they still like my husband very much and so I feel like a winner to have him.

His former father-in-law lives in town and we see him and call him at Christmas. I think he's nice and it's good to keep in touch. You don't stop liking a person just because there is a divorce.

We never see or hear from her family although I am sure they must miss their grandchildren. I think they felt when my husband got custody that that was the end of their relationship with the children though it was more their choice than ours.

Grandparents' Rights

Although many of the wives said that they were not averse to their husbands' keeping in touch with the first wives' families, it seems that divorce is the natural parting of the ways for the husbands and their former in-laws in the majority of cases. This raises the question of grandparents' rights, an issue which is becoming more and more prominent as the number of grandparents (about 70 percent of U.S. senior citizens have grandchildren) who are severed from their grandchildren, often on a permanent basis, rises along with the divorce rate.

Where do grandparents stand? The fact is that they are still part of the child's biological family even after the child's parents are divorced. One set of grandparents invariably loses out, however, when it comes to a close and continuing relationship with their grandchildren—the parents of the noncustodial spouse. In the 20 percent of the cases where the husband does get custody, his second wife will have to face the first wife's parents who want to see their grandchildren. For the second wife, the issue of grandparents' rights can raise particular problems. How much contact and under what circumstances should children in her care have access to their mother's parents? Will a continuing close association with these grandparents be good for the child, or will it prevent a healthy bond from forming between the child and the second wife?

There are currently grandparents' rights associations springing up across North America, intent upon lobbying for the right of grandparents to continue to have access to their children's children in the event of death or divorce. Legislation was introduced into the U.S. Senate this year in the form of the Grandparent Visitation Act, which would provide for grandparents to be able to petition their state courts for visitation privileges. There is, at the moment, considerable confusion about the status of grandparents' rights because the only comprehensive U.S. federal legislation concerning the subject of custody and visitation is the Uniform Marriage and Divorce Act. This act, while it does not mention grandparents specifically, has, on occasion, been used to authorize such visits in the absence of any specific statutes. In Canada such judgments vary from province to province.

Some grandparents' rights groups can unfortunately create a self-fulfilling prophecy when they espouse points of view such as the following which appeared in a piece of promotion literature from the Grandparents' Rights Association:

Grandparents are ignored by the judiciary. Parents lose their children and grandparents are not allowed to adopt, have custody or even visit. The worst circumstance is adoption by step-parents. Many state laws prohibit grandparent visitation after adoption. Maybe we should rise up as a body and start disapproving the marriages.

Needless to say, a second wife faced with this attitude on the part of her husband's ex-in-laws would likely request that these people stay out of her home. It is evident that such attitudes can only breed serious rifts in her relationships with her step-children and in her marriage.

Another question a second wife must ask herself is: will her own parents accept his children from his first marriage and are they willing to take on the role of grandparent to another woman's children? The situation obviously can get very complicated when, under optimal circumstances, there can be four sets of grandparents, all with different affiliations to different children, depending on whether the second wife had children from a previous marriage, whether her husband did, and whether they have a child from their current marriage. Individual circumstances will dictate just what the second wife will have to deal with when it comes to the issue of grandparents. In some cases the problems will be few, and everyone will manage to get along and accommodate all necessary visiting rights. In others it is just the opposite. Lately, more and more grandparents on either side say that their rights are being denied because this or that parent has moved to a different area and married again and doesn't want any more contact with them.

It is easy to see that when a woman becomes a second wife there are a lot more family members waiting in the wings than there are for a first wife. If a second wife's nuclear family is bigger as a result of her marriage, then her extended family is larger exponentially. In many cases, for the second wife, it is a question of accepting the whole package. Other couples handle the situation differently and some opt out completely from old family ties and friends in order to carve out a new life together. This may sound extreme, but some people cannot deal with the situation any other way. That is why you find so many husbands and their second wives moving to another city, or at least wanting to, just so they can begin at the beginning without all these other people in their lives. The important thing to remember is that although you have some responsibility, especially to family members, the most important thing is your relationship with your husband.

Foes

Last but not least, when it comes to what a second wife can expect to inherit in the way of people from her husband's first marriage, are the foes. "Foes" is a bit of an old-fashioned word, but "enemies" may be too strong. Foes are people who don't like you and go out of their way to let you know it, people who are responsible for persistent aggravations. Foes are people who will become your enemies because they were his first wife's enemies, or they may become your enemies because they were her friends.

We live in a small city where there is not a lot of good shopping. You know what I mean, one good place to buy dishes, one good place to buy furniture, etc. So, when we first got married I wanted to go out and buy some things for our home to start our life together with our own things especially since neither one of us ended up with much from our previous marriages. Anyway, I told my husband what I wanted to do and he said, "Well I wouldn't go here and I don't think you should go there, etc." The reason for all this being that his first wife had bought a lot of china and linen and glassware after they separated and told the stores to send him the bills. Which they did. He just couldn't pay them and so of course they are not about to let him (or his wife—me) buy anything else until he does. They are still calling up and demanding payment for things I have never seen and even though we could afford to pay them a little bit every month I refuse to pay for dishes and things that she is using. I didn't realize that when I got married her bad debts would somehow be transfered to me.

There are the second wives who are on the receiving end of torrents of feelings, most of it negative, from people who feel they are entitled to an opinion on the situation although they are not friends of the couple involved. More often than not, they were friends of the first wife, or club members, or old girlfriends from school. None of them will ever forgive him, and certainly not you, for what's been done to that "wonderful woman."

In my case, I wanted to join the local ladies' fitness and social club and as it happens it was the same one (there is only one good one in our town) that she belonged to before the divorce (she is now remarried and living in another state). Anyway some of her old buddies were still there and they singled me out on the first day. I couldn't believe it when they asked me how it felt to break up a perfect marriage. If only they knew. Anyway, from then on I got a heavy dose of the cold shoulder from their little group. It's O.K. by me, but I still feel that it's none of their business.

My husband's ex-wife was always a little weird (his words). I think she got one foot stuck in the sixties because she still dressed and acted like a hippie. After they got divorced she took up with all sorts of odd people and started acting like a teenager again, hanging around rock clubs and smoking dope. She met a guy, a musician, during this time who was heavily into drugs and as it turns out gay and a borderline alcoholic as well. She married him about a year ago and both of them have really gone down hill since then. I think in a way she married the worst possible person she could find as a way of getting back at my husband for divorcing her. But, people who knew her when she was married still stop me on the street sometimes to ask me if I am pleased that I have driven her to such depths. I tell them that it's nothing to do with me. We all make our own choices but I know there are a lot of people out there who blame me for what happened to her and who hate me for it.

Friends, family, and enemies, too, make up our social milieu; as such, their feelings about us and the way we live our lives have an affect on us. Second wives are either loved or hated, welcomed or ignored, depending on any given person's opinion of the new marriage. The important thing to remember is that these judgments are based on a second wife's placing in a marriage, not her worth as an individual. Those who are interested in knowing her as a person will give her a chance. Those who are interested in proving to her husband that he has made a mistake will never give her a break. They are best ignored.

6 Sex and the Second Wife

"I never realized what I was missing before!"
Second Wife

GOOD SEX MAY not make a bad marriage better but bad sex is the major reason that men give for straying from their first marriages, sometimes all the way to the divorce courts. That is why sex in the second marriage is so important. Second wives have the image of being promiscuous women who hunt down other women's husbands, using sex as the weapon. This is quite the opposite of the truth, as has been mentioned before. The truth is that the great majority of second wives and their husbands report that they are very happy sexually in their second marriages, perhaps more so than in any previous relationships.

This chapter has been included so that we can examine the reasons for this sexual satisfaction. What is it about being a second wife, or having a second wife, that leads almost invariably to a contented sex life? Are second wives more faithful than first wives? Are their husbands? What about the harem syndrome, and does your husband have a sexual hangover? All these areas will be dealt with in this chapter. There is one more subject related to sex that must be discussed under the heading "sex and the second wife." It is directly related to the second wife and to the sex life of the family as a whole, as well as to that of the individual marital partners. It is incest.

95

Sexual Fidelity and the Second Marriage

Sexual fidelity is more likely in the second marriage due to increased experience, greater sexual knowledge, and the desire not to "risk" jeopardizing the second chance by being sexually promiscuous outside the marriage. Whereas in the general population there is a rise in infidelity as the marriage partners grow older, there is a decrease in infidelity in the same age group if they are married for the second time. For the general population infidelity peaks for women between the ages of thirty-five and sixty, during which time 69.2 percent report having had extramarital experiences, and for men between the ages of thirty and fifty-four, during which time 48.9 percent indicate that they engaged in affairs outside marriages. It is precisely at these ages that most people marry for the second time and report that they have not had, nor are they interested in having, extramarital liaisons. This is, as we will see, the case for both husbands and wives.

One can speculate, perhaps, while their contemporaries, who are still engaged in their first marriages, are beginning to experience the so-called mid-life crisis and desire change, those involved in second marriages are just at the point in their lives where much is new in their sexual lives and marital relationships. They have just committed themselves to life with a different partner and are not as likely to look elsewhere.

Satisfaction and the Second Wife

Sexual satisfaction in any relationship is a combination of experience and the genuine desire for one person to please the other. It comes as no surprise, therefore, to find out that 86 percent of second wives found their sex lives to be satisfying. Compare this with the percentage for women in general: In a recent survey conducted by *Cosmopolitan* magazine only 46.1 percent of the women respondents said their sex lives were satisfactory. What, then, makes second wives so sexually content?

Yes, I would say our sex life is very satisfying. My husband appreciates me as a sexual person. We are never bored with each other.

Our sex life was very good until recently but I think that my husband prefers to please himself, as in his first marriage, so things are slipping a bit.

I'm very happy. We both try to please each other, although I would say that he tries harder to please me than I do him.

It's great! We seem to sense each other's needs and try to satisfy them.

Very satisfying. He is always attuned to my needs. He's a warm and loving man who isn't afraid of my affections. He's great.

Our sex life could be more active but we work at making it good constantly.

Most of the time everything is just fine although I think that unmarried men seem to be more considerate during and after sex. My husband doesn't spend as much time as he could on that part of it. I think perhaps that he's been married (first and second times) so long that he's a bit jaded.

Our sex life is very satisfying. I think it is up to the couple to decide and discuss what they both need and what they want in a lover.

I couldn't ask for more. I never realized what I was missing before!

Yes, and its getting better all the time. He definitely tries hard to please me sexually and I love him for that. I'm very happy with our physical relationship.

Many wives, when talking about their own sexual satisfaction, mentioned that they felt their husbands "tried harder" to please them and were generally more caring and affectionate toward them. More husbands also were willing to discuss what pleased their wives, and much of the embarrassment about sex, which often clouds younger relationships, were gone by the time the second wives came along. With better communication between the husbands and wives and more willingness to talk and experiment with different sexual techniques, is it any wonder that second wives say they are more satisfied?

Aside from the husband's improved attitude toward sex, the second wife can also take advantage of his physical maturity. Older husbands, while they may be slower to arouse, are not as likely to reach climax as quickly, and, therefore, this allows the time necessary for their wives to become aroused too. Older husbands also are less likely to place the entire emphasis on the sex act itself, but rather, they appreciate the added pleasures of foreplay and of cuddling and talking before, during, and after, which often adds greatly to the feeling of closeness that many women need, but often fail to get.

As one gets older, expectations about sex and its place in a relationship change. Women know what to expect from sex and from their partners by the time they reach their thirties. They know themselves better and are more aware of their own needs, which allows them to be more comfortable with sex. In addition, since woman are supposed to reach their sexual peak in their early thirties, many second wives are at that point in their lives when they are, theoretically, more ready and able to enjoy their sex lives. They are also more likely to be mature enough to recognize that just because the initial sexual flush of a relationship wears off, it doesn't necessarily mean that love has gone out the window. This is a normal occurrence in the progress of a relationship, one which should give way to a deeper and more lasting bond between the couple. If women in their thirties (those who are becoming second wives in ever-increasing numbers) have been married before, they may have already had their children. Birth control and procreation are not as likely, then, to play as much havoc with their sex lives as they might in the lives of their younger contemporaries.

All in all, it appears that second wives can count on having more fulfilling sex lives with their partners than first wives. They are older, wiser, and, like their husbands, probably more likely to handle all aspects of their marriage with kid gloves because experience has taught them its value. Not only is sex within the marriage reported to be more satisfying for the second wife, but sex outside of the marriage, which is on the rise for women in general, is less prevalent among second wives.

Infidelity

Infidelity and the Second Wife

Infidelity has diverse meanings because there are more ways to be unfaithful to someone than simply by having sex outside of marriage. Our definition of infidelity is more akin to the idea of adultery, but without the negative overtones that religious and legal institutions ascribe to it. For the purposes of this book, it will be as defined as the existence of a sexual relationship outside of either a marriage or a long-term commitment to live together.

While some cultures still punish infidelity harshly, especially for women, ours has seen a considerable increase in the incidence of sexual relationships outside of marriage over the last four decades among both men and women. This phenomenon is due largely to two things, both of which relate directly to women. Improved methods of birth control allow women to enjoy sex more (and have more sex) without the fear of unwanted pregnancy. The development of a more permissive attitude toward sex generally in society has allowed women to acknowledge their sexual needs and desires. Sex is no longer only a man's game. With the birth of a female sexual identity, it is not surprising that the bonds of a relationship, which were sufficient to constrain the female partner in the past, are loosening, and women are looking for sexual partners outside of marriage. The philosophy of the sexually active singles lifestyle, which has developed over the last two decades in particular, is now spilling over into the married lifestyle, and results in more people of both sexes seeking sexual liaisons outside of their marriages.

Recent studies show that 54 percent of married women have had one or more sexual experiences outside their marriages as have 47 percent of married men. The statistics on infidelity have not changed much for men in the last thirty years (Kinsey found that approximately half the men in his famous study had extramarital affairs), but they have more than doubled for women. Kinsey found that only 25 percent of the women in his study had had extramarital liaisons. These figures represent the behavior of the male and female population in general. They are not representative of the behavior of second wives and their husbands, as we shall see.

Our study showed that 75 percent of second wives had not had or considered having an affair outside their marriages. In answer to the question: Since your marriage have you ever considered having an affair? Why? these are typical of the responses given.

No. And that surprises me because that is what destroyed my first marriage. I am very satisfied here.

The idea only enters my head when some guy puts the move on me. My husband and I didn't exchange rings and this sometimes creates a problem. I've never seriously considered an affair. I'm happy now and would be crazy to pursue an extramarital affair. Yuck!

I have considered it but never done it but not because there is anything wrong with our marriage. I don't want to mess it up but having an affair would make me feel alive.

No. I wouldn't even think of it. I'm perfectly satisfied.

Sometimes when I think of all the problems we have had (money, kids, etc.) I feel like finding someone else and starting over. It would be so nice. I don't think I could do it though.

No, I have regretted the marriage at times but know that he would be lost without me and I couldn't build my happiness on his unhappiness.

No! I don't need another man to complicate my life!

Some of the wives, of course, did say yes.

Yes! Because I have needs that are not being fulfilled sexually, etc. I want to be desired, to feel like a woman. He's much too shy and straightlaced. So very traditional. Twice in four months is not enough for me. It may have been for his first wife.

Yes. Definitely. I feel I am being taken for granted. There doesn't seem to be any spark left. Everything is so routine.

Yes. My husband is not always there when I need him.

I do. I feel the need to have someone else in my life the way he has his first wife. Their relationship is not sexual but they have a closeness from being parents and shared experience that we lack in our relationship. I would like someone to pay attention to me the way he pays attention to her and their kids.

There seem to be two separate schools of thought here. On the one hand we have the second wives who are faithful talking about the "risk" factor of having an affair and how it is not worth taking the chance of breaking up their marriages. On the other hand there are those second wives who feel that their needs, whether sexual or otherwise, are just not being met by their current marriages and who feel the need to express their discontent or seek fulfillment outside the marriage. How do their husbands feel about infidelity?

Infidelity and the Husband

Of the second wives surveyed, 73 percent said their husbands, to their knowledge, had not had nor considered having an affair since they had been married for the second time.

> *No, I think he has found the happiness and security he was looking for with me.*

> *No, he has not and would not consider it. He is very conservative and traditional.*

> *No. I am sure he would not. He was faithful to his first wife, too.*

There were husbands, however, who did.

> *He dated one girl and tried to have an affair but he couldn't carry it off. Too much guilt, I suppose.*

> *I think he probably has. Men need to fantasize and have more different experiences than women.*

> *Yes, he had an affair with his ex-wife.*

> *I think he probably has. He's human after all.*

Infidelity and the First Wife

In spite of the fact that the majority of second wives felt that their husbands had been faithful to them and would continue to be so, many were aware that their husbands had been unfaithful to their first wives. Forty-three percent said that their husbands had had at least one affair while married to their first wives. This is convergent with the figures for the married male population in general.

Why would husbands tend to be more faithful to their second wives than their first? A recent study by Anthony Pietropinto, M.D., and Jacqueline Simenauer about male sexuality *(Beyond the Male Myth)* showed that men admitted what would most likely cause them to stray into extramarital relationships were, in descending order: poor sex at home, 26.7 percent; exceptionally attractive woman, 24.8 percent; fighting at home, 18.4 percent; and finding a woman who understands them better, 10.8 percent. Since 56 percent of the second wives said that their husbands had not been sexually satisfied in their first marriages, and, moreover, 80 percent said that their husbands enjoyed sex more with them than with their first wives, it is perhaps understandable why more men would be faithful to their second wives than their first.

Aside from the fact that he used to go to hookers occasionally, I suppose you could say he was faithful to his first wife.

He was faithful to his first wife for a while at the beginning of his marriage out of duty more than anything, but it did not last and he had several affairs.

My husband was faithful to his first wife and he has been faithful to me. In fact, when we first met it was difficult for him to adjust and "unmarry" himself from her to begin a new sexual relationship.

I think my husband was sexually satisfied in his first marriage more out of ignorance than anything else. He didn't know how much better things could be, but weren't we all like that the first time round? If you asked him today he would probably say that he wasn't sexually satisfied in his first marriage because now he knows better.

I know he wasn't sexually satisfied in his first marriage because he says his first wife used to think sex was a chore and he jokes about it being every Saturday night whether he wanted it or not. He couldn't afford to miss the opportunity. It's different with us. We both enjoy sex and he knows I want him whenever he's ready.

There is much care and love in our relationship plus maturity and experience. He did not have a good sex life with his first wife. She was too young and had children right from the beginning of their marriage.

I know he is happier because we both like a lot of sex. To his first wife it was just something a woman had to do to hold a man and to have babies. Sex was not for recreation.

My husband says his first wife wasn't much good at sex and that was why he ran around on her since shortly after their marriage. He always tells me that I turn him on. I guess that's why he was faithful to me and was not to her.

It would seem that a "better" sex life is what keeps a husband faithful to his second wife; but better is a very subjective term. Perhaps it is not so much that the sex itself is any better *per se*, but rather, that the partners themselves are better at it. Sex is one of those things that does improve with additional experience, not to mention that an attitude tempered by maturity may be the real reason that sex in a second marriage is "better" than it was in the first. There are other aspects as well. If both a husband and wife have been married before, there is often a need to make up for past mistakes. They have learned from their previous marriages what to do and what not to do. Sex in youthful marriages is often expressed as a selfish need (particularly by the inexperienced male) and the desire for self-gratification is paramount. Unfortunately this often leads to a never-ending circle of selfish-husband-frustrated-wife-cold-wife-frustrated-husband. Fortunately by the time they are married for the second time most men (and women) have had enough sexual experiences to know how to please their partners and themselves. They understand the importance of a healthy sex life in a marriage and are more apt to take the time and effort to ensure that this is true of their marriages.

Infidelity: The Harem Syndrome

There is one aspect of sexual infidelity that is peculiar to second marriages of which a second wife should be aware. Nearly 10 percent of the second wives in the survey said that their husbands had been unfaithful to them with their first wives. This can be a more shocking revelation than finding out a husband was having an affair with a stranger. The reason is quite simple. There is inevitably a sense of competition between the second wife and the first, particularly in the beginning of the marriage. Because the second wife may often feel that the first wife may try to lure the husband back, the existence of a sexual bond between the old partners is a tangible threat to the marriage. It signals the husband who has not truly "left" his first wife. If the husband has been seeing a stranger, the second wife can always rationalize, "I am his wife and he will come back to me, to our home and to our life," but, if he is seeing his first wife, his second wife can only think, "I am his wife—but so was she!"

Why do men who leave their first wives still seek out a sexual relationship with them after they have remarried? Part of the reason is the harem syndrome, of which we have already spoken. Unfortunately for these men, our society does not permit a man to have more than one wife (legally) at a time. Some men manage to circumvent these regulations, however, by remarrying while keeping their previous wives available. As well as ego satisfaction there is the consideration of male territorial imperative which must be taken into account under these circumstances. Some men honestly feel that once a woman has been to bed with them, she becomes their property. (This attitude does not seem to apply in reverse.) When men like this marry for the second time, they truly feel that their first wives are still their territory. Others convince themselves that it's not like doing it with a stranger, a more sophisticated example of the same territorial imperative.

There are compassionate ex-husbands who rationalize that their first wives are all alone and have no one else but them, but beneath this, the result is the same. The husband runs both households and presumably both women's lives. It is a convenient way of maintaining control.

Of less concern, perhaps, are the 'for-old-times'-sake' husbands who like to insist that they are unfaithful with their first wives for nostalgic reasons. There was a small but significant number of reports of this type of behavior in the survey. Husbands who found themselves in a familiar city or social environment in the company of the ex-wives (for a child's wedding, for instance), sometimes allowed themselves to revert to their old relationships for a few hours. In these cases the second wives involved tended to be less troubled and more understanding. These cases were easier to deal with, perhaps, because the encounter usually represented a one-time occurrence, not an on-going threat to the second marriage.

In each case these men and women are not simply hurting the second wives involved, in fact, the damage done may be greater to the first wives. The husband's continued presence prevents a first wife from starting again and creating new relationships. This is often the intention, although it may be a subconscious one. The potential second wife would be well advised to take note, at the beginning of a serious relationship with a divorced man, of just how close he seems to be to his first wife. If he is still involved with her (in any way, not just sexual) the astute woman will not be hardpressed to detect his feelings. His conversation and his behavior will give him away. Does he refer to her regularly? Are they in frequent or daily contact? Are they still "friends," do they socialize? In a sense a continuing involvement with the first wife is much easier to detect than an affair with a stranger, because the second wife is already aware of the first wife's presence and should be equally aware of the possibilities for intimate involvement. Do not be naive enough to expect that, just because they are divorced, all contact of a physical nature is necessarily over. If you do suspect something is going on between them, take action.

For the second wife a husband's infidelity has different implications than it did for his first wife, as many second wives will admit. While a first wife may convince herself that it is just a passing fling (or one of many passing flings), a second wife knows that her husband has already left one wife. While the first wife may choose to believe that he will come home again after he gets it out of his system and that he would never leave them (the kids, the house, the car, etc.), the second wife knows he has done so in the past.

This is not to say that, once a man has been unfaithful to one woman, he will go on being unfaithful to other women in the future. Infidelity, for most men, is the result of a particular set of circumstances, not a predetermined behavioral pattern. The thought that their husbands are capable, based on their knowledge that they have been unfaithful to their first wives, may cross the minds of second wives, but they also know that their husbands are less likely to be unfaithful to them. Most men are not prepared to risk their second chance at marriage for the sake of a passing fling. They do not have the emotional or financial reserve to go through the breakup of a marriage again. Also, their more mature attitude toward sex places it in its proper perspective relative to the value they place on their relationships with their wives. If you want to look at it another way, a man who has an ex-wife, a second wife, and possibly two sets of children really has very little time to fool around. Whatever the reasons, the second wife can be secure in the knowledge that her husband is much more likely to remain faithful to her than to his first wife.

Is There a Sexual Hangover?

In order to find out if their husbands' past experiences, particularly their past married experiences with sex, had had any effect on their current sexual behavior, we asked the second wives if they thought their husbands' first marriages had contributed significantly to the shaping of their sexual habits. The responses were almost evenly divided, with 41 percent of the wives saying yes and 46 percent saying no. The remainder said they had no idea or had never really thought about it.

> *I think his first marriage did affect his attitude because he is more appreciative of me as a sexual person because she wasn't much of one.*

Yes. Their sexual problems led to his being more aware of how to please me and how to take care of a woman's needs.

I'm sure that after thirteen years it must have had some effect on the way he sees himself as a sexual person.

Yes, from his first marriage he developed a desire to love and be loved. He was ready when we married to give and to receive.

His first marriage left him feeling very restricted and we had to work at making him feel more free and able to express himself sexually.

Yes, his first wife was very submissive sexually and I think he thought I should be that way too, although it is not my nature.

He was very disappointed with sex in his first marriage and so he didn't put much effort into it with me until he realized how different it could be.

Yes, she totally complied with everything he wanted and I think that made him very selfish sexually. He does not know how to give and take.

There were, of course, wives who felt that their husbands' former marriages did not contribute to their later sexual behavior.

No. He knew all about sex long before he married her but I do believe that he was never compatible with anyone before me.

It had no effect at all. He was a stupid lover then. He is a stupid lover now.

For those second wives who felt that a husband's experience with sex in his first marriage did have an effect on his approach to sex in his second marriage, the opinions were divided as to whether or not this experience was beneficial. Husbands who had a good sexual experience the first time 'round came to their second marriages with positive attitudes toward sex. While free of the youthful limitations of their first relationships, they were replete with a rewarding sexual maturity that benefited their second marriages. Many of the husbands who did not enjoy fulfilling sex lives with their first wives were so happy to experience this with their second wives that they used their skill in addition to their renewed enthusiasm to create a close and satisfying sexual bond with their second wives. There were, of course, second wives who felt that their husbands brought negative habits or attitudes about sex into their new marriages. For these women, it was necessary to work harder at achieving compatible sex lives than if they had married men who had not been previously married, but they were far fewer in number.

Incest

You may wonder why I chose to include a section on incest in this chapter. Most people shy away from talking or even think-ing about incest. It is, after all, our oldest and most deeply ingrained sexual taboo. Most societies shun incest and those who commit it when they are discovered. For this reason most people prefer not to discover it when it is going on in their own homes. It is estimated that 75 percent to 90 percent of child molestation within the family is never discovered, and even when it is, it is often hushed up and smoothed over for the sake of keeping the family together.

For the second wife incest is a problem of growing concern. Women with children, who are about to become second wives or who already are and may have suspicions that something is going on in their families between their children and their husbands, must be aware that they and their families are in a particularly high-risk group. It is also necessary for them to know that they are not alone. Incest is a problem that thou-sands of second wives have to face and it is going to grow as more and more women remarry.

No questions on the subject of incest were included in the questionnaire for *Second Wife, Second Best?* because it was felt that most of the respondents would probably be unaware of the problem or at least unwilling to admit to themselves or others that it existed in their own families. The information presented here, then, is based on studies done by researchers who have investigated this area of family life.

What is Incest?

Legal definitions of incest vary considerably from place to place and often do not include sexual activity between stepparents and children beyond a certain age. For instance, in English law, intercourse between a man and his stepdaughter is described not as incest but as "unlawful sexual intercourse," and even then applies only if the daughter is under sixteen years of age. Research in the field of child abuse often classifies incest as "sexual activity involving genital contact between people too closely related to marry." This definition, however, does not necessarily cover the behavior that can go on between stepparents and their stepchildren. For our purposes incest is defined as "sexual contact of any sort (intercourse or otherwise) with a child or children of either sex by a member of the child's family, either with or without the consent of the child." The question of blood ties is not a part of this definition for the simple reason that an act of incest by a stepparent who is acting as the child's regular parental figure is just as damaging and traumatic for the child as an act of incest with its biological parent.

The Incidence of Incest

Most of us tend to think that incest is quite rare these days except among certain backward and isolated groups. We also have a preconceived notion that incest is a lower-class aberration, that is, closely linked with limited intelligence and poverty. This is not true. Incest is with us in every facet of our society, at every educational, economic, religious, and social level.

Although actual figures on the incidence of incest have been difficult to ascertain in the past, in the last few years researchers have begun to isolate statistics on cases of sexual abuse of children from general child-abuse data. Part of the problem is that, until recently, there has been little effort to break down these statistics into family and non-family members and even less to compare the frequency of incidence in natural fathers to that in stepfathers. Now, however, the issue is beginning to receive the attention it deserves.

Since many researchers use the terms "child abuse," "child sexual abuse," and, less frequently, "incest," almost interchangeably in reporting their findings, the following figures will be given using the researchers' own terminology. The American National Center for Child Abuse and Neglect in Washington estimates that the annual national incidence of child abuse is between 60,000 and 100,000 *reported* cases. The American Humane Association in New York estimated a total of 200,000 to 300,000 cases of female-child molestation alone (including unreported cases) annually. Of these, at least 5,000 were estimated to be father/daughter incest. A more recent study done in 1978 on the subject of incest found that 16,000 new cases of father/daughter incest occur each year. As recently as 1983, a study made in Toronto, which was prepared for a special committee on child abuse, found that one out of every four girls, and one out of every ten boys, will be sexually molested during childhood—mostly by their parents, relatives, and family friends.

A study by Herbert Maisch, one of the foremost researchers in this field, found that 90 percent of the offenders were fathers or stepfathers. Evidence, so far, seems to suggest that children of both sexes (it is becoming more frequent to find that a father who assaults his daughter sexually will also assault his son sexually) are more at risk from stepfathers than from their natural fathers. David Finkelnor of the Department of Sociology and Anthropology at the University of New Hampshire, another noted researcher in the area of child abuse, in a study published in 1981 found that a stepfather was five times more likely to sexually victimize his stepdaughter than was a natural father. Other researchers have commented that it is not unusual for some men to choose women with teenagers or young children for the express purpose of seducing those children. If they succeed, sexual interest in their wives usually disappears, as it was the children who really interested them in the first place.

Studies have shown that sexual abuse of male children by fathers or stepfathers has a much lower incidence. In a study done in 1978 of 266 male college students, only four participants reported having had incestuous experiences with family members, usually with adult males. Variations of incest beyond father/daughter or stepfather/daughter incest, then, are rare. Sibling incest and mother/son incest are more prevalent than father/son or stepfather/son incest, accounting for 13 percent and 4 percent of reported cases respectively.

It is clear, then, that incest is a problem usually associated with adult males and young females and is likely to be more common between stepfathers and daughters than in any other combination of parent, stepparent, and child. The mean age of the female victim is approximately 10.2 years, which tends to suggest that, Nabokov's *Lolita* notwithstanding, incest is usually a male-instigated activity rather than the seduction of an adult by a promiscuous teenager. The reasons postulated for this behavior run the gamut from the sexually repressed and emotionally immature male who cannot relate comfortably to a woman his own age, to the cold and distant wife who is only too happy to abnegate her sexual responsibilities in favor of her daughter while still keeping her husband in the home. There are many theories on the treatment of incest, some focusing on the individual, and some on the family as a whole. It is not the intent of this book to delve more deeply into the subject except to note that it would seem that in many cases, the husband is allowed to continue his activities with one or more of the children and that the wife is usually aware of what is happening (although she may try to deny it to herself, perhaps for fear of losing her relationship with her husband or out of economic necessity) but prefers not to acknowledge it. The children, too, often become silent participants. They may be afraid of punishment, or they may be so young that they may think that such behavior is the normal course of events, despite their own unhappiness.

It is unlikely that incidents of incest are limited to just one or two occasions. Once the behavior has started, it tends to continue for years, usually until the child involved is grown and leaves home. Even then the father or stepfather may turn to younger members of the family to take the place of a child who has left. Incest is not uncommon in our society. Studies show that one out of every one hundred women has had a sexual experience with her father or stepfather. That is only the tip of the iceberg. Second wives are more affected by this problem because the proximity of an "unrelated" female child in the household allows those so inclined to convince themselves that it's not really incest because they are not related by blood. The incest taboo breaks down under this reasoning and the taboo against pedophilia seems to be relaxing as young girls are held up as objects of sexual interest in advertising and throughout the media.

Is incest between stepfathers and daughters on the rise? Researchers have acknowledged that, yes, incest is a much more widespread problem than we have previously acknowledged. They also are beginning to give greater consideration to the phenomenon of stepfather incest because, with the rising divorce and remarriage rate, it is becoming increasingly prevalent. In a recent survey on sex and women in the 1980s, *Cosmopolitan* magazine reported that the majority of letters received on the subject of incest involved young girls and their mothers' new husbands. One fourteen-year-old respondent, who was molested by her stepfather-to-be from the age of six, said, "I never wanted to tell her [the mother] about Sam. She loves her new husband and I do not wish to make her feel alone again."

In a similar case an eighteen-year-old girl was molested sexually from the time she was twelve by her stepfather. When she announced she intended to get married, her stepfather told her mother about the relationship "to get even" for the desertion. They were divorced, and the girl is permanently scarred by the sexual abuse and the feelings of guilt she has about being "responsible" for breaking up her mother's marriage. This letter to Dear Abby typifies the dilemma.

> *Dear Abby:*
>
> *For a 27-year-old woman, I've been through a lot. I attempted suicide three times and was institutionalized twice because I was so filled with guilt and self-loathing I didn't think I deserved to live. I am now recovering with the help of a therapist who has helped me realize that I was the victim.*
>
> *My problems began when I was sexually abused by my stepfather from the time I was 8 until I was 14. I never told anyone until my younger sister became pregnant by him when she was 13. Because of her testimony and mine, Dad was sent to prison for seven years. My mother divorced him.*
>
> *I just learned that he is out on parole and going to marry a young widow with two small daughters. I don't know if she knows about Dad's record but if she doesn't and he molests her little girls I would never forgive myself for not warning her. Should I be the one to tell her?*

Conservatively speaking, according to Finkelnor, over one million American women have been molested sexually by their fathers or stepfathers and approximately 16,000 cases occur each year. In 40 percent of these cases, the offense was not a one-time occurrence. Fifty-five percent involved the use of force.

These facts are not intended to be alarmist or sensational. They are intended to bring to light a situation of which the second wife, in particular, must be aware because her children are more likely to be victims of incest than the children of a first wife.

7 Feelings and the Second Wife

"Though we all disguise our feelings pretty well,
What we mean by 'Very good', is 'Go to hell'."
                                        Noel Coward

THERE ARE FEW situations in life that can evoke the flood of feelings that marriage does. Most of us marry for a variety of reasons, not least among which is the desire to love and be loved and to find happiness and fulfillment with another human being. These feelings are a part of life's rewards, and in our culture particularly, where we choose our own mates, most of us expect our fair share of the wonderful feelings that are supposed to accompany being in love and getting married. Second wives are no exceptions.

It became clear, talking to the women involved in the survey, however, that there were other emotions at work for the second wife besides love, happiness, and contentment. While we all experience unpleasant emotions in our lives, most of us, at least in the carefree, early days of marriage, are not ready for these "bad" feelings. Unfortunately many second wives have to deal with more than their share of anger, jealousy, resentment, and guilt. Most are totally unprepared, and more than a little ashamed, that they have these unpleasant feelings intruding on their expected happiness.

Feelings such as these can be overwhelming to the second

115

wife because they catch her at a most vulnerable time—the beginning of her marriage—when her life is in a state of change and she is trying to adjust to it. Unless she is prepared to face up to them, they can work to undermine her marriage. This is not to say that all second wives experience this, but many reported that they passed through a stage in their early married lives where these emotions did indeed prove to be a problem. We all have preconceived ideas about negative feelings; we are often taught to suppress these feelings in childhood. Second wives, too, carry the burdens of their early learning with them into their adult relationships; hence, they are prejudiced against these emotions from the start. This does not help them to deal with these feelings when they occur. Aside from being an uncomfortable psychological state, it is also socially unacceptable to display jealousy, anger, and/or resentment, particularly for women.

Second wives, often more than other women, are convinced that they should not have feelings like this, either because many of them have gone through so much to marry their husbands (his messy divorce, her messy divorce, or the death of a spouse). They feel somehow their achievement of the marital state should not be fraught with any more anxiety, or they believe society's point of view that being second is not really as good as being first, and hence, they have to try harder and not complain if things don't go just as they planned.

It is not difficult to see that when these emotions surface all the rationalizing in the world will not stop them. It is very important for second wives, and women in general, to be comfortable with the idea that, yes, these are my feelings, whether others think they are right or wrong. This is very seldom the case and, more often than not, we do silent battle with ourselves in trying to deal with our emotions, while at the same time pretending to others that everything is just fine.

Anger

Of all the emotions discussed by the second wives in the survey, none was so strongly felt, nor so strongly denied (at least in the beginning), as anger. More wives admitted to feelings of anger than any of the other frequently felt negative emotions. Not only were they angry at their individual circumstances, they were also afraid of the anger itself and its possible consequences.

Exhibiting anger is one of the biggest taboos our society establishes for women. It is most definitely *not* a desirable feminine characteristic, and as such, it is something that society tries very hard to discourage in its female members. The old saying "hell hath no fury…" illustrates this attempt to keep the burgeoning tide of female hostility at bay. Society makes it abundantly clear to us from childhood that expression of anger is unattractive in little girls or big ones. Should a genuine expression of anger occasionally find its way to the surface, it is often indulgently explained away, by men and women alike, as being a consequence of Mother Nature's monthly cycle or the hallmark of impending hysteria. Anger today, like sexuality in the Victorian era, is simply not something that a lady is expected to express.

Living with this anti-anger cultural baggage is all right — if you don't happen to be the one who is angry. In this circumstance — that is, when you are not the angry party — you too may be in favor of censoring expressions of anger; after all, it does rock the collective boat. But when we don't confront anger and instead keep doggedly trying to ignore it, or hide it, or call it something else, we perpetuate an already bad situation. Many of the wives in the survey who freely admitted to feeling anger about aspects of their situations as second wives also said that they felt a certain sense of shame because they harbored these feelings. Anger is treated like a social disease, and like a social disease, it won't go away if you ignore it.

Anger may well come into play during the courtship, but it is, more often than not, pushed aside at this time in favor of more rewarding feelings such as love, happiness, and sexual arousal. Many second wives admit that they did feel angry about some of the aspects of their courtships, but most put their heads in the sand and hoped the anger would dissipate because they wanted very much for the relationship to continue to grow. Most of the second wives subscribed to the false but common belief that the uncomfortable feelings would go away "after they were married" when "things would be different."

This did not necessarily happen, however, and those who were angry before they were married often had even more cause to be angry afterward because "things did not change"; in fact, sometimes they just got worse. What was bearable or possible to ignore during the courtship phase may suddenly become all too real and a much heavier burden for the second wife when she realizes that those little problems she had before her marriage are now a lifetime consideration and cannot be quickly dealt with and dismissed. On the heels of this unpleasant revelation usually comes the inevitable realization that many of the expectations the second wife had about marriage and her role as a wife bear little resemblance to its reality. Suddenly, as a wife, she may be putting up with weekend visits from unruly stepchildren, midnight calls from his ex, or pressure from members of her own family who don't want to see their daughter devote her life to "someone else's husband." As one second wife said, "It's as though they changed the rules after I started to play the game. Suddenly I went from being his lover to wiping his kids noses and going to hockey practice. My dream of what our life would be like together wasn't this." The reality of being a wife to this particular man certainly did not match what his second wife expected. Whether or not she was right or wrong in her expectations is immaterial. What matters is that she had expectations, they did not come true, and she is, as a result, angry, disillusioned, and bitter. During the courtship, the niggling, little twinges of anger she felt when his weekends were taken up with junior league practice she may have been able to minimize with the "after all, they are his kids" rationale. Often after marriage, however, this minimizing rationale no longer satisfies; it may be modified in the mind of the new wife to "they may be his kids, but I'm his wife; doesn't what I want matter?" The periodic twinges of anger may become a slow, steady burn.

Like the other wives in the survey who experienced considerable anger, this wife could not avoid participating in the other half of the anger/fear paradigm. Being a well-conditioned woman, subject to our anti-anger cultural baggage, she immediately sought to suppress her anger because not only was she genuinely fearful of the consequences were she to express it, but she was not all that sure she was entitled to her anger in the first place. Denying or subverting anger in the second wife's case can work well for a time, especially since there are so many more pleasant emotions on which to dwell. Continuous refusal to confront this emotion, however, is ultimately counterproductive. Just when you think you have managed to banish this sinister presence from your life, you start to feel tired, listless, emotionally low. Self-esteem slides, and depression sets in. That unmentionable, inexpressible anger has found an object at which to direct itself—you.

This cycle was experienced by many of the second wives in the survey. First came denial of anger, then recognition and suppression, and finally, depression. In several studies on women and drug use, researcher R. Cooperstock suggests that women are more likely to take their negative feelings to a doctor as a means of coping with them. The doctor, as part of a society that sanctions freer expression of emotional problems for women, tends to prescribe a higher portion of mood-altering drugs for them. In another study J. M. Rogers claims that women seek prescriptions for these drugs because they feel lonely, anxious, dissatisfied, and/or unhappy. He attributes the increase in drug use (and also in visits to physicians because nine out of ten women obtain drugs with a doctor's prescription) to the fact that people have been convinced that psychological and social problems have medical causes and chemical solutions. Depression, social inadequacy, anxiety, marital and familial discord, and our inability to cope with them, are seen to be medical problems. In a study done in Scotland in 1972 concerning differences in attitudes and perceptions of male and female patients, physicians reported that 96 percent of their female patients raised the problem of marital discord with them frequently, as opposed to only 51 percent of the male patients. It is obvious, then, that women tend to seek out (or are encouraged to seek out) professionals such as doctors, psychiatrists, and marriage counselors to help them deal with marital problems. Second wives are no different.

Women have fewer socially sanctioned outlets for expressing and dissipating their anger than men. In most cases they cannot even discuss their feelings with their friends or families because to do so would elicit a round of I-told-you-so's or ruin their carefully erected façades of domestic bliss. They are, in many cases, left to deal with their anger alone, particularly if they are not willing to take the plunge and seek professional help.

This subterranean tide of surging emotion motivated many of the women who participated in the survey to turn to professionals for help. Finally, they could admit to someone, an objective third party who would not blame or condemn, that they truly were angry and that they didn't feel they should have to put up with the situations that were making them feel that way. They were also extremely gratified to learn that the feelings of shame they had been fighting for so long were experienced by many others; that is, they were not alone. Also, in commiting their feelings to paper, many of the wives were able, for the first time, to focus on what it was that was making them angry.

Filling out the questionnaire enabled me to get a great many matters off my chest. Matters which I can usually only discuss with my best friend who is also a second wife. I couldn't possibly tell my family of course. They would think I was just complaining. I'm really afraid of somebody saying I-told-you-so. Everybody expects you to know what you're getting into but I honestly didn't realize it would be this difficult.

It felt really good filling out the questionnaire. After four years there are still a lot of problems, a lot of feelings of anger, resentment, confusion, hurt, etc. It feels good to get some causes down on paper. Having my side heard for a change instead of hearing so much about the poor abandoned first wife trying to support a family, etc. I have often felt so alone with my feelings to the point I almost hated myself. I know a lot of women must be going through the same thing as me and feeling the same way. It's time we were heard.

I filled out the questionnaire because it gave me a chance to get rid of some of my anger. It helps me to deal with it a little better, seeing my feelings on paper. I realize now that they are my feelings and I am entitled to them. Until this came along I always felt I was the only one with these problems. That maybe I was doing something wrong. My husband told me to go to a psychiatrist or something, that there must be something wrong with me because I was having trouble adjusting to being a second wife. I almost believed him.

From these quotes it can be seen that there are two distinct responses to the anger that second wives experience. The first response is self-directed and may be paraphrased as: "There must be something wrong with me. I shouldn't be angry. My husband is really a wonderful guy." The second response is directed outward, at sources other than the self; for example, "It's all his ex-wife's fault. If she'd just leave us alone everything would be OK." Many of the second wives in the survey followed the first of these responses and blamed themselves. They were essentially confused about their situations as second wives, primarily because being a second wife is a relatively new phenomenon in our society and the rules and guidelines for behavior are somewhat fuzzy and ill-defined compared to those for wives in general. There are few predetermined reaction patterns. Appropriate behavior is gleaned by trial and error, more or less.

In spite of what many people may think, behavior that seems to work fine for the first wife is often condemned as inappropriate in the second wife. If a first wife finds out that her husband is spending some of their money on his mistress, society agrees that she is not only entitled to be angry but to express it. If a second wife finds out that her husband is spending some of their money on gifts for his ex-wife, however, she is supposed to keep her feelings to herself. She still feels the anger rising inside of her as any woman would, but what to do? The self-directed women turn upon themselves because they do not know what else to do. The other-directed women are more likely to turn their anger outwards, and although they were in the minority in the survey, they were also the women who reported generally happier marriages.

One of the reasons that women generally refrain from expressing their anger at its inception is that they have been delegated with the responsibility of "keeper of the relationship." It is the woman who is considered ultimately responsible for maintaining happiness and contentment. Although by day she may be busy climbing the rungs of the corporate ladder, on weekends and at night, she is still, more often than not, the one who is expected to give just a little bit more toward maintaining the emotional stability in the marriage. After all, *he* probably has another family and mortgage payments on somebody else's house to worry about. If, therefore, anyone is unhappy in the marriage, including herself, it follows that she is not doing her job well enough.

In her efforts to keep the marriage running smoothly, the second wife often carries the burden of her unexpressed anger with her. As one second wife said, "It was like walking on egg shells twenty-four hours a day. I was really afraid to let him see just how angry I was because I wasn't absolutely sure that I had any right to be angry in the first place. After all, I married him and supposedly I knew what I was getting into. But I didn't." Although this wife admitted to her anger, it is unlikely that she will try to do anything about it for the time being, because she is still questioning her rights to her feelings and is concerned about how to express them to her husband.

It is apparent that many second wives spend a considerable amount of time worrying about their anger and trying to avoid it. It is, therefore, time the point was made that anger need not be a 'bad' thing; it can be a constructive, rather than destructive, emotion. It is a symptom of something being wrong in the marriage, and if you want the marriage to work, you should find out what is wrong and fix it. If you use anger as a tool to try and improve your marriage, then you can discover the weak areas and, one hopes, strengthen them. If, on the other hand, you continue to let anger fester, it can only make both you and your relationship sick. Anger is a warning and should not be ignored. It is also important to realize that love and anger can co-exist. They are not mutually exclusive emotions, and just because you love someone is no reason to feel that you cannot be angry with them when necessary.

There are a few things to remember should you decide to bring your anger out in the open. First of all don't expect your husband to intuit when you are angry and why. After all you've been doing such a good job of covering it up that you probably have him completely convinced that you're happy. Don't compound the problem by getting angry at him for not knowing when and why you are angry.

If his ex-wife is driving you up the wall, don't assume that if he loved you, he would naturally realize this without your telling him. He may not be around when she does whatever it is that angers you and so may genuinely be unaware of your feelings. He may not interpret her actions the same way you do. Just because they're making you homicidal is no reason to expect he shares your point of view. He may prefer to delude himself into believing that you don't really mind her 3:00 A.M. phone calls, which, because they are to him, he may reason, do not really involve a confrontation between you and her. He may be afraid to mention her actions to you in case he stirs up a hornet's nest. If you get the feeling he is withholding information from you, whether for these reasons or for some others, and it makes you angry, tell him. In fact, in all the foregoing situations, ultimately the most constructive course of action you can take is the same: Tell your husband what is bothering you.

In telling him you are angry and why, you will be shifting some of the responsibility for your anger onto his shoulders.

While your load may suddenly be lightened, his will be heavier. The next question is, therefore, will he be receptive to your confession and to what degree? There are various possible outcomes to the reasonable expression of your anger. He may see your side immediately and agree to tell her to stop calling first thing in the morning. This is possible, but not likely. He may agree that you have a point but may also defend her actions with any number of reasons. (Does he really expect you to believe she's afraid of the dark?) He may ask you if you have run out of Valium. In any event, he will then realize how you feel. If he chooses to ignore this knowledge, your relationship has more problems than just your anger.

If you are lucky enough to be wedded to the husband who sees your side immediately, read no farther in this section. You are happy and have a husband who is totally committed to you. Your anger should dissipate naturally. If you are married to the husband who agrees you have a point but defends his first wife, be aware that he still hasn't quite broken the emotional bonds with his ex. You may have vented your anger for the time being, but you have problems to work out. Beware of the husband who chooses to ignore or deflect your outpouring. He is willing to risk undermining your self-esteem in order to prevent confrontations with you and/or his ex-wife at some future date. After all, if he convinces you that your feelings are unworthy, you will likely keep them to yourself and stop bothering him with what he sees as *your* problems.

Jealousy and Resentment

These emotions are not always as easily perceived as anger, although there may be elements of both in anger. Those who experience these feelings may have trouble admitting so even to themselves because of the unpleasant connotations with which they are generally associated (pettiness, avarice, childishness). When was the last time you heard anyone say "I'm jealous," or "I'm resentful," especially in front of people they care about and whose opinions they value? Women have greater difficulty with these emotions, particularly with jealousy, because, inaccurately, they have been labelled as "feminine" weaknesses. Automatically this puts them in the category of less important feelings and not deserving of serious attention. Jealousy and resentment have not recently caught the popular imagination to the same degree as have other more powerful emotions, such as anger. They are less frequently the subjects of exhaustive studies and rarely come up in conversation. In short, jealousy and resentment, which erroneously are often attributed to the weak, are out of vogue. The woman who freely and frequently says "I am jealous of his first wife" or "I resent the money he gives her" is not likely to get much sympathy or many offers of help.

Feelings of jealousy do not start out in life to be such a terrible thing. In our early years they are likely to be manifested as sibling rivalry. Slightly more than 40 percent of the wives in the survey came from families averaging three or more children. Many were also the oldest children in their families and felt their first pangs of jealousy when the family started to expand. Suddenly they were forced to share parental affection. Jealousy of this type and at this level serves a very basic need, the need to survive. In the face of increased competition when the family grows larger, jealousy causes the older child to vie with its siblings for the life-sustaining attention of the parents. As Dr. Karen Horney, in her study *Feminine Psychology*, states, "In earlier days the claim to monopolize the love of father or mother met with frustration or disappointment and the result was a reaction of hate or jealousy. Hence there always lurks behind this demand (that of monopolizing the affection of a loved one) a certain hatred which often breaks out if the old disappointment is repeated."

The players may change, but the situation is the same for the second wife. Instead of vying with her siblings, she may now have to do so with her husband's children, or his ex-wife, or all of them. In the words of Dr. Horney: "When we realize upon what deeply rooted instinctual basis the claim on monopoly takes its stand we also see that if the present ideal justification for it were taken from humanity we would at all costs in some way or another find a fresh one. Sometimes one of its constituent elements may play an overwhelmingly great part in the instinctual economy, or all those factors we recognize as motive forces in jealousy in general may contribute. In fact, we might describe the demand for monogamy as an insurance against the torments of jealousy." This can be a particularly difficult situation for the second wife who was an only child, and as such, had never had to share parental love, and now finds that she must share her husband's love. Dr. Eugene Schoenfeld, a San Francisco psychologist, says of jealousy, "Normal jealousy is a warning signal that something is wrong in a relationship. Many people believe it is instinctive. And, it can be very useful."

There are two types of jealousy that a second wife may face. She may experience either one or both, depending on her particular circumstances. The first type, suspicious jealousy, is based primarily on the fear of sexual or romantic competition. Second wives, more than other women, are faced with this possibility because their husbands were (and sometimes still are) romantically linked with another woman. The second type is a little more complex, in that it is less specific in its focus. This type of jealousy is related to how you feel about your position relative to a third party, with respect to the amount of affection, credit, approval, and attention that the third party receives from someone you consider to be "yours."

In the case of suspicious jealousy, many second wives experience the unspoken fear that their husbands still have some feelings for their ex-wives or still find them sexually attractive. It is true that such fears are not always groundless, and what is even more true is that many husbands encourage their second wives in this feeling and feed the jealousy. It, no doubt, is gratifying to their egos if their second wives are jealous of them and their first wives. Many people take jealousy as a sign of love. Jealousy is not constructive, however, when it makes people insecure and unsure in their relationships. It must be remembered that second wives are often particularly insecure in their relationships without any added pressure.

The second type of jealousy often arises out of aspects of the husband's relationship with his first wife other than the romantic or sexual. This usually has to do with the way he spends his time and/or money and usually involves his children—a primary cause of jealousy in many second wives.

My husband's children live with his first wife but they are both involved in hockey so all season long he is constantly involved with taking them at all hours to practice and games. The hockey schedule is ridiculous. It affects what little social life we have. Constantly! Because he is so tired from driving all over the province with the hockey the quality of time we have together is affected. If I were going to choose another husband I would pick one without children.

In either case, jealousy is a perfectly normal manifestation of the fear that we are about to lose someone or something very important to us. Jealousy is common in second wives (and ex-wives) because, just as in childhood when they had to share their parents' love and affection with siblings, they have to share time, attention, and financial security in their marriages with someone else. Children usually adapt easily to having siblings with which to compete; but wives, whether they be first or second, do not. As psychologist Judith Bardwick points out in her book *Psychology of Women*, women generally seek more of their identity from their marriages and as such are highly motivated to see that relationship work out: "In the early years of marriage women are not as secure in the stability of the affiliative relationship and are motivated to succeed in the relationship because it is their major source of self-esteem.... Women continue to perceive the world in interpersonal terms and personalize the objective world in a way men do not. Notwithstanding occupational achievements, they tend to esteem themselves only insofar as they are esteemed by those they love and respect."

While you may not agree that women still seek their identities in their close relationships rather than in their careers, it is still true today that women often expect more in the way of personal fulfillment from their marriages than men do. As a result they are more likely to dwell on the possibility and implications of losing their husbands' love and affection. This is even more true for the second wife who is marrying a man with a doubtful track record in the marriage game already; one woman has lost him; might not two? Especially in the case where the husband left his first wife to marry his second, there is often the thought at the back of the second wife's mind that "he fooled around on his first wife and he might just fool around on me."

It is for these reasons that jealousy can have such a powerful hold on the second wife, especially in the early years of marriage when she is still getting to know her husband. Jealousy can cause even the sanest of us to do silly and destructive things in an effort to hold onto what we are afraid may be slipping away. If you are aware of the pitfalls of harboring jealousy, you will be in a much better position to deal with it, that is, to control it rather than letting it control you.

Resentment is similar to jealousy, but not nearly so tinged with romantic, if unflattering, connotations. Resentment is less localized and more likely to be concerned with the general state of affairs. For example, the second wife may not be jealous of the first wife's house, in that she herself would care to possess it, but she may deeply resent the fact that the first wife has a house, while she and her husband, who are paying the mortgage on that house, live in a small apartment. Resentment is predicated on a sense that something is unjust and that the state of deprivation arising from that injustice should not be borne.

Resentment, like jealousy, is more likely to be exhibited by the second wife because she has very possibly become part of a highly structured situation that she had no hand in creating and which may not conform to her standards of fairness. Whatever her reasons may be, whether they stem from a divorce settlement that is too demanding, an ex-wife who is too demanding, or a lack of acceptance by her husband's family, the second wife often cannot help but harbor resentment. She may not only be living in a world the creation of which was none of her doing, but she may also be powerless to bring about acceptable changes.

Resentment, unfortunately, is something that usually must be borne alone. A husband is not a good listener when it comes to discussing the finer points of a wife's resentment. He may be caught up in some covert resentment of his own, or if he finds out that you feel certain aspects of the situation are unjust, he may feel guilty or responsible for inflicting this mess on you in the first place.

Resentment is largely a situationally based feeling (i.e., it generally takes something outside the person to generate it), and in order for this feeling to subside, the environment must be changed. For some women, changing the environment means getting a divorce, but for most it is a question of trying to adjust the marriage so that those things at the root of the resentment are physically or temporally experienced less frequently. If it is his children you resent, the logical solution is to try and see them less often. If it is his family or friends, remove yourself from their company. In other words, try to limit your own contact with the things that trigger your resentment—"out of sight, out of mind" often works very well. If you focus your attention elsewhere, you may find your feeling of resentment diminishing in importance. It is, after all, difficult to dwell on the positive aspects of your marriage and feel resentful simultaneously.

Other Emotions at Work

Anger, jealousy, and resentment may be the emotions most frequently mentioned by second wives, but they are by no means the only ones. There are many others, depending on the situation, that range from niggling little feelings of annoyance to overwhelming sadness.

Let's consider hurt for a start, which tends to be a rather ill-defined feeling and is completely person-specific, that is, the things that hurt one person may not faze another. Hurt is often the antecedent of anger for second wives, as for others. When a second wife's expectations *vis à vis* marriage seem to have been thwarted, she often begins to think she is not being treated as a "real" wife. When she looks around for the cause of all this discomfort and realizes that her husband, the man she loves, is the source, then she feels hurt.

> *I know that this probably sounds silly, it really isn't a BIG problem compared to what some people have, but Nick has managed to hurt me in a number of small ways since we have been married. Though I forgive him for the big things but I find it very difficult to forgive him for these little misdemeanors, so perhaps they're not so little after all.*
>
> *In our first year of marriage, when I guess I was feeling a little extra sensitive, he forgot my birthday. No big deal and I just let it go by but, when I got a bill from the florist a couple of weeks later and realized that he had remembered to put flowers on his first wife's grave on her birthday, well, I felt really hurt. I just didn't understand how he could remember her and not me.*

No matter how insignificant these little betrayals of love may seem to others, if they are important to us, then we have a right to feel hurt. This wife's response is typical in that, even though she is willing to admit that this action or rather lack of action by her husband hurt her, she manages to make excuses for him all the same. Witness her use of "I know this probably sounds silly" and "it really isn't a big problem." Part of the problem with hurt is that so many women question whether they are right to feel the way they do.

Many second wives are caught up in the daily struggle of the love/hate paradigm. They love their husbands but hate the situation. This uncomfortable circumstance may go on for years because they feel that they would be even more unhappy if they left. It is a very difficult situation because either way the second wife loses something. If she goes, she loses her husband, and if she stays, she loses something of herself.

I left my husband about a year and a half ago. And when I did, I found that feelings, very bad feelings that I had managed to push to the back of my mind, have once again surfaced. He just could not break the bond with his first wife. So, they are going to try again. I miss an adult relationship and I would like to get married. After all, time is marching on.

In either case, the second wife is apt to experience feelings of sadness and loss, similar to what she would experience were a loved one to die.

The last feeling to be discussed is more of a state than a feeling. It does not go by any particular name, but rather, it is a symptom of a particular set of circumstances. It is that uncomfortable feeling which most of us experience from time to time, of being left out or ignored. Many women, as second wives, do not get to participate in their husbands' lives as fully as they would, if they had been their first wives. They report that, especially in social situations and so-called family events such as Christmas, graduations, and weddings, they are frequently made to feel that they do not fit into the program. Sometimes this is done intentionally by members of the husbands' families, who are trying to make the point that they disapprove of the new wives. Sometimes it is a simple matter of there being no clear rules of etiquette to follow which might allow people to deal more comfortably with a social situation that may include the first wife, the second wife, and even children. For the second wife, such occasions can be difficult and even humiliating experiences, unless she has the full support of her husband. Often a husband, in order to maintain the status quo, will allow his second wife to be passed by, thereby reinforcing her discomfort. The question of where the second wife fits in is something that should be answered early in the marriage to avoid difficult social confrontations later on. Every couple will have a unique way of dealing with this problem, but unless it is dealt with, it can only lead to hurt feelings and aggravation for both partners in the marriage.

Guilt and the Husband

Feelings of guilt are something with which any second wife should be prepared to deal. Few second wives in the survey admitted to feeling guilty themselves, but many said that they knew their husbands felt guilty about the breakdown of their first marriages.

> *I know my husband feels guilty about leaving his first wife. He is always phoning her to see if she's alright or if she needs anything. He bends over backwards to meet her slightest demands. He even gives her more money than the court ordered. I've tried to talk to him about this but he tells me that he still feels responsible for her welfare and, after all, she's all alone.*

The lot of the divorced husband is not a happy one, particularly for those with a profound sense of duty and responsibility. The Christian ethic tells us that while it is perfectly permissable to seek one's own happiness, it is not permissible to do so at the expense of others. Given the make-up of a disintegrating marriage, it is nearly impossible for one party not to find new happiness at the expense of the other. Somebody has to be the one who leaves, and that person, no matter how much he or she may have wanted to get out of the marriage, will, no doubt, assume a certain amount of guilt for being the one to call it quits. This guilty feeling is only exacerbated if that person feels in any way responsible for the breakdown of the relationship.

What is it about men that makes them able (and likely) to assume so much guilt so easily? Just as the second wife may be seething with unexpressed anger because she may view it as her responsibility to maintain a harmonious household in spite of her feelings, so, too, her husband is constantly chastened by unexpressed guilt because of his failure to maintain his previous marriage. Although women are silently charged with keeping the marriage on an even keel on a day-to-day basis, men are held ultimately responsible for its success or failure. Many men still see themselves as the protector, the provider, and the head of the household. When things go wrong, the first person to whom they look for an explanation is themselves. If the marriage didn't work, then they must have failed in some way. If a man feels he is not allowed to fail, he must exact some sort of punishment, and guilt is often the device used.

Whether or not anyone was to blame for the breakup of the marriage, it is the husband who ultimately feels responsible because he lost control of the situation. If he is the one who left, he feels guilty because of the emotional harm he has caused a women he once loved, and if he is the one who was left behind, he questions whether or not there was some essential short-coming on his part that drove her away. If he is a father, the prospect of being a long-distance daddy, of abnegating his responsibilities as a parent and possibly "scarring his children for life" only adds to his burden of guilt.

Although we may have invented no-fault divorce in the legal sense, morally, as a society, we still seek to place blame for a broken marriage. Often the husband accepts the role of the guilty party, in part because legally he is the one who is pun-ished financially in the divorce process. A man may allow himself to participate in a settlement heavily weighed in favor of his ex-wife (the guiltless spouse) because through self-denial, he assuages his guilt and makes his retribution public. Unfor-tunately there are few circumstances where self-denial affects only those who feel guilty. It usually spreads to those closest to us. Thus, many husbands will gladly agree to payments that are really more than they can afford and give up the house, the car, the boat, or even the business, thereby punishing themselves financially but also punishing their second wives and new families.

Society, too, gives a helping hand in inflicting punishment on the guilty by creating legal and social situations that serve as negative reinforcements for the husband. Whether he is culpable in the breakup of the marriage or not, he is usually expected to leave his home, his friends, his social support systems, and do without the creature comforts that he has come to expect in life. By creating this kind of negative reinforcement, society identifies a culprit for the broken marriage and exacts punishment. Without these social sanctions, marriage as we know it would become a thing of the past and people might drift freely from one relationship to the next. Since marriage is the economic and social basis of our culture, it is necessary to try and preserve it. The financial constraints, which the courts inflict at the time of divorce, prevent the partners from marrying and divorcing too many times because to do so would be economically prohibitive.

Not every new second wife is aware of guilt when she marries. She may look for symptoms of guilt in her new husband, but not every man wears his tortured heart on his sleeve. There are those husbands who prefer to suffer their guilt and do their penance in silence. This is, at least, what they think they are doing. But as with most suppressed emotions, however, guilt has a way of surfacing when least expected.

> *I was sure my husband was having an affair. He would say he was working late and then I'd call and he wouldn't be in the office or he would "go to the store" on weekends and come back two or three hours later. I was hurt. We had only been married for a little while and I couldn't understand after all we had gone through to be together why he would suddenly want another woman. It was purely by accident that I found out that his secret little rendezvous were with his ex-wife. Nothing sexual was going on but he would go over to her house and fix the plumbing or put up the storm windows, things he had been doing for her for years and which he felt he must continue to do because she depended on him completely. He didn't tell me because he thought I would be mad. I was, twice over. Once, because he was doing these things and twice, because he was sneaking around and causing me to expect the worst.*

The second wife may expect to deal with three different manifestations of guilt. Besides displayed guilt (giving gifts, paying more alimony than necessary) and secret guilt (doing these things without letting your second wife know) there is a third type of guilt commonly found in this situation—shared guilt. With shared guilt the husband manages, through various means, to transfer some of the heavy burden of his guilt to his second wife. Sharing the load makes it easier for him to cope but also brings about the unfortunate consequence of sharing the punishment, too. People who like to share their guilt often think along lines such as, "If I hadn't fallen in love with her then I'd still be with my first wife and I wouldn't feel guilty. Because she made me love her she is partly responsible for my guilty feelings and so should share them."

I didn't feel guilty about breaking up my husband's first marriage. He told me over and over when we were going together that he felt nothing for her anymore and that it was all over. I know he used to run around on her the whole time they were married and sometimes he'd get drunk and beat her up. But, now, every time we fight he never fails to remind me that if it weren't for me he'd still be with her and his kids. He says it's all my fault that he left her, and now he can't see his kids anymore.

Shared guilt is often the worst kind because it brings two people into a situation which is extremely unhealthy for their relationship not to mention highly unfair to the second wife. Many second wives are not even aware that they are sharing their husbands' guilt because it is often not expressed openly. The husband is unlikely to say to his new wife, "Honey, help me share my guilt," but he may well say "Honey, we can't get by on my salary alone. Both of us are going to have to work if I'm going to make payments to her. You know she can't go out to work yet because she has to stay home and take care of the kids." Or perhaps it may be more like this: "Dear, we can't afford to go on holiday this year if I'm going to send the kids to summer camp. I know it's not part of the settlement, but I don't like to think about them cooped up around the house all summer after all they've been through."

Few, if any, second wives will argue with the logic of these arguments because, at the back of their minds, is always that little suspicion that if it hadn't been for them, he would have gone back to her. Also the idea that the child from the broken home is suffering on her account can be a powerful argument for making her own needs seem selfish.

This all may sound rather grim, but married couples play these games all the time. It's just that second wives have to play these games differently and in accordance with a different set of rules. Manipulation of this sort is not always conscious, nevertheless the results are the same. One of the first things any second wife should be prepared to ascertain is just how guilty her husband feels about his first marriage, and how he is going to handle that guilt. A little guilt is to be expected, but if it seems that you might become a victim of that guilt, take the advice of this second wife before you marry.

I insisted that my husband go back to his first wife before we got married if there was any possibility of their reviving their love. I didn't want our marriage soiled by a huge load of guilt from his first marriage. I gave him every opportunity to reconcile with her and when I was sure that he didn't really want to and that there would never be any recriminations or remorse on his part then I felt free to marry him.

8 Coping and the Second Wife

"The North American marriage idea is one of the most conspicuous examples of our insistence on hitching our wagons to a star. It is one of the most difficult marriage forms that the human race has ever attempted."   Margaret Mead

THE WAYS IN WHICH women in general and second wives in particular cope with the stresses of married life have not been given much consideration to date and have certainly received no serious attention within the medical community. Women were supposed to derive a considerable amount of their satisfaction, not to mention their identities, from their married state, and so it was inconceivable that this state itself, regardless of the partner, could be the primary source of any genuine distress. Indeed, it was the poor unfortunate who failed to nab a man by the time she was thirty who was deserving of our most concern. After all, what could be worse than being an old maid?

Too often women have been their own worst enemies. Many of them still share in the view that women should, in order to be mentally healthy, socially acceptable, and personally content, be married. In order to be successful at being married they must be feminine, nurturant, submissive, complaisant, sensitive, and rarely assertive, competitive, outspoken, self-involved, or angry.

137

Obviously the times and these attitudes are changing, and women are beginning to realize that their roles as wife, mother, and nurturer can be fraught with tensions and dissatisfaction. If this is true for wives in general then it is more so for the second wife. As well as the problems that plague marriage in general in the 1980s, there are those unique to a woman's situation as a second wife.

We must acknowledge that the typical feminine dictum that happiness is achieved through dependence and self-sacrifice is largely a fanciful concoction of our patriarchal society. This attitude is responsible for many of the problems that second wives in particular have to face. It also prevents those women who are eager to talk to someone about their problems (doctors, lawyers, priests, etc.) from finding a sympathetic ear. This letter to Ann Landers will serve as an example. It concerns a second wife who married a man with three children from his previous marriage.

> *I made it plain when we were married that I was not going to comply with his divorce decree that said the kids were to be with us every other weekend. I don't have any children and I don't want any.... I have disliked children since I was a teenager. Only recently have I had the courage to let it be known. What did I get? Kids dumped on me on the weekend—or for an hour which sometimes meant till the next day. Now that I have decided to be outspoken and rude, if necessary, I get a lot of static from my mother-in-law. My doctor said I was not cut out to be a mother and to quit trying. So, how can I get this across to my husband's family?*

The reply from Ann Landers read:

> *From the way you write I can't imagine you having any trouble getting anything across to anybody. Why did you marry a man who was obligated to take his children every other week when you hate to have them around? You walked into this mess with your eyes wide open. Sorry I can't be supportive but I see nothing but trouble ahead.*

Unfortunately this response does not deal with the problem itself but with the presentation of the problem. The writer, who seems to have held back her feelings for some time from the tone of her letter and who has released them in a rather forceful flood of harsh words, is being dealt with in the same fashion that she complains her mother-in-law and her doctor dealt with her complaint. Instead of accepting the possibility that the situation may be truly unbearable for this second wife, and given this, that she has a problem deserving of some sympathy and constructive advice, Ms. Landers turns the tables on her and blames her for her problem. People often assume second wives knew what they were in for, and so any problems that arise are their own fault. Most second wives don't know in advance, however, and many will insist that no one can know until one has been through it. A psychologist, whose husband was a psychiatrist (in their careers they dealt almost exclusively with the problems of stepfamilies), once commented that she and her husband thought they were going to breeze through the whole second-wife situation because their specialty was remarriage and blended families. They found out after they were married just how incredibly difficult the situation could be, and as she said, if they, as professionals in the area, had difficulty handling it and encountered many unexpected problems, then how could the average couple be expected to manage? Perhaps a more appropriate answer to Landers' correspondent might have been: "If you went into your marriage with a pre-voiced arrangement that you would not participate in his bi-weekly custody visits and your husband accepted this, and, if his custody rights limit him to every other weekend, then (on those occasions and those occasions only) when the children come to visit, let them visit with him and you do something else. As long as your arrangement with your husband did not require you to accept equal parental responsibilities, then don't—and don't let others try and make you feel guilty about it. You are as much entitled to not like his children as they are entitled to not like you."

Most of the feelings kept hidden by second wives are those

which society in general frowns on in women because they are not considered appropriately feminine qualities. Today it is still not acceptable to some that a woman admit she is angry, that she dislikes her husband's children, or that she resents the support payments he is making to his previous family. These feelings are wrong because they go against the perceived feminine role of self-sacrifice. Many second wives feel so guilty about their feelings that they cannot bring themselves to discuss them openly with others, and if they do, they are often censored or dismissed as being trivial.

How do second wives cope then? Feelings and situations do not go away just because they are ignored and many second wives (and women in general) behave in a variety of ways to help them cope.

In the following pages, the commonly used coping mechanisms will be discussed. It is important to note that the ways these wives cope are not always beneficial. In fact, some of them can be quite destructive. Many coping mechanisms are subconscious reactions to the particular situation and are often not recognized by the individual as such.

Projection

The subconscious use of projection as a coping mechanism is seen fairly frequently in the second wife because it often occurs in situations where people feel particularly vulnerable. Projection is described as the attribution of one's own unacknowledged feelings to others. The case of Pat, a twenty-nine-year-old bookkeeper, will serve as an example. She had been married to John for three years. John is forty-eight years old and a successful businessman. He had been divorced from his wife of twenty years for the past five years. He is the father of two children now age twenty-one and twenty-four.

When I first met John I knew that he was divorced and that he had children from his previous marriage. I also knew that they were practically grown up and so I didn't really anticipate any problems with them. I didn't actually meet them until after John and I were married but I became aware through things he said and the fact that they wouldn't come to our wedding that they didn't want me around. The first meeting was a disaster. They were rude and unfriendly to me. Evidently their mother had had a few things to say about me and of course they had listened to her. After that I became very uncomfortable with them and in the end I told my husband that I didn't want them in our home. I made things very difficult for John. I realize now that I was simply reacting to my fear that they would dislike me by rejecting them more than they were rejecting me. I understand now that I was very unsure of my position in John's life at the time and the least little bit of resistance from them caused a much larger reaction in me. I was convinced they hated me when in effect it was me who disliked them because I was afraid they would dislike me and cause their father to turn against me.

Pat is one of the few women I to whom I spoke who has come to terms with her method of coping. She realized she was projecting her own feelings of insecurity and fear of rejection onto John's children who, it turned out, didn't really care one way or the other about Pat. In doing so, she created an uncomfortable situation between her husband and herself (the very thing she was afraid would happen if the children rejected her) and between herself and his children.

The fear of being rejected is not unusual for the second wife. After all, in many cases, she is taking on her husband's pre-formed social set (friends, family and children), and her anxiety over their possible lack of acceptance can easily lead her into projecting her negative emotions onto those around her. All second wives should be aware of this possibility. As a way of coping, seeing your own negative feelings in others will only make matters worse. A little reserve and caution is not a bad idea in the beginning, but to be too cautious and suspicious of his friends and family can only prejudice the outcome of your relationship with him.

Hypochondriasis

Hypochondriasis is probably the most well known example of subconscious coping behavior. Hypochondriasis is the transformation of reproach toward others arising from stress or unacceptable aggressive impulses into self-reproach, initially, and later into complaints of illness. This coping mechanism permits the individual to belabor others with his own pain or discomfort instead of making direct demands upon them or in place of complaining that others have ignored his wishes.

The very nature of hypochondriasis is suggestive of the socialized feminine approach to stress. It typifies acceptance of the feminine role of dependency, inner-directed rather than other-directed coping behavior, and the use of manipulation of others rather than direct confrontation of the problem. Particularly in the past, hypochondriacal behavior was one of the few ways that women had of getting the upper hand. It provided both a coping mechanism and a pleasant attention-focusing device and was most often used in their dealings with men.

Unfortunately the memories of this type of feminine manipulation still linger. Society still expects a certain amount of feminine fraility to be part of a woman's identity. Is it any wonder, then, that women still continue to use illness as a method of control and as an outlet for unacceptable feelings? Illness, after all, generally nets sympathy, care, and concern. It also prevents one from having to cope immediately with an undesirable situation. The following are examples.

Martha, a forty-five-year-old homemaker, is married to Gerald, who is approximately the same age and an engineer by profession. They have been married for eight years. Both were married before, for five and ten years respectively. Martha is an apparently robust woman who appears to be in good health, but she is frequently ill with one thing or another, although she rarely suffers from the same ailment twice and is never seriously ill. She spends a lot of time going to doctors for tests to discover what is wrong with her. She is convinced she is not a well person.

I don't know what it is but I always seem to catch everything that is going around. I never feel really well even when I am not sick. One morning last year I woke up covered with hives. I've never had hives before. After that I had trouble with my back and had to stay in bed for a few weeks. It always seems to be something.

Further discussion with Martha reveals that these bouts of illness or allergic reactions are usually triggered by some stressful event related to her marriage. The hives, for instance, appeared shortly after Gerald went to his daughter's wedding in another city with his ex-wife, and the back problems began when Martha thought he was spending too much time with his sons. It is also evident that Martha feels quite competitive with Gerald's ex-wife. She is convinced that if she is not the perfect wife to him then she will "lose" him, just as his first wife did; so, although she strives to be "the perfect wife" in other ways, she also tries to manipulate Gerald by being dependent on him through her various illnesses. How could he leave a sick woman? Worrying about her, how much time can he spend thinking about his former family?

A similar example is that of thirty-two-year-old Janice, a merchandising manager, and her thirty-five-year-old husband, Alan, a salesman. Janice reveals through her interview that she has a great deal of unexpressed hostility. As a second wife, she has run up against experiences she feels are unfair and with which she has trouble coping. Indirectly she blames Alan for being responsible for bringing this stress into her life. Although she insists that she loves him, she admits that were it not for him, a lot of the stress would be removed from her life. He is the source of both her emotional support and her emotional upheaval.

I can't understand it. I know that Alan loves me and yet he doesn't love me enough to put me first in his life. I still have to take a backseat to his kids and his ex is still hanging around demanding this and that. And he goes along with all of their demands. I get so mad. Sometimes I think I can't cope with it any more. And why should I have to? I would love to have my husband all to myself, to have a life of our own without all this interference. I really love him. Why can't he see that this situation is becoming unbearable for me? Sometimes I wonder if he loves me enough to care that it bothers me. Or maybe he just thinks he can have everything his own way—me, her, and his kids, one big happy family.

Janice is caught in a dilemma. The person whom she loves most and from whom she gets the most satisfaction is also the one who is the cause, at least in her eyes, of most of her misery. This is a difficult situation, to be sure, and like many women, Janice is incapable of expressing her anger directly to Alan. She is afraid of the consequences and also isn't sure that a direct expression of her feelings would solve anything. She feels that "if he really loved me he would 'know' what is wrong."

Living with this inner turmoil has produced a variety of hypochondriacal reactions in Janice. She, too, gets sick, but unlike Martha, whose illness did not interfere with her eternal search for perfection, Janice allows her sickness to interfere with her daily routine. She is often too ill to cook dinner or clean the house. Frequently she does not feel well enough to make love. In this way she is, through her illnesses, making a statement to Alan. Indirectly she is telling him she is angry. Alan doesn't see this, however; he just thinks she is frail. The problem continues.

Reaction Formation

Reaction formation is typified by behavior diametrically opposite to an uncomfortable instinctual response. This coping mechanism includes overtly caring for someone else when one wishes to be cared for oneself, or expressing an emotion completely opposite to one's true feelings. A good example of this type of coping behavior is Jane's. Jane is twenty-five and her husband, Phil, is thirty-four. They have been married for two years and have no children from their own marriage. Phil has a little boy from his first marriage to Karen.

When I married Phil I felt uncomfortable about his relationship with Karen. She was still a big part of his life. They saw each other often and had several business interests in common. Worse than that he still liked her as a person and enjoyed her company. I was jealous, I suppose. Why couldn't she have been the sort of ex-wife who made a pest of herself and whom he could have come to dislike? They were both so civilized about the whole business of their divorce and his marrying me. And, I couldn't handle it. It wasn't the way I expected things to be. I mean he even invited her and her new boyfriend to have dinner with us on our first wedding anniversary. I suppose I could have gotten used to all this eventually but I really didn't like her as a person. If she had been anybody else I would have had nothing to do with her. In spite of my feelings I found myself becoming very friendly to her even though deep down inside I wished she would just get lost. Phil thought this was just wonderful. We even ended up going to her wedding. I just kept smiling and smiling and being nice. The whole time I kept wondering what I was doing. I really couldn't stand the woman and here I was acting like her best friend. I became really quite disgusted with myself and began to examine my reasons for acting the way I was. Of course, it was true that part of it was to please Phil, but part of it too was that even though I was dying to tell her what I really thought I just couldn't bring myself to do it. Maybe I was afraid of what Phil would say and maybe I was afraid of the strong emotion I was having. I had never really disliked anybody I knew before. These strong negative feelings were something totally foreign to me and I didn't know how to deal with them. I think towards the end I really began to hate her. That's an awful thing to have to admit but it's true.

Jane's strong feelings of dislike were too much for her to handle, so she rechannelled them into more acceptable feelings of apparent friendship. Although Jane was able to see through her feelings and come to terms with them more sensibly (she no longer sees Karen and has told Phil how she feels), her reactions were similar to those of many women. She was conditioned all her life not to feel anything like hatred. She was caught in a bind when she had these feelings.

Ruth's is yet another example of reaction formation. She is thirty-one, and her husband, Bob, is fifty-one. They are currently in the process of getting a divorce.

> *I knew when my husband asked me to marry him that part of his reason was to have a wife twenty years younger than he was who he thought he could satisfy sexually. I had never been married before and I married him because I loved him, or thought I did. I'm not a very sexy person but I knew that sex was very important to my husband so I began to act very seductive and sexy around him. Sometimes I felt silly but always did whatever he wanted and let him know how much I enjoyed it. I used to lie to him about what a wonderful lover he was (he wasn't). It's true what my mother said. If you're number two you have to try harder. Also I thought if he thought I was just as interested in sex as he was he wouldn't go wandering like he did in his first marriage. He did.*

Again, we have a second wife exhibiting behavior contrary to her true impulses. From looking at his dissatisfaction with his first marriage, Ruth felt that the way to keep her marriage together was to become something she essentially was not. Her behavior was a conscious effort and not a subconscious one, but it is doubtful that she could have kept up her false persona indefinitely. If the marriage had lasted, there would have come a time when she would have reverted to her normal sexual behavior and she would have had to confront an even more complex situation. This example is not unique to second wives. It is true that, in cases like this, the second wife can be tempted to use her historical perspective of the first marriage to try to second-guess her husband's desires rather than allowing them to reveal themselves naturally. This is not a good idea.

Suppression

Suppression is the conscious or semi-conscious decision to postpone paying attention to a conscious impulse or conflict. The mechanism includes minimizing acknowledged discomfort (i.e., "looking for the silver lining" or "keeping a stiff upper lip") and postponing, but not avoiding, the problem. Perhaps the most famous example of this type of behavior being used as a coping mechanism is Scarlett O'Hara's reaction to the final departure of Rhett Butler. After he leaves, she promises to "think about it tomorrow."

Suppression is not a denial of the situation, but merely a postponement of any significant action for the time being. There is no effort to avoid a confrontation permanently, just to gather one's resources or faculties first. Consider these two examples. Louise, a forty-two-year-old homemaker, is married to Jerry, a truckdriver of almost the same age. They have no children and have been married for four years.

Before we married, my husband tried to sell the house he lived in with his first wife (she left him). I really didn't want to live there as I felt the house would always be her place and not mine. I was very uncomfortable with the idea but because of the way the real estate market was at the time we couldn't sell the place and so after we got married I moved in. I still feel uncomfortable sleeping in the same room where they slept but it's a nice house and well-located. At least we don't have to live in an apartment, but someday I would like a home of my own though Jerry is quite happy to stay where we are.

Brenda, age thirty-one, has been married to Dave, forty-two, for three years. Dave is well-known in the town where they live, and so was his first wife. Brenda moved into the town shortly before she met Dave.

Whenever my husband and I go out we seem to run into people who knew him when he was with his first wife. That wasn't so bad, but then he would just sort of forget to introduce me and I would stand there feeling like a piece of the furniture. I'm sure that most people didn't know I was his wife. They probably thought I was his mistress or somebody he just picked up. That really used to hurt. Once, while I was standing there while he talked to another couple,

*the man looked right at him and then at me and asked how his wife
was. I could have died. I tried to talk to him about this but he says
I'm being overly sensitive and I told him that he is rude and
inconsiderate. Anyway, now whenever we get into a situation like
that I just wander off the minute they start talking and come back
when the conversation is over. I know that's not the best solution but
it works for the time being and at least Dave and I don't get into
unnecessary arguments over it. Still, sometimes I do get mad when I
think about it, but I just clam up and try and shut it out of my
thoughts.*

Both Brenda and Louise are exhibiting typical signs of suppression. Each has a situation which she finds uncomfortable (both
are things experienced by many second wives), and each recognizes what makes her feel this way, but neither has done
much about it, and Louise, in particular, is "looking for the
silver lining" in saying that at least they don't have to live in an
apartment. "Making the best of a bad situation" is what women
in general are told and taught to do with life's difficult situations; second wives, obviously, are not exceptions.

Passive/Aggressive Behavior

Passive/aggressive behavior occurs when aggression toward
another is expressed indirectly and ineffectively through passiv-
ity or by inflicting it on the self. This coping mechanism also
suggests a so-called female approach to problems. Consequences of the old idea of woman as "the weaker sex," particularly when in concert with any significant degree of economic
dependence, often demand that, rather than directing their
aggressive feelings against the source, women turn them in
upon themselves.

If suppression as a means of coping may be paraphrased as
"looking on the bright side," then passive/aggressive behavior
goes one step farther. It is a matter of accepting the status quo
without trying to dress it up, as witnesses the case of Joyce, a
thirty-eight-year-old part-time secretary. Joyce and Harold
have been together for four years. They are not married though

she would like to be. They live as a married couple. Even though Joyce works part time she is basically being supported by Harold and has been since they started living together.

Harold says that he is embarrassed to get married now because he feels that with his two children about to get married it wouldn't look right. I think that's a poor excuse. I think it's just that he's got everything he wants and has it his own way, so why should he change just to please me?

Joyce is hurt and angered by Harold's behavior. She hides her anger behind a sarcastic sense of humor and often describes herself to others as nothing more than "his cleaner, his cooker, and his hooker." In fact, from talking to her it would seem that she derives a perverse sense of pleasure from describing herself thusly to others. In doing this, she is directing her anger at Harold toward herself and degrading her position as his common-law wife in front of others. The reality is, that by trying to demean herself in this fashion, she is punishing herself rather than Harold.

This type of coping behavior is, to say the least, unhealthy for the woman involved. It often exacerbates the problems at hand by lowering an already diminished sense of self-esteem. More dangerously, it possibly reduces her worth in Harold's eyes, as well. Rather than moving her closer to her goal of marriage, it is quite probably moving her in the opposite direction.

Displacement

With displacement the woman redirects her feelings toward a relatively less significant person or object other than the one which is arousing her feelings. For instance, many women take out their hostilities toward their husbands on their children or perhaps their co-workers.

It is extremely difficult for a woman to direct her negative feelings against her husband because, while he may be the source of her aggravation, he is also probably the source of her emotional or financial support. Many women, in addition, cannot accept the existence of two sets of conflicting emotions about the same person at the same time, so it is easier to redirect their anger onto someone or something else which will not retaliate and, therefore, increase their tensions. As a method of coping this, too, is not particularly helpful, although it does prevent the destructive inner-directed feelings of some of the other methods.

Like the other methods of coping we have discussed, it fails to directly confront the problems at hand. It is at best a temporary way of maintaining stability, and it also prevents the husband from seeing his wife's true range of emotions which includes real feelings women have been conditioned to believe can result in the loss of love.

Sublimation

The indirect or attenuated expression of instincts *without* adverse consequences or marked loss of pleasure is known as sublimation. Examples of this type of behavior are most often seen in our society in the expression of aggressive impulses through competitive sports. Unlike other neurotic defenses, sublimation allows one's defensive instincts to be channelled to a specific activity rather than to be dammed or diverted.

Sublimation is probably the most overt method of coping. One's feelings are acknowledged, modified slightly, and directed against a relatively insignificant person or goal, so that satisfaction is the result. With displacement, one's feelings are acknowledged, but are redirected with *no* resulting satisfaction. A good example of sublimation in women is the stereotype of the wife who, when she is angry with her husband, spends all day cleaning the house from top to bottom. By doing so she is dissipating her anger, and at the same time, she receives some satisfaction from having a tidy room.

With specific application to second wives, it is easy to imagine the "perfect" second wife who channels all her feelings and energies into making her husband happy in every sense of the word. She is super wife, determined to be "better" than his first. In effect her own anxieties about being seen as less capable than the first wife drive her on to be even more capable than she may have been otherwise.

If he tells her that his first wife always wore flannel nightgowns to bed, she may go out of her way to wear nothing but Frederick's of Hollywood. If his first wife was a good cook, she will take gourmet cooking classes. In these ways, she is sublimating her anxieties about being not as good as his first wife by being much better at whatever her husband feels is important. Hence, in the chapter "Sex and the Second Wife" you will note that many second wives went out of their way to be understanding and "good in bed," especially if their husbands were less than enthralled by their first wives in that area. Not only will sublimation help to curb a second wife's anxieties, but her achievements will result in a mental pat on the back from which she can derive some small pleasure.

Sublimation is a coping mechanism particularly applicable to second wives because of the feelings of competition (often unexpressed) that they may feel with the first wife. Under the circumstances, is it any wonder that many husbands report that they are much happier in their second marriages?

Dissociation

As a method of coping, dissociation is probably the most widespread way of dealing with problems. The use of drugs and/or alcohol in order to numb unhappiness or blot out anxiety or distressing emotions is a part of our daily lives. Dissociation is described as the drastic modification of one's character or one's sense of personal identity to avoid emotional distress.

The role of women in our society creates in many the characteristics commonly attributed to drug and alcohol dependents. Because they are invariably defined on the basis of their relationship to others (husbands, children, friends), women have been treated as a race of children. It is the roots of this patriarchal attitude that programs them to define themselves as dependent, passive, fragile, empathetic, sensitive, nurturant, yielding, and receptive. The internalization of these characteristics by women is a very effective means of social control because, if one can be led to believe in one's own inferiority, then it is that much easier to accept the status that goes with that inferiority. If this is true for women in general, then how much more true can it be for second wives who are in a disadvantaged position compared to other women, let alone to society in general?

Given society's attitude to women and to second wives, is it any wonder then that when a woman has trouble accepting her role or rebels against some of its inequities, she is often told by those around her (husband, family, friends) to seek out professional help to help her cope with her problems? More often than not, she will find her doctor exhibits the same attitudes that trouble her in the first place. When researchers in the field of drug and alcohol dependency have been asked to compare female traits to male, they list such things as more nervous, unstable, neurotic, socially dependent, submissive, fearful, emotional, and passive.

Studies into the use of psychotropic drugs (tranquilizers) found that 24 percent of all prescriptions written were for this type of medication. Seventy percent of these prescriptions were for women. Ninety-five percent of the users of these drugs received them by a prescription in their own name from a licensed physician. Twenty-five percent of the female population in North America will have taken a psychotropic drug within the last two weeks.

What effect do these drugs produce in the women who take them? Essentially they are used to reduce emotional reactions and relieve mild anxiety, tension, or agitation. But, the so-called paradoxical effects of these same drugs include sleep disturbances, rage, personality changes, as well as skin rashes, nausea, and dizziness. Worse still, prolonged use of these drugs can lead to physical dependence and serious withdrawal reaction. Regular use of so-called minor tranquilizers induces tolerance, making increased doses necessary to produce the same effects. Chronic users run the risk of becoming physically and psychologically dependent on the drugs and unable to cope without them.

Other researchers have shown that women are the victims of deceptive advertising by the drug industry. Millions of women are hiding behind a chemical curtain that not only does not shield them from anxiety and depression, but exposes them to more serious illnesses. They go to doctors complaining of harmless ailments, anxieties, and fears and encounter doctors who have been exposed to ads such as a recent one circulated in medical journals for a popular tranquilizer, which shows the drug being dispensed to men for the relief of muscle pain and to women for the relief of emotional problems. Is it any wonder that when women seek professional help, instead of understanding they get a diagnosis of emotional illness and a prescription?

It is too often true that the use of these legal drugs goes hand in hand with the use of alcohol as a method of counteracting stress. The increase in the rate of alcoholism among women was a staggering 60 percent between 1969 and 1979. It is evident that the changing roles of women are leading to increased stress and pressures. One of the newer roles to emerge out of the last few decades is that of the second wife who faces tensions that are on the one hand unexpected, and on the other hand unacknowledged as yet by society as being real problems.

Researchers have found that crisis situations, which relate to the family in particular and the woman's role of wife and mother, can trigger the use of drugs and/or alcohol as a means of coping far more often in women than in men. In the case of the second wife, the seeking of solace in one sort of bottle or another often relates directly to thwarted expectations regarding marriage. We marry to start a new life and frequently find ourselves trapped into dependence, financially and personally, in a situation that does not meet our needs. We sometimes experience devastating guilt when we demand of others what they feel they have the right to demand of us. As second wives, we often harbor underlying resentment and anger at being treated as second class, as might members of any oppressed group. Daily life often confers on the second wife a greater than normal allotment of emotional upheaval and material inequity. There are many reasons why second wives often have a particularly hard time being confident, independent, and aggressive. In a very real sense, they are constantly treading on unbroken ground. There are few people around who will say to them "Yes, the same thing happened to me and I handled it this way." Should we try to express our feelings we are often censored for not exhibiting the correct female behavior.

There is a double bind created by the stress associated with being a second wife *and* the tension of dealing with this stress within the norms of acceptable female behavior. Women are not discouraged from seeking relief through drugs and alcohol. They are, to a certain degree, in keeping with the fashion of the times. We seldom take seriously the "ladies who lunch" even if it includes too many martinis. Yet the use of drugs and alcohol can be the most permanently damaging means of coping we have discussed.

The trivialization of women's problems and concerns in our culture affects all women adversely, but it can be particularly harmful to second wives. So few of our professional people have stopped to consider what it must be like to be a second wife and what the potential problems are. Very few of our professionals have stopped to consider what it is like to be a second wife and that being one may cause problems. A therapist who specializes in marriage counseling for women told me that, despite the fact women are seeing her specifically regarding their marriages, the subject of their husbands' previous marriages is often introduced only after many sessions, although it may prove to be the most significant factor behind their present emotional state. Some therapists to whom I spoke expressed surprise that a second wife could have any problems that would be different than a first wife's. At this point second wives are left to cope more or less on their own.

Coping is defined as successfully handling a problem. As you can see from these examples, coping is perhaps the wrong word for the way these second wives have been dealing with their respective situations; few of these methods have successful results. Most of the coping mechanisms we have discussed are, at best, ways of avoiding coping with the real problems involved. As such they are not as destructive, however, as these last two methods of dealing with the stresses and strains of being a second wife. The first of these is divorce, which will be dealt with in Chapter Ten. Divorce is the final method of removing oneself from an untenable situation. When something can no longer be denied, ignored, or turned into something else, leaving may be considered the only alternative left. This obviously will not save your relationship, but at least it may save you. More and more second wives are taking this way out.

The last alternative, which often comes on the heels of some of the other methods and frequently precedes divorce, is the use of physical violence. Physical violence is generally triggered by a culmination of stressful events. When all the other coping mechanisms fail to ease the pain, and especially when drugs or alcohol are involved, physical violence can erupt. These two cases, taken from recent U.S. and Canadian newspapers, typify what can happen.

> *A thirty-two-year-old woman was charged with attempted murder of her fifty-six-year-old husband after shooting him in the back while he slept. Police said that the shooting followed a domestic argument over the husband's son from a previous marriage.*

> *A forty-seven-year-old man was convicted of the murders of his second wife and stepdaughter after he bludgeoned them to death following a domestic argument over his son from a previous marriage. "I just kept hitting them and hitting them and hitting them," he said. He said his wife, who had been drinking heavily that night, resented the time he spent with his son. He also said that he had been aware that she had been unhappy for some weeks before the murders but "it was an anger that you couldn't get at....I didn't know the reasons for it."*

These tragedies can happen when second wives are afforded little credibility and given even less help for their problems. A paternalistic pat on the head and a prescription will never be a solution. "But you knew what you were getting into when you married him" leads only to the question so many second wives have asked. Did we?

9 *Money and the Second Wife*

"You can be as romantic as you please about love, Hector, but you must not be romantic about money."

George Bernard Shaw

UNFORTUNATELY MOST WOMEN do not take Shaw's advice. They are very romantic about both love and money. This is partly their own fault and partly that of a society that has ingrained in them for centuries the idea that they mustn't bother their "pretty little heads" about the sordid matters of finance, and that as a reward for their ignorance there will always be men around to pay their bills. Ibsen's Nora is a perfect example of the female attitude toward money. When her husband asked what she wanted for Christmas, she asked him if, rather than a gift, he could give her money, so that she would have some of her very own and not have to rely on him for every cent. Nora was ahead of her time in appreciating the power that money can give, and also, the total dependence born of the lack of it. The fact remains, however, that she still had to ask her husband for it.

A century has passed since Nora was created, but things haven't really changed very much for women in regard to money. Most women still rely on their husbands to handle the family finances, content in the belief that they will take care of them. By abnegating their responsibility to take care of

157

themselves and refusing to learn to understand financial matters, which effect their daily lives in a large way, women are leaving themselves open to being taken advantage of. Why is it that more older women live at the poverty level than any other group of comparable size? First of all, society has helped to push them into an old women's ghetto by using them to bring up the next generation and then tossing them on the garbage heap once the task was done. They themselves are responsible in some ways for their plights, however, as are all the single mothers and other women living close to the poverty level because they have never bothered to find out about their finances and have always relied blindly on some man to take care of their interests. Why do women still persist, to this day, in covertly condoning their own financial dependence, whether private or public?

Part of the reason is that women who show any overt interest in money, in its acquisition or maintenance, are thought to be mercenary, scheming golddiggers, and certainly lacking in femininity. No one faces this attitude more than the second wife because many people think that she married for money anyway, so there is already a strike against her. The second thing, which keeps women from learning about their own finances, is men. The reason here is simple. Once women are privy to the mystical knowledge of money and how to make it, what will they need men for?

Slowly, women are taking more notice of their financial situation. They must approach with confidence the issue of family finances (and I don't mean just balancing the household budget) to protect themselves and their children. For the second wife this can be of even greater importance. The following sections on Marriage Contracts, Assets, Taxes, Wills, Insurance, and Pensions are not meant to be the last words on the subject. What they are intended to do is to point out areas where second wives need to be knowledgeable and one hopes they may dispel any irrational fears about the world of personal finance. Second wives must learn to handle their own financial affairs or risk becoming victims of their own ignorance.

Marriage Contracts

Until recent times marriages between people of substance were regulated not only by the state, but by individual marriage contracts, so as to preserve the family wealth in the event of a divorce. The idea of marriage contracts being the privilege of the wealthy dates back to our oldest written legal system— *The Code of Hammurabi* (written by a Babylonian king in the 18th century B.C.)—where the privilege of contractual marriage (i.e., legal marriage) was reserved for the propertied classes only. Aside from preserving family wealth, marriage contracts were also used to lay down the rules of inheritance, marriage settlements, doweries, and where nobility was involved, rank. We must remember that marriages of old were made, more often than not, between two families rather than two individuals, and the foremost ambitions of the families were not the happiness of the couple involved but the financial security and proper succession of the inheritance.

Today's marriages are based almost entirely on the opposite. We marry for love and forget about money, at least in the beginning. It is often not until the marriage comes apart that the question of who owns what becomes important. By then, it is often too late because the lines of communication are severed, and the battle lines are drawn between the people involved. It is then that a marriage contract would be most practical. In spite of the fact that marriage contracts can protect the rights and outline the duties of both parties, most people find the idea of combining love and money distasteful, if not immoral.

There was a time in the not-so-distant past when marriage contracts *per se* were not recognized by the courts since there was usually a reference in the contract to the event of separation, and these clauses were considered to encourage the breakup of marriages. Even today there are still many people who feel that if you go into a marriage planning for its eventual demise you are not ready to marry; if you truly loved each other, you could never consider the possibility of divorce. Members of this till-death-do-us-part society are resisting the reality of a 50-percent divorce rate. Under these circumstances, you cannot afford to rely on love to get you through, because the person that you're absolutely dotty about today could be the man who kidnaps your children in an attempt to gain custody five years from now. The practical among us may acknowledge that what marriage contracts lack in romantic terms they more than compensate for in the throes of divorce. Even so, it is still often difficult to raise the subject with your loved one. Many of us are loathe to be labeled mercenary. This is compounded tenfold if we are marrying men with more money than we have. Many people, in addition, do not understand exactly what marriage contracts are and often tend, therefore, to associate them solely with divorce. They can, however, be useful in other ways, because they can contain any sort of guidelines for the marriage that suit the couple involved, with a few minor exceptions. They are also a wonderful way of clearing the air and laying all the cards on the table *before* it is too late.

If marriage contracts are a good idea for first wives, they are almost a necessity for second wives. First of all, by defining your obligations and contributions to the marriage and those of your husband, you avoid any misunderstandings at a later time. Will your prospective mate be expected to look after his children for three months every summer while his ex-wife is off traveling? What is your role? What will that three months cost you? Is his medical insurance transferred into your name? Who is going to pay for his children's orthodontist? Having a marriage contract lets a second wife know just what she is getting into. It will help her clarify how much her husband earns, how much he pays to his ex-wife and children, and for how long, and just what her expected contribution will be. All this may seem unnecessary when you are head-over-heels in love, but it won't help your relationship to find out after five years of marriage that all his life insurance is still in his first wife's name—and that it is going to stay that way. Second wives have to look out for themselves more carefully than first wives because no one else is doing it for them.

Once you have agreed to have a marriage contract remember that it can be as simple or as complex as you care to make it. It does not necessarily require the use of a lawyer, although common sense would dictate that if a Rockefeller were marrying a Getty it would be a good idea. If you do decide to consult a lawyer, it is better if each party goes to his or her own lawyer because an otherwise legal contract prepared by one lawyer for both parties could be challenged in court on the grounds that undue influence was exerted by the more powerful party on his or her attorney, or even that a conflict of interest existed on the part of the attorney should it come to litigation. As with other written contracts, there are certain requirements that a marriage contract must fulfill before it is deemed valid. It should contain:

1. Offer and Acceptance (evidenced by signatures of both parties).
2. Adequate consideration (something promised in return for the other party's promise).
3. Legal consideration (a promise of sexual favors in return for support or exchange of property is illegal).
4. Clear and reasonably exact terms with little ambiguity or vagueness.
5. Absence of unconscionability (must not be grossly unfair to one party or the other).
6. Absence of duress, coercion, or undue influence.
7. Full and fair disclosure of all relevant facts, assets, and liabilities.

A contract in this form must be signed by both parties. While it can be entered into before the actual date of marriage, it cannot take effect until the marriage itself takes effect.

Advantages of Marriage Contracts for Second Wives

Given the increasingly wide discretionary powers of the courts these days, when it comes to division of property and support, marriage contracts can be very helpful to the second wife. You may wish to have clarified from the beginning, and in writing, just whose name major assets will be in. In the event of divorce, you way also want to know exactly where you will stand with respect to support, or you may wish to protect any assets that you, as an individual, acquire during your marriage. For instance, if you knew that you were going to inherit a valuable piece of property or a painting, you may want it to be declared solely your asset and not an asset of the marriage. Similarly if as a second wife, you come into the marriage with property from a previous marriage, you may want it clearly stated that that property remains yours and yours alone. The matter of custody and support of children, either from your marriage or from a previous marriage, may also be outlined. The more details you include in your marriage contract, the less chance you have of facing emotionally and financially expensive litigation later on.

In most cases marriage contracts are binding, unless they are specifically contrary to the public interest. You cannot include matters relating to birth control or exchange of sexual favors, for instance, because to do so may give the impression that the contract is based on sexual favors and, therefore, is invalid. Judges may override the provisions of a marriage contract if they deem them to be unfair, or if they lead to one spouse being dependent on public assistance.

Whatever terms you agree to will be enforceable for the next ten, twenty, or thirty years depending on how long your marriage lasts. Make sure that you can live with them over the long run and that the contracts will be equally satisfactory to you in the event of any future changes in the marriage.

Assets

Any asset that is in the husband's name is accessible to his former spouse's claims. Generally speaking, it is best that any property acquired during a second marriage be put in the second wife's name if there is concern that the first wife (or children) may try to acquire interest in such property. Putting assets in the second wife's name can circumvent the problems that may arise from wills and questions of succession because the assets involved are not part of the husband's estate. They are part of his wife's estate, which is a step toward putting them out of the reach of his former family.

Another reason for putting assets in the second wife's name is that should the husband default on his support payments to his ex-wife or children for whatever reason, and there was a separation agreement or court order pursuant to which the husband is required to pay money to the first wife (or children), the first wife may get a judgment from the court against the husband for a specified sum of money. Armed with such a judgment the wife has all the rights that any judgment creditor has against a debtor. These include the right to seize and sell real estate or any property owned by the debtor. A judgment creditor does not have a right to seize and sell real estate, however, until one year after the judgment has been granted.

The final reason for putting property or assets in the second wife's name is that a separation agreement, which affords support to an ex-wife or children, does not necessarily terminate on the death of the husband. It can be applied against his estate after his death, whereupon the necessary assets may be seized and sold to satisfy the financial obligation of the agreement, regardless of what the man's will might indicate.

It would seem, then, that in order to protect the second wife and any children of that marriage from the financial responsibilities incurred during first marriage, most husbands would be well-advised to put major assets in their second wife's name. But do they? Our study showed that 61 percent of the husbands did not put any assets acquired during their previous marriages in the first wives' names, but 63.4 percent did put at least some of the major assets acquired during their second marriages in their second wives' names. Twenty-seven percent put assets in neither wife's name, while 20 percent put assets in both the first and second wives' names. Only 9.7 percent put assets in their first wives' names, but not their second.

This suggests that while the majority of husbands did not put assets in their first wives' names, they had a change of heart when they married for the second time. This may indicate that the husbands are showing concern for the security of their second wives (and children) by protecting them financially. It may also indicate that by putting these assets in their second wives' names, they are enjoying some small revenge on first wives who stripped them of their assets during the divorce. At the same time they are making it perfectly clear just where their loyalties now lie. The statistics do not indicate that a husband who was "burned" by his first wife will be very reticent to part with ownership of major assets to his next wife since less than 10 percent of husbands, who gallantly put assets in their first wives' names, refused to do so a second time.

In the face of our current legal climate, which seems to favor first wives over husbands or second wives, and in order to recognize the financial contribution of the second wife to the marriage and secure her position, it is advisable to put major assets in the second wife's name rather than face the possibility that, at some time in the future, the first wife or children may try to attach assets to which they are really not entitled.

The Tax Man Cometh

When you marry a divorced man or are planning on living with one until he is divorced so that you can then marry, it is a good idea to be familiar with his tax situation because it will affect your financial position as a couple. Tax laws, like divorce laws, vary from place to place. Also, like divorce laws, many tax specialists believe that current tax laws are years behind the times when it comes to reflecting the realities of our society. Although the concept of fault was supposedly removed from divorce laws in the 1970s, it is still an element of the tax laws. Tax-wise, divorce can be just as much a crushing blow, especially to the husband, as the emotional impact of the marriage breakup. Quite simply, tax laws are anachronistically punitive. Not everyone, of course, loses in the case of a divorce. The government usually does nicely. In fact, in the United States, approximately $500 million per year finds its way into government coffers as a direct result of divorce-related taxes (approximately $100 million of which is on alimony alone). Part of this problem is based on people's lack of knowledge about the tax implications of getting divorced. When your world is falling apart, it is rather difficult to turn your mind to saving yourself from the tax man. Another aspect of the problem is the inflexibility of these tax laws that tends to turn people's personal crises into a source of additional government revenue. It is, therefore, important for a second wife (or soon-to-be second wife) to provide some objective insight into what is happening to her husband's financial position because they will both bear the brunt of decisions made at this point for years to come.

Tax and Property Settlements

In the United States, the tax laws are so structured that a husband who gives up (or is forced to give up) his share of the family home can be hit with a heavy capital gains tax on the increased value of the house during the time he owned it. The tax is due immediately upon the divorce being made final. The IRS regards the transfer of the house to the wife as a sale, even if, technically, she has not bought it. The same is true when a husband and wife exchange assets of equal value (for instance, she gives up her interest in the family business for his interest in the house). The tax man regards this not as a swap, but as two separate sales, and consequently two separate taxable events taking place, in the forty-three states where assets of the marriage are not automatically jointly owned. The husband, therefore, is left paying tax on half the increased value of the house, and the wife on half the increased value of the business. If the wife has no money of her own, of course, it is usually the husband who ends up paying both lots of taxes.

Divorcing couples in community property states do not have to pay taxes on a equal exchange of assets because the division of co-owned property (the property of the marriage is so regarded) is not a sale in the eyes of the tax man. If either the husband or the wife uses separate property (such as individual bank accounts) to pay off a half interest in a community asset, however, this then becomes a taxable event. The paying off of an obligation in installments after the divorce is also considered a taxable event.

For most divorcing couples, timing is an essential element in avoiding paying too much tax. Any sale should occur after the divorce because there are punitive tax rules applied to the sale of property between related parties (so don't bother trying to switch assets and then get divorced in the hope of avoiding taxes). After the final decree, assets will be taxed at the lower capital-gains rate, and this is, therefore, the best time to "sell" them to your former spouse. The point is that a husband, who is trying to be a nice guy and let his former wife and kids stay in the family home, usually gets hit with a whopping tax bill when he "sells" the house to her at a time when he (and his second wife) can least afford it. In Canada, there are tax consequences when a husband transfers his share of the family home to his wife upon a separation.

Tax on Maintenance and Child Support

In the United States alimony and maintenance payments are taxable to the recipient (usually the wife) and deductible for the party who pays (usually the husband), as long as these payments are made under a decree of divorce or a separate maintenance order; under a written divorce or separation instrument; or under a written separation agreement or decree of support. If a husband is simply paying his ex-wife an amount of money every month without one of these written documents, he cannot deduct those payments. Because of this, it is not unusual for ex-wives or separated wives bent on revenge to hold off getting it in writing as long as possible because, once it is, they will be taxed on the amount of money they receive.

Payments for the support of minor children are neither

income to the recipient nor deductible for the paying party. Because of this, the amounts of child support and alimony should be clearly delineated and fixed in the final divorce decree. In the no-alimony state of Texas, child-support payments are often padded to provide for the ex-wife as well, thereby offering the husband no tax break.

In Canada both alimony (paid while the marriage continues to subsist) and maintenance (paid after the marriage has been dissolved) are deductible to the payor as long as there is a written agreement to that effect. Third-party payments (i.e., mortgage and utilities), when they are of direct benefit to the receiving spouse, are also deductible to the payor and taxable to the recipient. As for minor children, payments for their support are taxable to the parent in whose custody the children are (usually the wife) and deductible for the paying party.

In Great Britain any payments under a court order or binding agreement for the maintenance of the wife or ex-wife are deductible to the husband and taxable to the wife. Tax must be deducted from payments of alimony and maintenance at 33 percent except that no tax must be deducted from payments up to an annual limit of £1,092 where payments are made by one party to the marriage for the benefit of the other or for the maintenance of a person under the age of twenty-one. Voluntary payments are neither deductible nor taxable. And maintenance payments made directly to the children are taxable to them and deductible to the payor. If the divorce is effected in a foreign court, no tax is deductible from the resident of Great Britain who is paying, but if the recipient is in the United Kingdom, tax on the amount received will be required.

Alimony or maintenance payments in both Canada and the United States must be periodic in nature in order to be deductible. Generally this means that they must be paid in a fixed amount over an indefinite period of time, or an indefinite amount for a fixed period of time. Temporary rehabilitative alimony, therefore, is not deductible to the husband or taxable to the wife.

Lump-sum settlements (a one-time, agreed-upon amount), even if paid in installments over a period of years, are not deductible by the payor or taxable in Canada. For this reason many men who could pay a large sum of money for a one-time payment to their ex-wives prefer to make periodic payments. In the United States the payments of a principal sum over an extended period (up to ten years) has a deduction limited to 10 percent of the principal sum in any given year.

One more point of interest: neither the cost of the legal fees in a divorce (generally born by the husband), nor the cost of legal fees for enforcing an order for support are deductible in Canada. This is inspite of the fact that, up until recently, a wife could deduct the cost of taking her ex-husband back to court.

Marriage Penalty Tax

Because such a large percentage of second wives work, compared to the total population of wives in general, it is wise to be aware of the so-called marriage penalty tax, or sin subsidy, before you decide to go from just living together to being legally married. Since 1969 when Congress, in an effort to equalize the tax burden between singles and marrieds, introduced what became known as the marriage penalty tax, many couples who otherwise would have said "I do" prefer to say nothing at all. Under the tax system of progressive rates, the first tax dollar of the second income (i.e., the wife's) is taxed at the same rate as the last tax dollar of the first income (i.e., the husband's). The tax tab for a married couple with two incomes, therefore, is substantially higher than for two single people who are living together. This piece of legislation has caused quite some outrage in the last ten years. Some couples have even gone so far as to get divorced because of it. Starting in 1983, any couple with two working members can now deduct the first 10 percent of the first $30,000 of the second income. The higher the couples' tax bracket, the greater the saving. In an effort to overcome previous inequities, new inequities have been created, however, because the full tax deduction is available only when each spouse earns a minimum of $30,000. Statistically speaking, these couples are not in the majority.

This is just another example of where the laws have failed to keep up with the times. By creating this tax penalty for two-income families, they failed to take into consideration that, in this day and age, the two-income family is a necessity, not a luxury, particularly if you are a second wife.

Wills

The making of wills is a subject that most people avoid. Either they find the subject itself distasteful because it is, of necessity, associated with the death of a loved one, or they feel that wills are only for the rich, and their relatively meager possessions do not need a lot of expensive legal claptrap in order to be properly distributed posthumously. Women in particular shy away from the subject of wills because many feel that they have nothing of any great value to leave behind. They just assume that their husbands will "take care of that sort of thing."

Until recently, this may have been true. Except in the cases of the wealthy, men were generally left to deal with the subject of wills because they were the ones who had the property to dispose of. Times have changed, however, and now the subject of wills is something that should be investigated thoroughly by all women—and particularly by the second wife.

Wills concern the second wife in two ways. Firstly she should find out if her husband has a will and, if so, what is in it. This is not being mercenary; it is being practical. Most wives assume they will receive the bulk of their husbands' estates, but the second wife particularly would be well-advised to verify this. Secondly she should think about having her own will to take care of her family and dependents, because her family and her husband's family are not necessarily one and the same.

The fact of the matter is not all men make wills. In the event that your husband dies intestate (without having made a will) then you, as his legal wife, will be entitled to the first $75,000 of his estate. After that, depending on how many children are involved (from first or second marriages), as his wife, you will be entitled to one-half of the residue of his estate if there is one child, or one-third the residue of his estate if there are two children or more. You must be prepared, though, if you are a second wife and your husband dies intestate, for the eventuality that other people, besides you and your children, will have a claim on his estate. If he has been paying alimony or child support, then the recipients of these payments, as his dependents, will also have a claim on his estate. Without a will specifically declaring his intentions about the dispersal of his estate, there could be years of costly court battles between you and other family members. This is not to say that if he does leave a will and bequeaths all his possessions to you, his second wife, that his first wife and children cannot contest it or that the courts cannot override it. They can. By leaving a legal will, however, he will make things much easier for you in court, because the judge will subsequently be able to take into consideration his wishes in the matter. As a second wife, therefore, you should encourage your husband to make a will, because the more people who feel they have an interest in his estate, the harder it will be for you to retain what he may have wanted you to have.

In one case the husband took care to leave a legal will. Although his children from his first marriage contested it, his widow is in a much better position than she would have been had he died without leaving his instructions. The husband was a reasonably well-off retired businessman at the time of his death. He left a will providing that his second wife, a woman in her sixties, could live off the proceeds of his estate, while the two children from his first marriage, who were in their late thirties, would share equally in that income when she died. The children both took their stepmother to court charging that, as executrix of the estate, she was mismanaging her responsibilities by trying to sell the estate and force a settlement. In addition, they wanted her to pay back the $178,000 she had received from the estate over the past nine years. The case is still pending, but it shows what a second wife can expect, even when her deceased husband's wishes are clearly stated.

Over 85 percent of the husbands in the study had made arrangements for their estates should they die. It was interesting to note that while a far smaller portion of the second wives had also made wills, there was a distinct difference in the attitudes of the husbands and the wives regarding to whom they would bequeath their possessions. Over 50 percent of the husbands left their estates to their second wives and children (from either one or both marriages and usually divided equally). Another 32 percent left everything solely to their second wives, and 15 percent left the estates only to their children with no provision for their second wives. For the second wives it was quite another story. A full 40 percent of the second wives left everything to either friends or other relatives, instead of their husbands. This is understandable when you think that many second wives do not have children from their marriages and do not want to see their possessions revert to their husbands' families should the husbands die after inheriting their estates. They preferred that their belongings be divided among people for whom they cared. Only 25 percent of the second wives left their estates solely to their husbands, while 28 percent left them to their husbands and to children of the marriage between the second wives and their husbands jointly.

As for the ex-wives, it is significant to note that none of the husbands in this survey made any provision for their ex-wives in their wills. Ordinarily, unless a contrary intention appears in the will (such as a will contract, which makes the husband's will irrevocable and, therefore, means that he cannot change it to include new beneficiaries or exclude old ones should he remarry), the devise or bequest of a beneficial interest in a man's property to his former spouse is revoked, and the will is construed as if the former spouse had died before him.

With respect to the children from the marriage for a second wife, it is most important to note that whether the deceased was testate or intestate, if he has not made adequate provisions for the proper support of his dependents (i.e., children from either marriage who are being supported by him), the court, upon application, may order that such provision as it considers adequate be made out of the estate for proper support. This means that all the husband's minor children are theoretically treated equally with respect to support, and that he cannot leave everything to one set of children and ignore the others. This does not mean that all children must share equally in the estate, only that adequate support must be provided for them while they are minors. If such an application for support is made, the court may make an order suspending, in whole or in part, the administration of the deceased's estate until the matter is settled. It would seem, therefore, to be to everyone's advantage to get the matter settled as soon as possible. The question of need versus want is integral here. Those who merely want some of their father's estate have been known to hold up the proceedings until they have forced those in need to acquiesce to terms that they may otherwise have refused.

No application for support can be made after six months from the time a will is probated (if there is a will), or until the court has granted letters of administration (if there is no will). Letters of probate and letters of administration empower the executors (administrators of the estate) named in the will or the appointed administrators to manage and distribute the estate. Those included among dependents who have a right to file a claim against the estate are: parents, children, siblings of the deceased, and the deceased's spouse. The definition of spouse in this context includes a person whose marriage to the deceased was terminated or declared a nullity. A divorced spouse, therefore, can be a dependent entitled to claim against the estate. A common-law spouse may also be regarded as a dependent. As with support payments, the court may order payments to be made in a lump sum, periodically (with either a limited or unlimited number of payment periods), or the court may order the possession or use of specific property by a dependent in order to fulfill the need for support.

One point, which it is essential to make about wills, is that the court's attitude today concerning the inviolability of wills is quite different from what most people commonly perceive it to be. This quote from a judgment made in 1870 illustrates the way most people feel the law approaches one's last will and testament.

The English law leaves everything to the unfettered discretion of the testator on the assumption that though in some instances caprice or passion or the power *of new* ties *or artful contrivance or sinister influence may lead to the neglect of claims that ought to be attended to, yet, the instincts, affections and common sentiments of mankind may be safely trusted to secure on the whole a better disposition of the property of the dead and one more accurately adjusted to the requirements of each particular case than could be obtained by the stereotyped and inflexible rules of the general law.*

In essence what this says is that left on their own, morality and common decency will assure that the person making the will will do the right thing by those who are his dependents, even if he has married again. It is clear that the pendulum has swung to the other extreme in today's courts, where the "stereotyped and inflexible rules of general law" are commonly applied to wills often disregarding what the testator has laid out. Be well-advised when making out a will, then, to keep in mind that, regardless of what you may want, the law may deem it necessary to intervene. This is particularly important to the second wife because while her husband may have left everything to her, the courts can insist that his estate continue to support his other dependents (i.e., his first wife and children). In that context it should be acknowledged that while minor children may grow up and no longer require support from your husband's estate, his ex-wife is entitled to the support she has been receiving possibly for the rest of her life.

Many people are in awe of wills because they are legal documents and because they are so, people often feel that they cannot make a will without the costly advice of a lawyer. This is not necessarily the case. Allowing for certain basic parameters, a will can be made by anyone, anywhere. In order to be valid, a homemade or holograph will can be in one of two forms. It can be an English-style will, which is written in anybody's handwriting (or typed or printed), but which is signed by the testator (the person making the will). The signature must be witnessed by two people, neither of whom is to benefit from the will, present at the time of the signing. A holograph will is wholly in the testator's own handwriting and, as such, does not require the corroboration of witnesses. In either case what must be clear are the identity of the giver, the identity of what is being given, and the identity of the person who is to receive it. The intention of the will must be clear and in writing before the court will consider it valid, but it does not have to be a complicated legal document unless the person making the will has a lot to bequeath to many individuals. In that event the advice of a lawyer is best sought.

It is important for a second wife to consider having a will of her own made, particularly if she and her husband put assets acquired during their marriage in her name or if she has dependent children from the marriage. Wills are not a morbid subject. They are a necessary piece of business that one hopes will make things easier for friends and family if something happens to you. Also, as a second wife, you should make an effort to find out about your husband's will. Don't you make the same mistake made by the second wife who found out only after her husband died that he left everything to his former family. It is better to be prepared.

Insurance

A recent full-page ad in a national news magazine from Imperial Life Insurance Company had a banner headline which read: *MARRIAGE USED TO BE ALL THE LIFE INSURANCE A WOMAN NEEDED.*" The ad went on to point out: "with marriage came the assurance that you would always be taken care of." Today, it suggested, when one in three marriages ends in divorce, "more women are opting to take care of themselves." Would that that were the case.

Today most first wives are still being "taken care of" by their ex-husbands' insurance. Life insurance is being incorporated more and more by lawyers into divorce or separation agreements. This means that husbands must keep up their life insurance payments, and ex-wives and/or children remain the irrevocable beneficiaries. It also means that the husband cannot change the beneficiary of his insurance policy—ever.

This has definite connotations for the second wife and her children. Most men cannot afford to pay for dual insurance, that is, for each family. Since they must continue to pay for their original life insurance policies and cannot switch beneficiaries, their second wives are often out of luck. Husbands, whose insurance policies are work-related benefits and who otherwise cannot afford additional outside coverage or for other reasons would not normally consider it, may be forced to do so in an effort to provide some sort of coverage naming their new spouses as beneficiaries. Otherwise, their second wives would be unprotected in the event of their deaths, but their first wives would not. Second wives would be wise to investigate their husbands' life insurance situation and to consider, if they have dependents of their own, taking out their own life insurance policies.

As with wills, many women do not feel they need life insurance because they are not the major breadwinners in their families, and their deaths would not unduly deprive the families of support. This may be the case for the first wife, who stayed at home to raise the children (depending on what dollar value you wish to place on her role as a homemaker), but for the second wife, who works and whose income is an integral part of her family's financial support, the possible dent in the budget caused by her death or disability could be significant. The second wife with children should also consider that, if the husband's life insurance already names the children from his previous marriage as beneficiaries, she would be well-advised to take out some life insurance naming her own children as beneficiaries in the event something should happen to her, because they cannot expect their father to be able, for example, to put all the children through college on his salary alone.

Many women avoid the subject of insurance because they do not understand the various types of policies and their benefits. The way to best match your requirements to what is available is to do some shopping around. Here is a brief rundown on what to look for in insurance.

What Kind of Insurance?

A working woman who has dependents to support may need to consider these possibilities:

1. She may want life insurance to replace her income if she dies.
2. She may want an insurance policy which would pay off a mortgage or other debts.
3. She may want to have some sort of disability insurance in case she is sick or disabled for a time (or permanently) and unable to work.

Once she has decided why she needs insurance, she must decide on the amount of insurance required and the type.

Calculating the amount of life insurance you need does not have to be complicated once you have decided why you need it. Start with an assessment of your net worth. List all the amounts of money available on your death including any funds from private or public pension plans, the value of your investments, and your savings and bank balance. If you own a house and intend that it should be sold on your death, then include that too, minus the amount still outstanding on the mortgage. From your total assets, deduct your total liabilities. What is left is your estate. Usually only very large estates are subject to succession duties. If yours falls into this category, include those duties as a liability. Your insurance policy generally will not be subject to tax, but it may be included as part of your estate and as such bring the total value into the bracket subject to succession duties.

Once you have calculated the value of your estate, the next step is to determine how much your dependents need, if you are no longer there to support them. Subtract this amount from any other income source you may have. The result is the balance you must provide through insurance. There are many suggested formulae for determining what your total life insurance coverage should be. One of the most widely used is simply to multiply your annual income by five.

Once you have decided how much, it is time to decide what kind of insurance will best suit your needs. It is much better to go to an insurance agent already armed with some idea of what you need. Remember, agents work on commission and they may be tempted to sell you more insurance, or more expensive insurance, than you really need. There are two basic types of policies: term and whole life. Insurance agents get a much bigger commission on whole life, but it is more expensive for the policy holder, so it is important for you to understand the difference. Term insurance provides protection for a specified period of time only. If you die within that period, the insurance company pays out. Once that period is up, however, your insurance protection is finished. Term insurance is ideal for the woman who wants to provide income replacement for her dependents for a limited period of time, or who wants to cover the amount of her mortgage in case she dies before it is paid off. Whole life insurance is the type of policy that pays a lump sum on your death, no matter when you die, so the premium you must pay is much higher. Many people will argue that term insurance is all anyone really needs, and as a woman, when statistics show that you will most likely outlive your husband, you can probably best meet your insurance needs with a term policy.

Term Insurance Policies

There are a variety of term insurance policies. A "level term" policy means that the amount of coverage remains the same throughout the period of the policy, but the premiums themselves may escalate because, as you get older, the risk that the company will have to pay out increases. A level term policy may also be "renewable." This means that at the end of the policy term, you have the option to renew the policy for a further period without taking a medical exam. The premium may go up if you renew, however, and there is a limit on the number of times that you can renew. A term policy may also be in the form of a "decreasing term." This means that the amount of your insurance will decrease each year, but the premiums will stay the same. This is a suitable policy if you are taking out insurance to pay off your mortgage in the event of your death as it can be arranged that the term of the policy coincides with the term of the mortgage, so that, as the mortgage decreases, the amount of the insurance decreases proportionately. Term policies may also be "convertible," which means that you have the option to convert them to whole life before the expiration of the term, without taking a medical.

Some policies offer a combination. You may be allowed to start out with a level term, change to decreasing term on any policy anniversary, and move back to level term if you want to or change to whole life. This ability to change or increase your insurance coverage without taking a medical may be significant, especially as you get older and more medical problems are likely to develop.

Term insurance and whole life insurance may also be participating and non-participating. This means that you may or may not be able to share in your company's profits. It is necessary, naturally, to pay a higher premium for a participating policy.

Whole Life Insurance

Whole life insurance may also be referred to as straight life, ordinary life, permanent life, or cash value insurance, but all mean the same thing. The policy pays out when you die unless you cash it in first. If you buy whole life, the premium will remain the same throughout the term of the policy (i.e., your life) even though the risk factor may increase as you get older. This is made possible by charging more than the company needs to cover its risks in the early years and less later on. Naturally your premiums will be lower the younger you are when you take out the policy. Young women have the lowest premiums because they are expected to live the longest and have more opportunity to pay.

With whole life insurance, as your premiums accumulate your policy builds up a cash value. This cash surrender value, as it is also called, is the amount of money you get back if you decide to give up the policy. With whole life, you can borrow up to the amount of the cash value from the insurance company at a fairly low interest rate. Remember, though, that the insurance company is actually only lending you your own money, and if the loan is still outstanding when you die, they will deduct the amount you have borrowed from the value of the policy before paying out. Cash buildup value is very slow for insurance policies and you are usually required to leave your money in for a minimum period (two years) before borrowing it back. If it's savings you want, you would do better opening a savings account at the bank because the rate of interest you will get from the "savings" through your policy is usually at least two percentage points below what you could get by investing in a long-term savings plan, such as a guaranteed investment certificate. Remember also that if you keep the policy until you die, the insurance company will only pay out the face value of the policy and not the amount you have paid in. This can represent a considerable difference, particularly if you take the policy out at a fairly young age.

As with term policies, there are variations of whole life policies available. Limited payment life is one alternative, for which you pay premiums for only a limited period of time. The premiums, naturally, are higher, but such a plan is suitable for the person who expects to earn the bulk of his or her income over a few short years. Single premium life is a whole life policy you pay for in one lump sum. Endowment policies are a form of permanent insurance that pays out at a particular maturity date (i.e., you could buy an endowment policy to pay out when you are sixty-five to provide you with a lump sum upon your retirement). Such policies are very expensive, however, and are really more of a way of saving than of being insured.

Disability Insurance

Every working woman should consider having disability insurance above and beyond what the various government plans allow, particularly if she has dependents. Private disability insurance for women is a notorious area of discrimination, but many insurance companies will try to convince you otherwise. The fact remains that insurance companies will often not offer private disability insurance to women, and those that do may charge a woman double what they would charge a man for the same coverage. Often, it is only women with high incomes who can afford such coverage. For those women who work out of their own homes and who are full-time homemakers, it is virtually impossible to get any kind of disability insurance. The reason for this discrimination is that disability premiums are based on rate of claim, and women claim disability far more often than do men. Men have *longer* periods of absence due to disability, however, and they also have a far higher incidence of serious illnesses such as cancer and heart disease.

Some companies do offer disability insurance for the working woman as an adjunct to life insurance. A typical policy provides for disability payments to begin after a waiting period of three months. It charges a twenty-five-year-old woman 40 percent more than a man of the same age for the same coverage, and at age forty-five 30 percent more. This is predicated on the belief that if it is too easy for a married woman to get disability payments, there will be less incentive for her to return to work because, after all, she has a husband to support her. This typifies the popular point of view about women not really needing to work or to have insurance because they will always have men to look after them. It does not apply, in most cases, to the second wife who *does* need to work and who likely marries a man a little older than herself whom she cannot realistically expect to always be around to look after her or her dependents. Although the situation with respect to disability insurance is grossly unfair at the moment, if your salary is as essential to your family's maintenance as your husband's, and many second wives will tell you that it is, it is a good idea to shop around and see what kinds of disability insurance you can come up with — just in case.

Housewives, of course, are out of this picture because it is considered difficult or impossible to determine an income base for their disability payments. It is difficult, apparently, to determine and pinpoint when a homemaker first becomes disabled and when she can return to work. It would seem that a good criterion for making such a determination is to take into account how long and how much the family must pay for someone else to do her work. The typical disability policy provides benefits for the first two years that the policy holder is unable to perform his or her regular occupation, and after that, benefits are related to whether or not the policy holder is capable of any other kind of work. This, too, is difficult to determine, according to the insurance companies, in the case of a housewife.

Pensions

The issue of pension benefits is usually something that most people do not think about until they near retirement age, but the second wife should consider it much earlier because of the presence of the ex-wife. More and more, today's courts are awarding pension rights as part of divorce settlements. This is done in order to improve the financial situation of the wife who has not worked outside the home, and who, therefore, has no pension benefits of her own. Generally speaking the portion of the ex-husband's pension awarded to his ex-wife is usually half, based on his contributions while they were living under the same roof. Many lawyers will attempt to incorporate pension benefits into a separation agreement, but even if the ex-wife relinquishes her claim to those benefits, the courts are more often taking the position that they will not enforce such a release. If a husband fails to pay support to his ex-wife according to the court order, then all or part of his pension may be awarded to his ex-wife to account for that support.

Recently one ex-wife tried to have her husband's company pension garnisheed to cover back support payments. The company's lawyer, however, argued that a garnishee order could only be levied against the man's salary, and since he was no longer employed by the company, the pension could not be considered as salary. The woman lost her case. This does not apply, however, to government pensions. There are two ways an estranged wife can approach getting a share of her husband's company pension. First, if he has not yet retired, but has accumulated a pension fund either privately or through group insurance, she may gain access. If he is already retired, she may attach the pension directly, but as we have seen, this does not usually work very well. Theoretically, divorced wives cannot attach a man's pension, but there are movements afoot to change that law, and we can expect that, in the near future, a man's pension will also be fair game for his ex-wife, even if it was not part of the original divorce settlement.

As a second wife this may have direct implications for you, especially if you are married to, or even living with, a man who is retired or is about to do so. Older people generally have to be satisfied with a lower standard of living, but if you and your new husband are reduced to living on half his pension while his ex-wife lives on the other half, then things will be even more economically strapped. This will change in the future as more working wives have pensions of their own, but for the moment, the situation definitely favors the first wife because she is supposedly entitled to a share of the pension since she did not work outside the home during her marriage. If the second wife who was previously married did not work outside the home during her first marriage, she is still not entitled to part of her former husband's benefits if she remarries or lives common-law with another man. What you have is one wife living on half a pension, and the husband and his new wife living on the other half. It would seem that any man retiring under these circumstances should make sure that his second wife is still young enough to work.

There are many things about money that a second wife needs to know to protect her interests and those of her dependents. Asking about these things does not make her mercenary; it makes her a practical woman who is concerned, intelligently, about her own financial position and that of her family. Remember—ignorance in this area does not bring bliss, but it may bring disaster.

10 *Divorce and the Second Wife*

"If marriages do not last forever, then why should divorce."
                                        Jean-Pierre Aumont

DIVORCE IS AN ISSUE that faces the second wife in two ways. Firstly, as a second wife she inherits the outcome of her husband's previous divorce (keep in mind that 84 percent of the husbands of the second wives surveyed were divorced from their first wives). Although the courts will tell you that the object of divorce is to see that "both parties are fully restored to their former state," any second wife will tell you that this rarely proves to be the case. Unlike marriages, divorces can last quite literally for a lifetime and even longer. Secondly, the second wife may have to contend with the possibility of her own divorce. In the last few years the divorce rate for second marriages has increased from 35 percent to 57 percent. In 33 percent of the unions where the husband was previously married and the wife previously single, the breakup of the marriage occurs before the fifth wedding anniversary. This can be compared to only 19 percent of the marriages where both partners were previously single. In the survey for this book 40 percent of the second wives interviewed said that they had considered seriously, or had already started, the procedure to divorce. Their reasons, for the most part, were directly related to their status as second wives and not to any internal problems with personality conflicts or goal orientation that often plague other marriages and lead to the brink of divorce.

I am currently in the process of divorcing my husband because of his on-going affair with his first wife. It is not just the affair itself but the fact that he seems to think it's OK for him to do this because they used to be married.

I have seriously considered divorcing my husband because I am tired of playing second fiddle to his children. They make me feel like a servant in my own home and I can't get rid of the feeling that he places them first in his life over me.

I have considered divorcing him because of our severe difference of opinion about my two teenage children living with us. He doesn't want them and I keep telling him I am their mother as well as his wife.

Yes. I am in the process of divorcing him now. It is too hard to compete with the memories of his first wife. I can't live in the same house with both of them, if you know what I mean. She's dead and has been for some years but to him she might walk through the door any minute.

Sometimes I have considered divorcing him. I would like to marry someone who had never been married before and start my life over fresh without all the hassles of his kids and his ex and the money problems they have caused us. It has really destroyed our relationship.

Yes, sometimes I think about divorcing him because even though we are married there is still the sense in our relationship that I am his mistress and she is his wife. We cannot shake it. It's as though we are not really married. There is no sense of permanence when you are married to a divorced man because there is always that thought that he might get divorced again. The whole concept of your marriage is different.

Is it any wonder that the subject of divorce is one in which second wives have so much interest? For those second wives who have never been married or divorced before, this chapter will serve as an explanation of just what they can expect should it happen to them, and for those who are marrying divorced men, it will serve to outline what has already happened to their husbands and how it might affect them and their marriages.

A Perspective on Divorce

Until recently divorce was difficult if not impossible to obtain in our society, and once it was obtained, those who were party to it were permanently tainted with the scent of failure if they were men, or stamped with the reputation of the "gay divorcée" if they were women. Divorce was not something that so-called nice people did because it negates the basis of our whole society—the family.

Historically our attitudes toward divorce have run the gamut from the unilateral repudiation popular in the Roman Empire, to the time of the Reformation when a valid marriage was considered immutable. It was either very easy or downright impossible, depending on where you were and whether the church or the state had the final say. Under the strict jurisdiction of the church, there was a feeling, which still exists today in some religions, of the irrefutable sanctity of the married state. We carry some of this belief into the present with the idea that for each one of us there is one perfect mate. It wasn't until the late sixteenth century that marriage jurisdiction passed into the hands of the state and civil divorce developed into a possible alternative, albeit not an easy one to procure. It wasn't until 1857 that divorce in England (much Canadian civil law is based on English civil law) no longer required an act of Parliament to become a reality. It is easy to see why divorce was not a very popular method of rectifying marital discord. It was around this time also (the mid- to late-nineteenth century) that the concept of a dual standard for husband and wife, insofar as grounds were concerned, became part of the law. A wife guilty of adultery could claim no maintenance after a divorce and the "innocent" spouse, who was usually the husband, had the best chance for custody. If a husband obtained a divorce from his wife on grounds of adultery, he was entitled to compensation from her paramour. Many systems prohibited a spouse who had committed adultery from remarrying for a certain period of time or from marrying the paramour involved; and so developed the concept of "fault" which, like it or not, is still very much with us today.

Fault presupposes that one spouse is innocent and the other, guilty. Until very recently only the "innocent" spouse could be granted a divorce. Fault, by its very implication, necessitated the process of adversarial divorce common in our culture today. One spouse is pitted against the other with the respective lawyers and witnesses lining up on opposing sides in order to decide who was really right and who was wrong, and, therefore, to determine which of them is entitled to the bulk of the "spoils" from the marriage. Because the courts do not generally have the time to dig down into the mire of the relationship and find out just who did what to whom and, therefore, achieve some form of titular justice, they tended to rely on the unspoken rule that the husband is the guilty party. After all, if he couldn't control his family's affairs, or if, God forbid, he was the one who left the family home for whatever reason, he must be to blame and should be made to pay accordingly. Many husbands understandably find this difficult to swallow, especially those who were not responsible for the breakdown of their first marriages. In the course of researching this book, I came across many irate husbands who complained that "*She* left me" or "*She* was the one who was always fooling around," and yet they find themselves still found guilty for the divorce. They feel this is because they are being punished by an unfair judicial system that levies on them inordinate financial burdens. Out of all this grumbling the idea for no-fault divorce evolved, which says, basically, that neither side was to blame, and the marriage just broke down as some marriages are wont to do. One hopes the day will come when this concept takes hold and divorce, consequently, will become a much easier and less inequitable process. In the meantime we still have to fight our way through the divorce courts, wounding our ex-spouses as much as we can in order to get divorced. This is when the trouble begins, not ends, as we shall see.

Divorce and the Second Wife

In spite of the trend toward easier and less painful divorces and the assertion by some experts that the rising divorce rate is not a repudiation of the married state as many alarmists claim, the courts and our legal system generally still approach the whole issue of divorce. as though it were the end. In fact, for most people it is merely a change of direction. Men do get remarried and have other families, and yet, rather than encouraging a severing of old ties if at all practicable, the current legal structure encourages constant contact between divorced spouses over custody, maintenance, and financial matters. Added to this, the revenge created out of the adversarial process provides a desire on the part of the "wronged" spouse to get back at his or her former mate. With the help of the courts, the so-called wronged party can ensure that he or she will be a constant presence in life of the former spouse and the new family.

Divorce in the 1980s

Part of the reason behind our system's encouragement of this constant presence is that society has changed its attitudes considerably in the last twenty years. No longer is the divorcée viewed as the immoral seductress of other women's husbands. Suddenly she has become the victim of the divorce and not the cause. The prevailing attitude in the 1980s is still "how could he do that to her?" The former shady lady of the divorce courts has now become the respected single parent trying to cope with raising a family on her own. Divorce laws and society's attitudes have not remained static. There was a time when divorce law blatantly favored the man. The children were seen as his property, as was everything else. He could divorce his wife for adultery, but if she wanted to divorce him, she had to prove adultery *plus* an additional ground, such as rape, sodomy, or desertion. If she was successful, she got virtually nothing from the marriage, regardless of how many years she may have worked in the home or, possibly, in the family business.

This was obviously a very unfair and one-sided state of affairs, which the legal system has gone a long way toward rectifying. Some would say it has gone too far and has moved from extreme to extreme, without considering the implications. While the changes in divorce law were intended to address the inequities faced by women, in many ways they have had the unfortunate effect of making the ex-husbands of these women unwilling martyrs. Rather than create a more just system of divorce, we have simply exchanged one victim for another.

In some countries, like Great Britain, the law is trying to change to reflect reality, but it is often a case of fighting an uphill battle against public opinion. A good example is the question of blame or fault, which fell out of favor in England in the early 1970s but which is now finding its way back into the divorce courts. When the Law Commission published its 1980 discussion paper "The Financial Consequences of Divorce," it was inundated by a flood of letters from spouses who felt that the transgressions of their former mates should indeed be reflected in financial settlements. A typical case was that of a Wimbledon insurance executive who came home one day to find his wife in bed with members of a pop group. When he divorced her, he was astounded to discover that she was going to receive one-third of his income, one-third of his capital, and one-third of the value of their home, which would have to be sold. The husband in question asked, "How can the law grant a meal ticket to a thirty-year-old woman when she was the one who was fooling around?" If he chooses not to make these payments, he must consider that there are currently around two thousand men in English prisons who have been jailed for refusing or being unable to make their maintenance payments.

In response the Commission recommended that the courts

should take the spouses' conduct into account where it would be "inequitable" to disregard it. This recommendation is now enshrined in the new Matrimonial Proceedings Bill, which is currently working its way through both houses of the government. This bill recognizes the equality of husband and wife by ending the woman's right to maintenance after the breakdown of marriage. As such, it has a similar philosophy to the North American idea of rehabilitative alimony. Both of these approaches to divorce and maintenance encourage the idea of support for minor children, but not for ex-wives. Needless to say, this piece of legislation, which is of obvious benefit to second wives, is stirring up considerable opposition from first wives and other interested groups. In fact, the Meal Ticket Bill, as it is being called, is bound to be unpopular in a country where only 11 percent of divorce court registrars felt that young, childless women divorcing after a short marriage should get no maintenance.

It is no secret that the divorce rate is climbing, and the face of divorce is changing. This is directly related to two important factors in our society. On the one hand, agitation from women's groups has caused the courts to take women and their problems into more regard in the divorce situation, and on the other hand, we are living longer. By the year 2000 some experts say that one may reasonably expect to have three spouses during a lifetime. The possibility of divorce, therefore, is greater for all of us and not just because we are in a dead-end marriage. People expect more from their relationships today. Marriage is no longer an economic haven for women or sanctuary for the raising of children. What is important is the quality of the relationship. As Bernard Farber said in his book *Family Organization and Interaction,* "Marriage is not maintained for orderly replacement but exists for personal welfare."

These situations are in direct opposition to one another. The legal system encourages women to "take their husband to the cleaners" and leave them, in some cases, financially ruined. The sociologists are telling us that divorce and remarriage are perfectly normal given our increased longevity, and we will be expected to marry more than once in the near future. The whole concept of marriage and divorce is in a state of flux right now as our legal systems try desperately to catch up with social realities. Into this complex and contradictory scene the second wife of the 1980s must fit.

Who Divorces and Why

It comes as no surprise that statistics show higher rates of divorce for those who married young, particularly if there was an unexpected pregnancy involved; nor is it surprising, given the previous discussion, that women are more likely to petition for divorce than men. Approximately 66 percent of divorce petitions are brought by women. This may be because women generally have less to lose financially by divorcing, and also the one who brings the action to court is less likely to be seen as the one at fault. Many husbands will allow their wives the courtesy of bringing the petition down. If a wife is a young mother with small children, she is most likely to file for divorce. As she gets older, the likelihood of her filing dwindles. In marriages of longer duration, involving older couples (those over fifty), it is usually the husband who files for divorce. This can be explained by the fact that as women age, they have more to lose in the divorce than their husbands because they are not as likely to remarry and are not as viable in the job marketplace. Many of the possibilities of employment that are open to younger women are closed to those over fifty.

When divorcing, most people rely on three major grounds: cruelty, adultery, and separation for not less than three years. The first two account for about 45 percent of all divorce cases and are not as popular as the third because they are harder to prove, and they imply direct fault. Separation, with its no-fault emphasis, accounts for about 40 percent of the divorce cases. Grounds vary for men and women, with men leaning toward separation and women toward cruelty. Age plays a part for both sexes, with adultery being more popular grounds for younger males, and separation for older people of both sexes. It should be noted that these are objective grounds established by the court, and they should not be confused with the subjective grounds that are the real cause of the marriage breakdown. It is interesting to note that only 58 percent of petitioning women who said that adultery was the real cause of their marriage breakdown actually cited it as grounds for divorce.

For the second-wife-to-be, the fact that separation is the preferred grounds can mean that she may meet her future husband while he is only separated from his first wife. In that case she will experience all the anguish and often the mud-slinging that attends the divorce procedure. It can also mean that if she is informed about what may happen, she can help her husband-to-be think clearly during a time of great stress and perhaps guide him toward decisions that will be in the best interests of their future as a married couple instead of conceding too much to his ex-wife in the vain attempt to "get it over with." For this reason it is vital that every second wife understand the divorce procedure and its inherent implications.

The Divorce Procedure

What is Adversarial Divorce?

As we have said, most divorces today are based on the adversary system. You and your lawyers, and your spouse and his or her lawyers, square off to see which side can get the most from the other. This attitude toward divorce, where it is seen as a gladiatorial contest, is responsible for many of the harsh feelings that arise in the divorce and linger for years after, infecting new relationships and scarring children.

For many of us divorce is likely to be the single most frequent and consequential connection between us and the legal system. We are more likely to end up in court for reasons of marriage breakdown and related issues than for any other major legal reason, civil or criminal, with the exception of minor traffic offenses. Divorce litigation is unique among legal actions because it is almost always accompanied by intense and intimate emotions being aired publicly. It is also rarely a clearcut business because, especially for couples with children, contact may continue for years to come, and old wounds will constantly be reopened. As we have discussed, a divorce action, by tradition, finds fault. One of the parties is rewarded and the other punished. This is complicated by the fact that usually one of the parties desires the divorce more than the other, and so there are feelings of rejection that have to be compensated for.

In this adversarial situation it is very difficult to find a constructive middle ground where communication and agreement between the parties is facilitated. Initially the wife may not really want the TV and the stereo and the husband may want her to have them both, but by the time his lawyers and her lawyers are finished, she will be demanding both and he will be trying to prevent her from having either. Many couples have said that they started out amicably enough in dividing up their belongings, but once they got embroiled in the legal procedure, they were at each other's throats in no time. If one considers that lawyers are in the business of conducting litigation and basically have no training in dealing with families in crisis, can we be surprised that our current legal efforts to dissolve a marriage must, perforce, create enemies out of people who once cared for each other? According to family mediator Dr. Howard Irving, "The adversary system as it applies to domestic relations falls short of the mark; it provides solely the knife to sever the nuptual knot. Furthermore, in every step the adversary system has the effect of deepening marital wounds and rendering the possibility of reconciliation increasingly more difficult."

For the woman who marries the divorced man, the residue of these legal battles will, without a doubt, be part of her life for some time. She is marrying a man who has been through the wringer and who, thanks to the courts, society, and his ex-wife, now sees himself as being at fault for the whole nasty business. Do not think that the first wife's lawyers have not played on the fact that this man is consumed with guilt in order to get a larger settlement for their client. It is their job to do so. Divorcing women do not usually have these problems because they are not the financial mainstay of the family and as such, more than their husbands, are more likely to be left both emotionally and financially intact. They also have the added benefit of being the righteous survivors of the divorce.

The Procedure

The process of divorce often starts with the creation of a separation agreement. This is a written contract between the couple in question whereby they agree to live separate and apart from each other. This agreement must be purely voluntary on both sides, otherwise it is not valid. A second wife would be well-advised to find out what her husband's separation agreement says before she marries, so that she will know where they are likely to stand financially in their marriage.

Usually it will contain financial provisions for what the husband will pay the wife and children and in what fashion. Payments may be made over a period of years, or in a lump sum, and may be seen to cease should the wife remarry or the children reach a certain age. Many husbands will quickly agree to pay a certain sum every month without thinking about what the future implications might be. First of all there is the matter of duration. A wife who does not remarry or does not marry a man who can ensure that she will continue to live in the style to which she was accustomed, can, quite literally, receive payments for the rest of her life. Even after her husband's death she will still be entitled to payments from his estate.

This may seem reasonable until you consider the implications for the second wife, as witnesses this recent precedent-setting ruling by the Supreme Court of Ontario. The court ordered a second wife to pay the first wife $1,300 a month in alimony. The second wife is forty-one and the first wife, fifty-three. The husband had recently died leaving everything to his second wife and some money to his two children from his first marriage. The first wife demanded that his estate, which he had legally willed to his second wife and which included their matrimonial home, a joint bank account, and some insurance, continue to pay her support. The courts agreed. In addition the court upped the amount from the original $800 a month the husband had been paying while he was alive. Any second wife would be wise to encourage her husband to try to limit the time he has to pay support to his first wife or, at least, to make sure that it is to cease upon his death.

After duration of payments, there is the amount of the payments to be given careful scrutiny. Most wives, or rather their lawyers, will insist on a variance clause. This stipulates that if a husband has a significant change in circumstance (raises, inheritance, etc.) his ex-wife may go to court and ask the judge to award her more money. In another recent Ontario Supreme Court decision, the court ruled that a doctor has to pay his ex-wife a lump sum of $15,000, plus $350 more in alimony, and $250 more per month for child support. The judge also included a cost-of-living clause in the agreement. The judge agreed that the doctor had become considerably more prosperous in the years following his divorce than during his marriage and that it was reasonable, therefore, to expect him to pay his first wife more. The doctor's prosperity increased largely due to his opening a clinic with his second wife, who was also a doctor.

Variance can work both ways, of course, and it does not always have to do with the husband earning more money. In 1974, for example, a dentist and his wife divorced, and he agreed to pay her $400 a month in support payments. Later that year she received part of her inheritance ($15,000), and in 1976 she received the rest of it (more than $500,000). In the ensuing years, during which he had stopped support payments but was raising their four children, she squandered all the money. Left with nothing, she ended up living on welfare. She went back to court and the judge awarded her $500 a month support from her ex-husband.

The point to be made here is that as long as the husband has agreed to make any sort of support payment, even if it is only one dollar a year, his ex-wife can go back to court and get "a raise." For this reason many husbands prefer to pay one lump sum at the time of the divorce and so be free of payments for the rest of their lives. Unfortunately not too many men can afford to do this. Variance clauses are intended, in theory, to work both ways (i.e., if a husband suddenly finds himself in dire financial straits, he can go to court and ask to have the order varied in his favor). It is not often, however, that the courts will reduce payments. In fact, a husband can be prevented from placing himself in a less advantageous position financially, such as taking a lower-paying job, even if he might derive more enjoyment from such a job. An engineer in California, for example, decided after his divorce that he wanted to change careers and buy a farm. The court ruled that his income *potential* was a certain level and the amount he paid his ex-wife was based on that amount. He would be expected to continue paying at that level, even though his actual income would be substantially reduced if he gave up his present position. He still is an engineer. While the courts expect men to live up to their financial expectations and not waste their money, the same, as we have seen, is not required for ex-wives.

Aside from financial provisions, the separation agreement probably also contains information relevant to child support and custody. Children's support payments are usually (although not always) fixed, until the children reach an agreed-upon age. This is usually the age of majority, although the agreement can stipulate that the payments continue while the children are still living at home or until they finish school. In addition to support, custody and access rights will also be included. It it very important to have these clearly defined, especially if the respective spouses are "at war" and willing to use the children as pawns in the divorce game. If the access rights are clear, no one will have the opportunity or occasion to say, "Pay me more money or you cannot see the children." It is also handy for the second wife, particularly if she is working, to know exactly when and for how long she will be expected to look after the children.

As far as custody goes, it is usually the mother who is awarded it, simply because today in our society mothers are thought to be more in tune to the needs and wants of their offspring, especially the younger ones. This popular belief, which is based on the presumed existence of the maternal instinct, predicates this attitude in our legal system as well as in our social systems. The unwritten right of the mother to her children is usually reflected in the mother's claim in custody cases. Social norms in this regard are so entrenched that there exists a common-law principle (the tender years principle) stating that children under seven should be with their natural mothers. It has only been in the last few years that fathers have been allowed to lay claim to their children in custody cases. This is in direct contrast to the laws of the early nineteenth century, which held the father to be the legal guardian of all children from the marriage, no matter how young. Today this is only half true; the father still has the legal responsibility for providing for the children, but it is the mother who has custody of them. Only about one-seventh of all fathers who sue for custody receive it. This figure has not changed in the last ten years.

It would appear that the concept of fault plays a role in who gets custody, just as it does in who pays. Fathers who petition for divorce are less likely to get custody than respondent fathers. Those most likely to get custody are petitioner mothers. Older fathers are a little more likely to get custody than younger fathers. Statistics indicate that invariably all children go to one parent.

The issue of custody has relevance for the second wife because she may have to deal with the situation where her husband is paying for children he may seldom see. In some cases husbands give up seeing their children entirely because the situation becomes too difficult. Many second wives will often feel that, directly or indirectly, they are responsible for him making this decision. The second wife, in addition, must cope with her husband's guilt at leaving his children and the out-of-pocket expenses involved. The children's presence in their mother's home will necessitate frequent contact between her husband and his ex-wife. The issue of custody can have a profound effect on the marriage of the second wife.

Lastly, separation agreements frequently contain provisions for life insurance, payment of debts, division of property, and any other issue that the divorcing couple feels is relevant to their particular situation. Separation agreements can be helpful in allowing the divorce to proceed as an uncontested case because all the major issues have already been settled before the divorce comes to court. This is a quicker and less expensive method than battling it out in front of a judge. The judge will look closely at its provisions when making final judgment. For this reason it is very important that the agreement is made with a cool head and clear view to the future because as a second wife, you and your husband will have to live with its consequences for a long time. Remember that a separation agreement is a contract like any other and it is enforceable in the same fashion. If payments are in default, a suit can be filed for a judgment entitling the wife to seize assets, garnishee wages, or even send her ex-husband to jail. A man in Toronto, for example, was jailed because he could not pay his ex-wife the $1,800 he owed her in back payments. The court ordered his salary be garnisheed in the amount of $644 a month (he earns $2,200 a month before taxes) to cover the arrears. His common-law wife said that she had been unable to raise the $1,800 to get him out of jail and had to borrow close to that amount from friends and family for lawyers fees and sheriff's charges since the arrest. On top of that, he lost over $1,500 in wages for the time he was in jail. His common-law wife said they had been unable to pay his regular support payments and were currently drowning in debt.

Property Settlements

Theoretically the ideal situation when a couple gets divorced is that they split up the property of their marriage 50/50, so that each will benefit equally from the effort of the marriage. In practice, however, even in the so-called community-property states, things do not always work out this way. As with all decisions, pertaining to divorce, both parties are still at the mercy of the courts, albeit within the jurisdictional guidelines set down by their particular legal systems.

As it stands one of the most complex issues to be sorted out upon divorce is who gets what. The "what" refers to the property of the marriage, which is generally defined as the house, land, money, stocks, furniture, jewellery, or anything else that could, theoretically, be liquidated.

There are several different legal approaches to the subject of property in a marriage. Perhaps the most well known and often cited is that of the community-property states. These include:

Arizona	Louisiana	Puerto Rico
California	Nevada	Texas
Idaho	New Mexico	Washington

In these states everything acquired during the marriage, regardless of whose name is on the title or in whose name the property is registered, and including any and all bank accounts opened during the marriage, is deemed to belong to both husband and wife. Gifts and inheritances are not included in most cases. This seems relatively straightforward, but in reality, one spouse's estimation of what the marriage property was worth is often completely different from the other's. In many cases spouses cannot decide easily on just what property was acquired during the marriage and what was not.

Returns on investments or property improvements can sometimes pose harrowing problems for lawyers and accountants who are trying to prove just how much of this extra value was due to the effort of the husband and wife during the marriage and not a result of something that happened before the marriage. Because of some of these difficulties with the concept of community property, couples do not actually split assets 50/50. What is more likely to occur is that they each get an equitable share. If a penniless woman marries a wealthy rock star, she is not automatically entitled half of the community property acquired during the marriage because she has not actually contributed to the acquiring of it to the same degree as her husband has before or during the marriage.

It is obvious that the trend for the future is toward community-property legislation. At the present time, however, most states still have separate property laws for husbands and wives. Separate-property equitable-distribution states include:

Alabama	Kansas	New York
Alaska	Kentucky	North Carolina
Arkansas	Maine	North Dakota
Colorado	Maryland	Ohio
Connecticut	Massachusetts	Oklahoma
Delaware	Michigan	Oregon
District of	Minnesota	Rhode Island
Columbia	Missouri	South Carolina
Georgia	Montana	South Dakota
Hawaii	Nebraska	Utah
Illinois	New Hampshire	Vermont
Indiana	New Jersey	Wisconsin
Iowa		Wyoming

Separate-property equitable-distribution states translate a property settlement as including all the assets of the husband and the wife acquired before or during the marriage, including gifts and inheritances no matter in whose name such assets are. At the time of a divorce, the property is divided equitably at the discretion of the judge. This can very likely mean that a wife with small children can be awarded 80 percent of the assets if those assets include the house (most couples' major asset). It can also mean that assets registered in a wife's name can be given back to the husband if the judge so orders. In both community-property and equitable-distribution states, the idea of fault often creeps in to color the judge's decision in favor of one spouse over the other.

There are some states, separate-property title-only states, which· include Florida, Mississippi, Pennsylvania, Tennessee,

Virginia, and West Virginia, where the judge doesn't even have to make a show of dividing the assets evenly. Marriage is not considered an economic partnership in these states, and whatever is in one spouse's name is his or her property—period. The other is not entitled to any of it. Husbands, therefore, who put their assets in their wives' names, for whatever reason, may be rudely surprised when they become divorced.

If you happen to live in a separate-property state there is nothing to stop you from crossing into another state where the divorce laws are more appealing to you and filing for divorce there. It is usually a simple matter of setting up residence and waiting for a short period.

In Canada the idea of separate property (i.e., whoever actually has title to the property is the owner and can do as he or she wishes) is often mediated by the "intention" of the parties should a dispute arise. For instance, assets purchased by one or both spouses but generally used by both in the course of the marriage (i.e., the house, the car) are regarded as a family asset. A "family" asset may have been purchased either before or during the marriage. It is essential to understand that family assets do not indicate joint ownership. Separate property still applies, but should a divorce occur, either spouse may receive a division of the family assets regardless of ownership. Only family assets that are in existence at the time of the separation are up for grabs. It is interesting to note, too, that family assets are divisible, but family debts are not and continue to belong to whomever incurred them. Again, with the division of family assets, a 50/50 split is ideal, but the actual split is left to the discretion of the judge who is expected to make an equitable distribution.

Alimony and Maintenance

Most people use these two terms interchangeably. The fact is that alimony can only be awarded while a couple is still married for the support of the wife by the husband. Interim alimony refers to the allowance paid after a divorce petition has been filed but before the divorce. Interim alimony can be awarded to either husband or wife. Maintenance is the payment made to the wife after the divorce.

The award of alimony is limited to cases where it is proved that the parties in question are living apart, and the husband has been guilty of adultery, cruelty, or desertion. It is awarded purely on the basis of need and has nothing to do with the merits of the case involved. It will do the husband little good to complain that he left his wife because she was promiscuous or an alcoholic. This may be a good argument at the time of the trial, but prior to the trial, the courts are simply concerned with the wife's financial need and not with who was right and wrong. The application for an award of interim alimony, because of this attitude, is a powerful weapon for the wife to use. She can hardly fail to get an order from the court if she can demonstrate need (which is not difficult) and the husband can do nothing to stop it. This is a good tactical maneuver on the part of the wife because the amount of interim alimony awarded seems to influence the amount of the final award by the judge. It is possible for the courts to vary an alimony order. It is generally the rule that if a divorce decree is silent as to maintenance, even if alimony has been paid up to that time, that no maintenance may be subsequently awarded. A decree dissolving the marriage effectively ends the alimony judgment.

Rather than allow an unknown judge to dictate an amount to them, many couples will go for a settlement because it is cheaper, faster, and more likely to reflect their own wishes. It has been said that a good settlement satisfies neither party. Logically speaking, it is better for a wife to settle for what the husband can reasonably afford and, therefore, will be willing to pay, rather than to squeeze every last drop out of him and be faced with the continuing possibility of having to enforce her judgment. The amount of payment awarded is generally at the discretion of the court and is viewed as being relevant to individual circumstances. The rule of thumb is thought to be roughly one-third of the husband's gross income, but it can be as little as one-fifth or as much as half depending on the situation. Some judges, of course, can go too far. In a recent Ottawa case, a Family Court judge ruled that a husband should pay his former wife and two children $1,800 a month support, which left him only $14 a week to support himself. This ruling was appealed and subsequently reduced to a more reasonable $800 a month.

Regardless of the amount, one rule which does apply is that a wife who has never worked and has no assets of her own is entitled to be maintained in the same circumstances as she enjoyed throughout her marriage. There is, however, no corresponding rule which states that the husband, too, should be allowed to live in the same style he enjoyed while married.

Support Applications

It is the intention of the law that all spouses are required to support each other when necessary, and that each has an obligation to try to support himself or herself. As a matter of fact, in the majority of cases, it is still men who support women, and the courts take this reality into account at the time of a divorce. The number of women currently receiving alimony and child support in the United States has gone up by 600,000 in the last three years alone. In spite of what many people would have you believe, not all husbands are bent on skipping over state lines to try and avoid their financial responsibilities to former families. Of the $9.9 billion due in support payments, $6.1 billion was paid. Almost two-thirds of divorced men *are* meeting their obligations in spite of their own personal financial hardships.

The financial dependence of women on their former husbands is changing, of course. As more women enter the work force and establish their own careers, there are more and more cases where the judge will order that no support be paid to the divorcing wife. These are still the expectations rather than the rule, however, and to assume that just because a wife works she will get no support would be foolish.

Considerations for Support

When the courts consider an application for support they take into account several things including: health, financial status, age, and the ability to be self-supporting of the parties involved, as well as the length of the marriage and the obligation to provide support to any other individual. A woman these days may receive recognition for her efforts as a mother and home-maker. In twenty-two states, the judge is required to take these aspects of the role of a wife into consideration when determining support. A monetary value may also be placed on the contribution of a housewife over the years she has been married. Some estimates put forward for this reckoning range from $6,000 to $18,000 a year. According to this theory, the longer you have been married, the more you should be worth in terms of support.

In spite of what the courts are allowed to take into consideration, there is still one thing that, depending on where you live, they are not allowed to look at when awarding support. That is fault. Marital misconduct or adultery is not grounds for denying your rights to alimony in many states. But in Georgia, North Carolina, South Carolina, West Virginia, and New York,* proven adultery automatically cancels the right to any support from a divorcing husband. Some states even take 'fault' a few steps further and include such things as being a nagging wife or a sloppy housekeeper in order to award little or no alimony. Some states, including Arizona, Delaware, and Hawaii, find "fault" in economic misconduct, and this can reduce the amount of your alimony, too. In spite of a more liberal attitude toward divorce, it is still difficult for a husband to get the judge to see his ex-wife as being at fault. For many men (and their second wives) this attitude is grossly unfair.

*Legislation is pending in New York to make adultery by either spouse a factor only and not an automatic bar to the alimony of either.

If proving fault during the marriage as a means for reducing an award for support is difficult, proving fault in conduct after the marriage is even more so. There have been several recent cases where the first wife has been living with another man, or even marries another man, and the judge still orders the support to continue. In the past most separation agreements contained a *dum caste* clause stating that the payments would only continue while the wife remained chaste. Since this was thought to be an interference in the possible forming of new relationships and rather unfair, it is now an unpopular idea. This, unfortunately, has given rise to a different form of inequity, as is witnessed by the case of a man from the Toronto area, who was ordered to pay $80 a week to his estranged wife in spite of her relationship with another man. The judge also ordered the husband to pay $100 a week to support his two children who were in his estranged wife's custody. The court ruled that the wife is entitled to permanent maintenance because her new companion is not supporting her. The estranged wife has just returned from a three-week trip to Europe with the man in question.

It is not always a question of cohabitation with another person. When the courts say they do not regard conduct as an element in issuing a support order they mean it, as is evidenced by the case of an Illinois woman, a practising psychologist, who pleaded guilty to plotting to kill her husband. She said she hired two men to do the job, but they, in turn, went to her husband, and he went to the police. She served two years of a six-year sentence. Upon being discharged, she divorced her husband and received half of his assets, some $300,000. Her lawyer pointed out that charges of misconduct have no influence on an individual's right to maintenance payments and property settlement.

In case you may think that orders for support do not contain a punitive element, consider the example of a man from Toronto ordered to pay $27,500 in child support to his ex-wife who married a convicted bank robber on the day the criminal was sentenced to five years in prison. She took the children to another city to be near her new husband in jail. The judge acknowledged that his decision would effectively strip her first husband of all his capital assets. The ex-wife, in addition, will also receive $32,000 from the sale of their matrimonial home.

What Constitutes Support?

The court can order financial support in the form of periodic payments, or lump-sum payments, or they may order that a trust be set up for the dependent, or any combination of the foregoing. They may also order the transfer of valuable property, such as the matrimonial home which is usually awarded to the wife, particularly if there are children involved. In one case involving a man who was a pilot, the court awarded his plane to his ex-wife as part of the settlement. She did not fly, and he was not allowed to use the plane. He also had to pay to have it stored. The court, in addition, has the power to make the payments retroactive to a time prior to the divorce and may order expenses for prenatal care and child birth. It may order that the ex-spouse be made the irrevocable beneficiary of an insurance policy and that health insurance be taken out in her name. Pension benefits also may be part of the support order. The court can order these payments to continue on after the death of the respondent and that they be secured against any property or asset should he go bankrupt. In the event of any specific order making the payments continue after death, they will last for only twelve months after the death of the respondent.

As well as being empowered to make an order permanent, the court may make interim orders to support until a full hearing or disposition of assets has occurred and may restrain the respondent from wasting or disposing of these assets in order to defeat the claim or order for payment. The terms of a domestic contract or separation agreement are not necessarily binding on the court. The court will make the order it thinks is appropriate under the circumstances, even if the contract were to contain a waiver of support.

Support and the Second Wife

These are the rules of divorce which supposedly apply to *all* wives, but common sense tells us that if a man has already been divorced once and is paying support and his first wife has possession of the family home, there is only so much to go around. If second wives generally cannot expect to live as well while they are married than first wives, they also can expect not to do as well should they divorce. Seventy percent of the second wives surveyed thought they would be worse off financially than their husbands' first wives had been if they were divorced. Only 13 percent thought they would be better off. This contradicts the popular belief that second wives are gold-diggers who are only out for the money, and once they get it, leave.

Our divorce settlement would certainly not be the same. She took everything, even his clothes, and left debts for him to pay. I would split the assets we acquired during the marriage and take only what I had before I married him and leave quietly.

My husband's wages wouldn't allow for him to pay alimony to two women so I guess I would be on my own.

Of course our settlement wouldn't be the same. My husband can barely keep his nose let alone his head above water as it is. He certainly couldn't afford to pay both of us.

I would never ask him for any support either financially or to solve problems for me. As far as I'm concerned divorce is the end and I would want a clean break.

I wouldn't want it to be the same. Although she is independent and has no children she still insists on sizeable alimony and he pays it because he takes his responsibilities very seriously. If I left I wouldn't want any part of him or his money. How can you start a new life if your ex-husband is still supporting you?

Of course it would be different. My husband would never be that stupid again. He learned his lesson about divorce with his first wife.

The only thing that would be different is that I would take no money and he asked me if we ever got divorced if he could have custody of the children because she got custody the last time and he just couldn't stand to lose his kids a second time.

Perhaps because these women have been through a divorce or lived in the wake of one, they can appreciate the repercussions. The second wives who were surveyed for this book invariably said that they thought they would be more fair or even that they would ask for nothing for themselves, only support for their children, should they divorce. Most of them realized that their husbands would not be able to afford to pay two lots of alimony or support and accepted that fact. There were a lot of comments about how badly the first wives had treated their husbands in the divorce, and most of the second wives were determined not to stoop to that level. They also were more lenient when it came to arranging for custody and access to the children.

What's New in Divorce

Divorce Mediation

Since conflict between married people and the dissolution of marriage seem to be an inevitable part of family life these days (more than 1.5 million marriages will end in North America this year alone), there is a growing awareness among those who want to ease the trauma of divorce of the benefits of divorce mediation. Essentially divorce mediation is the intervention of a third person (usually a qualified social worker or professional divorce mediator) who attempts to resolve the difficulties at hand by using his or her skills as a mediator, rather than by imposing the rigid opinions of the law on an already volatile situation. Divorce mediation can lessen the emotional harm and turmoil of the breakup of the marriage.

Divorce mediation never pits one person against another. The idea is to get the couple to reach rational compromises acceptable to both parties. Voluntary settlements worked out together by mutual agreement are not only more humane than forced litigation, they are also more practical. Research studies in Canada and the United States report a high agreement rate (75 to 80 percent) between divorcing husbands and wives following mediation. With mutual agreement neither party is made to feel they have won or lost, and no one is held as being at fault. Eliminating the blame factor can also help to eliminate the need for revenge and long court battles. Since the husband is not left feeling used, he is not likely to abnegate his responsibilities, thereby causing his ex-wife to chase him through the legal system as still happens in over 50 percent of the cases today. His second wife, too, will benefit from having a husband who has not been broken on the treadmill of our current adversary system.

Divorce mediation has the positive aspect of treating the family as a unit. It does not view the children as chattels to be bartered over in prolonged custody battles by vengeful adults. It allows the parents who know and love the children, in spite of their difficulties with each other, to decide what will happen to them, rather than letting a judge, who is unfamiliar with any of the family members and is, therefore, forced to base his decision almost solely on the negative information he has gathered about each parent during the course of the hearing (the parent against whom there is the least amount of damaging evidence being the one who "wins" the children), do so. It also allows the children themselves to have a say about which parent they would like to live with and does not necessarily encourage all children to go with the same parent.

The idea is to dissolve the marriage without destroying its members. Divorce mediation is not punitive and it is not as expensive as the current legal option. Only a small percentage of divorce cases go to litigation (close to 90 percent settle out of court), but this does not mean that they are settled with ease under the adversary system. Many cases settled out of court involve years of affidavits, letters, phone calls, and consultations. When you consider that lawyers' fees range from $50 to $100 an hour, it is no wonder that families can be driven to the edge of financial ruin by the costs involved in divorce. Those who do go to litigation can look forward to spending from $800 to $1,000 a day for each party. Add to this the fact that many men will get stuck with the bill for their wives' lawyers, as well as their own, and it is no wonder that they often grudgingly give in to exorbitant demands in order to achieve a quick settlement and avoid imminent financial disaster. Fees for a mediator are much lower (it has been estimated that the adversarial approach costs four times as much as the mediation approach), and the average number of sessions involved before a resolution is obtained is usually about six. It is easy to see why divorce mediation is becoming more and more popular in our divorce-ridden society. If divorce mediation were established on a more widespread basis, it would save U.S. taxpayers $9.6 million a year in legal fees. Many lawyers who make divorce their business probably shudder at the thought of losing so much potential income to divorce mediators, but what price can you put on the pain and suffering of the couple and the children who are involved in the battle of their lives?

Rehabilitative Alimony

The idea that a former wife is entitled to support for the rest of her life from her former husband is one of the biggest bones of contention second wives have with our current divorce laws. When you consider that the probability of divorce is at its highest for females at twenty-seven years of age (and for males at thirty) and that a woman's normal life expectancy is seventy-seven years, it means that if a first wife decides not to remarry or go to work she is entitled to full support for the next fifty years, with all the help and encouragement of our legal system behind her.

States such as Florida, Michigan, and California are now looking at factors such as the age of the wife and her demonstrated earning ability when considering what to award in the form of support. A young mother with small children may be awarded support until the children are of school age, at which point she will be expected to get a job and become self-supporting. Older women as well are receiving rehabilitative alimony in order to retrain themselves to enter the job market again after years as homemakers. Essentially, rehabilitative alimony is support paid for a set period of time, which allows the ex-wife to settle herself financially and place herself in a position where she is no longer dependent on a man.

Second wives obviously view this idea with a great sense of relief because it allows them to plan for a time in their future when their financial burdens will be lightened. Many legislators and policy makers, however, find the idea of rehabilitative alimony distasteful, to say the least. They firmly believe that once married, a woman, even though divorced, has the right to demand support from her husband and that forcing her to go to work is placing her in an economic and socially inferior position to her former status as wife and homemaker. Second wives, of course, look at it from another perspective. They feel that if they can go out to work to contribute to *her* support, then she should be perfectly capable of going to work and contributing to her own support.

Precedent-Setting Cases

This case has been before various California courts for the past three years. It is indicative of a new trend in divorce legislation which says that virtually anything, even if it is not tangible, is up for grabs when the time comes to end the marriage.

These are the facts. Mr. and Mrs. Sullivan married in 1967 while both were still attending university. When Mrs. Sullivan graduated, Mr. Sullivan went on to medical school. During the four years from 1968 to 1972, she says she provided the bulk of their income because he was still at school while she was working. She then took two years off to have their child and returned to work in 1975. In 1977 they separated. They were divorced in 1978 shortly after he set up his medical practice. Mrs. Sullivan was not awarded alimony because, as a financial analyst earning $35,000 a year, she was self-supporting and capable of living in the same style she enjoyed while married. She did receive $250 a month for child support. That was not to be the end of it. Mrs. Sullivan, 35, decided that she should be entitled to some compensation for her efforts in helping her husband get through medical school. In a precedent-setting Supreme Court case, she asked that her investment in her husband's education entitle her to part of its value when they got divorced. Her lawyers want Dr. Sullivan's degree declared community property, and a percentage of his income (10 to 20 percent) paid to his first wife. Dr. Sullivan and his second wife are fighting the case through every level of the courts, firstly because he said he contributed 70 percent of the financing for their marriage and, secondly, because he feels that the marriage is over and his ex-wife is not entitled to anything more than she got in their divorce.

In a similar vein, the Michigan Court of Appeals ruled this year that a man's law degree should be considered joint property because his wife helped him through school and is thereby entitled to a share of his earnings after their divorce. The three-judge appeal panel ruled that the law degree of the husband should be considered joint property. In an earlier decision, a lower court judge had awarded the wife $20,000 to be paid over ten years as a return on her contribution to his law degree. The higher court, however, ruled that the judge reconsider his estimate of what the law degree was worth by comparing it to what the husband *might* otherwise have hoped to make. The difference, then, adjusted on the basis of the couple's ten-year marriage plus the wife's contribution, should be divided equally between the husband and the wife. Needless to say, it would be considerably more than $2,000 a year. One has to question this logic and ask, if the man had trained for a less lucrative position (he had been a teacher previous to obtaining his law degree) how would the courts have then reacted? Would his wife be happy to deduct half the difference in the amount he was *not* now earning from her support payments? Is this husband being punished for having the talent and ability, not to mention the ambition, to give up teaching and go to law school? It is interesting to note that during the time the husband was in law school, the wife was earning $26,089 a year; one presumes that she is earning still more now. What might this woman's motive be in taking this to court? Might it possibly be revenge? It is not financial necessity. The woman did not even know, when she married the man, that he was going to be a lawyer, so it would be difficult to say that her financial expectations, at the time of marriage, had been thwarted. It sounds more than a little like opportunism.

The second wife, it seems, is also not immune to the far-reaching grasp of the first wife when it comes to the question of money. It is clear, as this case demonstrates, that judges are beginning to acknowledge the existence of the second wife because they are looking at her income when determining how much the husband shall pay to his first wife. These are the facts. In Chicago an Illinois court awarded an ex-wife an increase in her support payments based on the fact that the second wife was earning money, and this augmented the "family" exchequer. The second wife, who has two children from a previous marriage for whom she receives no support from her ex-husband, took exception to this. She was not allowed to be in the court room or to have any say in the matter whatsoever, even though her finances were being discussed and divided up for the benefit of her husband's ex-wife.

Similarly a judge in Ontario awarded additional support for a husband's ex-wife and children after looking at the salary of his live-in companion of two years. He did not, however, take into consideration the salary brought in by the first wife's live-in companion because the first wife claimed he did not contribute to her support.

Second wives, as we can see, are being drawn into the financial net spread at the time of the divorce by the first wife. It seems obvious that second wives should be prepared to battle for control of their own finances against possible appropriation by first wives. This may not be fair or equitable, but it is the way things seem to be going at the moment, and second wives, therefore, should be forewarned.

The final decision in the Sullivan case has not yet been handed down, and there will likely be costly appeals for years to come over this issue. As Dr. Sullivan has asked, where does it all stop? Evidently, with the help of the courts, it may well not stop—not ever. If it does not end for the husband, it will also be an on-going issue for his second wife.

11 *Second Wife, Second Best?*

"In this world second thoughts, it seems, are best."
Hyppolytus

ONE OF THE PURPOSES of this book has been to answer three questions: Does society as a whole, including all its social norms, laws, and customs, relegate the second wife to an inferior status? Do the husbands, children, families, and friends of the second wife treat her as a lesser wife because she is second? Finally, do second wives see themselves as being second best?

We have already seen how in some instances friends and family and especially stepchildren regard the second wife as not being on quite the same level or of the same value as the first wife. Society is the chief offender, however, because it has not kept pace with the times, and our laws and mores still view a second wife as an adjunct to a man's life, while offering the primary position to his first wife, even after divorce.

As a culture we find it very difficult to accept the fact that a man (or a woman, for that matter) can have more than one mate and more than one family during his (or her) lifetime. While the social reality may be more multiple marriages, this has not yet resulted in a swing in public opinion regarding second wives and their children. Some may think the answer to the question second wife, second best? is obvious, but it is important to point out not only how society feels about second

215

wives, but to look at how second wives feel about themselves. To this end we asked the question, "Have you ever felt second best or in second place because you were your husband's second wife?" The response was almost evenly divided, with 47 percent of the wives saying, yes, they had, and 52 percent saying, no, they had not.

I did for the first two years, but once I learned that he respected me I managed to put those thoughts out of my mind.

His mother is the one who really lets me know that I should feel second best. Whenever she comes over to our place she always says things like "When John was married," as though being married to me just doesn't count.

I feel second best because everything we own nearly is second hand. Our marriage is built on leftovers from both our previous marriages—nothing is ours alone, not even "our" children.

I feel second best because we have a much lower standard of living then he did with his first wife. She got practically everything when they were divorced and he had to start over with nothing. It's not the same as starting out with nothing when you are young and your whole life is in front of you. Starting out with nothing when you are middle-aged and are used to a better standard of living makes both my husband and I feel that we are second best and that our marriage just doesn't have the same value in the eyes of society.

His family and friends went out of their way to make me feel like a second banana but it didn't work because he always makes me feel number one.

I have never felt second best. As far as we are concerned we have always been married. There never was a first time or a second time except, of course, when you remember the children.

I think second wives as a group get treated second best not only socially but legally because everything that is possible is done to protect the first wife and children while nothing is done to ensure our rights as wives. Doesn't anyone think that divorced men are entitled to remarry?

Many second wives do not feel second best. Their married situations are not so very different from those of first wives, especially if there were no children from the first marriage and friends and family are supportive. Almost an equal number do have feelings of being second best which stem in large part from the reactions of those around them. Their husbands fortunately seem to be supportive and strive to convince their second wives that, as far as they are concerned, their second wives are first in their affections. Sixty-nine percent of the second wives said that they felt their husbands loved them more than their first wives, only 10 percent said they felt they were loved less, and 21 percent thought it was about the same.

I think my husband loves me more than his first wife. I accepted him, his faults, what he feels are his failures and agreed to raise his son. Plus, I was willing to move from another country to be with him.

I don't know whether he loves me more or not. Different times, different people, to meet different needs. I know that at one time he loved his first wife and that now he loves me. People change and situations change too.

I don't think it makes any difference whether he loves me more or less. The fact is that he is here with me and not with her. That's all that really counts.

I think he loved us both but in different ways and for different reasons. I just happen to suit his needs now better than she would.

I always thought that he loved me less than his first wife. I suppose because I look upon their relationship as his young romantic love but after reading this question, I asked him and was surprised to find out that he loves me much more than her.

Their relationship drained them both so much, especially all the hatred and fighting of the divorce, that I hardly think he has enough left in him to love me more. I never measure how much love or compare his love for her with me because I am not sure I really want to know.

He loves me less, of course!

I know he loves me more or at least he could if he did not waste so much energy on anger and guilt about her.

Some second wives were surprised at the answer to this question, others were very pragmatic about the whole issue, preferring to concentrate on the present and accept their husbands' presence in their lives as proof of their love. Even those who felt that their husbands loved them less did not express the sense that this made them feel second best, but rather, accepted it as the natural course of their relationships. This was particularly true of older second wives, or women who married for reasons such as security or to have fathers for their children, rather than for their own emotional satisfaction. What did cause second wives to have feelings of being second best were attitudes from people outside their marriages including family, friends, and legal and social institutions which, by their own prejudices against second wives, were responsible for feelings of low self-esteem in the women who had taken on this role.

When we asked what the basic problems a second wife should be prepared to face were, the substance of the answers was invariably directed toward sources outside the marriage itself. The problems that the respondents felt second wives should be prepared to face fell in these four categories.

Children from his first marriage	35 percent
His ex-wife	26 percent
Money and financial burdens	21 percent
Negative emotions resulting from his previous marriage	18 percent

Thirty-eight percent of the wives said they were prepared to face some of these problems when they got married, but 60 percent said they were surprised and, for the most part, not prepared for what they experienced as second wives.

I think that a woman marrying a man whose previous marriage ended with difficulty (i.e. bitter divorce or death) has to cope with the possibilities of sour or sorrowful memories. I think she has to remain strong and confident in her own personality and has to try to project as much warmth and understanding as possible to overcome these bad memories.

I think the three major things that a second wife has to cope with are children from his first marriage, financial strain and jealousy, mainly from his children and his first wife. Though I thought I was prepared to face these problems I realize now that they were, in reality, a complete surprise.

The basic problems that any second wife should be prepared to face are an interfering first wife—in our case just because she's nosy and likes to question the kids when she chooses to visit—and the children of the first marriage, whether you have custody or not. In my case, I was prepared to raise the children as my own as my husband had custody of them from the time she walked out, but I wasn't prepared for her interfering, lies, running me into the ground every chance she got, etc., when I was doing the job she didn't want.

The hardest thing is sharing him with the first wife and children and trying to compete for his attention with them. It is also difficult not to keep comparing yourself with his first wife and this came as a surprise to me because it was not that way before we married. It must be something to do with being his "wife" that makes me want to compare myself to his other "wife."

Less money due to his support payments was a big problem for us and so was the disruption of our household whenever his kids came to visit and as well, there was the "hands off approach" where they were concerned. She and I think differently about how to raise children and it was made clear to me right from the beginning that I was not their mother and my opinions were not welcome.

The biggest thing is never having enough money and the possibility, because of this, that we will never be able to afford to have children. It is difficult knowing that you can never really be number one in his life and it came as a surprise to me although I don't know now how I could have failed to not understand this in the beginning.

I was prepared to a certain extent for the problems of trying to get two sets of children to get along in the same house. But I never expected it to be this difficult. As it is, he defends his children and I defend mine and it goes on and on.

The financial planning in a second marriage is very much more complex because of his previous allegiances. Though this may not be a problem it is definitely something which must be considered.

I had trouble adjusting to the fact that although he is supposed to be divorced, contact with his ex-wife will always be necessary because of the children and the legal settlements, which you tend to think are final, but which can be changed at any time as new legal precedents are set and lifestyles change. For instance, each time we buy a new house, or take a vacation, his ex feels that he should be giving her more money too. My husband does not pay alimony but he pays child support and apparently if his first wife becomes ill for some reason and cannot work he could be called upon to pay her support for years after their divorce settlement was made. I was prepared to accept the support payments for his children, but I was not prepared to have her continually taking him back to court to get more money. Since we have been married, his support payments have been doubled!

It is easy to see why women can be unprepared for what can happen to them as second wives. Most of us have a fairly limited knowledge of divorce laws and custody situations, just as most people tend to think that divorce really ends a marriage or that the financial relationship to the husband's former family will remain more or less static. It comes as a surprise to many women that the more their husbands (and they themselves) earn, the more they may have to pay in terms of support. Unless you have actually experienced being a second wife, it is hard to imagine what the problems can be because we take the first-marriage scenario as our prototype for marriage in general.

To some women the reality of what it means in their cases to be second wives can cause considerable disappointment with their marriages. Most of the wives continue to love the men they married but would like to change the circumstances. That is why we asked, "Do you ever wish you had been your husband's first wife or that he had not been married before he met you?" Slightly over two-thirds of the women said, yes, they wish they had been their husbands' first wives. This gives an even stronger indication that it is' not the man but rather the situation that is the focus of most of the problems of being a second wife.

Yes, I most certainly do. I know, of course, that if he hadn't been married to her he would not be the same person I love now but sometimes I wish that he had just lived with her instead of being married and then there would be no legal hassles or responsibilities (and hopefully no children). It would make life so much easier for us now. We would have no big problems.

I wish I had been around when he was younger to teach him how to enjoy life. As it was he withdrew into his work to escape an unhappy marriage and I don't think he has ever really learned how to have fun and relax.

I feel that his first marriage damaged him irreparably and that even though we are together now there are still scars that will not heal and we both have to live with that.

Not every second wife would like to have been her husband's first. Some are candid enough to admit that they prefer being second in their particular situations.

I'm glad I wasn't his first wife. I don't think I could have handled him when he was young. And apparently neither could she!

What do second wives think they would have gained by being their husbands' first wives instead, aside from the obvious lack of financial burdens and ex-wives and children to complicate their lives? The advantages to being a first wife, at least as far as second wives are concerned, are more palpable than practical in many cases. The following are examples of what second wives felt they missed by being second.

Because of his previous experience with marriage, I don't always get the chance to be me. I'm very careful about not repeating her mistakes and sometimes I feel like me (the person) gets lost in the shuffle of wives.

I feel that I can never establish a truly close and happy relationship with his parents because I am his second wife.

It would have been so nice if we had free time together before taking on the responsibilities of a family (his) so that we could have travelled and gotten to know each other as people and not just two sides of a breakfast table with four kids in between.

I think what I miss most is the years we could have had together. I will miss growing old with him and because of our age difference I know that I am almost sure to be a widow. It is hard to accept and to live with but it is always in the back of my mind and sometimes other people can be so cruel when they bring the subject out in the open by saying things like "do you think you will marry again?"

In spite of the feelings that they have missed something, however intangible, 67 percent of the second wives surveyed said they would do it all again if they had the choice, as long as it was with the same men.

I would like to be more informed about his divorce, settlements, children, etc., but if it was the same man I would definitely do it again.

I would hope that I would not be so naive and trusting next time. If I had been more aware of what was involved and the potential problem areas, things would have gone a lot more smoothly.

If I loved him as much, I wouldn't care but I would try very hard not to fall in love with a divorced man with children.

I don't think I would get married again, period!

I might live with him but I don't think I would marry him if he was still paying alimony and child support. There's a lot to be said for being free of other people's responsibilities, both financial and emotional.

In spite of the disadvantages of being a second wife, it is encouraging that so many women come to terms with their unique problems as second wives enough to say they would do it again given the chance. It is easy to speculate, of course, what you would do given a certain set of circumstances when you know that those circumstances may never arise. But the fact that these women had enough faith in their husbands and their marriages to even consider opting for the same or similar situations again indicates that maybe there is something to be said for being second after all. What, then, makes it all worthwhile? Why did 80 percent of the wives surveyed say they considered their marriages to be happy, in spite of the additional pressures they experienced because they were second wives? Here is a list of the advantages of being a second wife according to the wives surveyed. The items are arranged in descending order of importance.

Older and wiser husband	20 percent
More ready to make the marriage work	19 percent
Husband more considerate	16 percent
Husband has learned from past mistakes	10 percent
Financial security*	5 percent

Here is what some of these wives said specifically about the advantages.

The husband understands what could go wrong because he has been through it before. He is more likely to be careful the second time around because two divorces would be very bad for his track record (and expensive) so he really wants this marriage to be successful.

The second time there is a healthier relationship based on mutual love, respect, and understanding. You don't get married just for sex and then find out that you're not really compatible after all.

Your husband has experienced living with a woman, a real woman, not some Playboy centerfold in his imagination. He doesn't expect you to look great in the morning with no make-up and hair in curlers. You don't have to be perfect because he knows you are

*There is more financial security in marrying a man with an established career than someone who is still in school or just beginning a career, particularly if there are no children involved or the ex-wife has remarried.

fallible. It is much more relaxed than trying to live up to that image of the sexy siren twenty-four hours a day.

Men often mellow when they are older and you can take advantage of that. I think that they are much easier to live with and generally less demanding.

We are both older and wiser. I think there is a sexual advantage because we are both more caring and willing to experiment than we were when we were younger.

If you can make it through the trials and tribulations of being a second wife you know you have a good marriage.

During the process of researching this book it became clear that in spite of the way second wives are perceived by those around them, they, more often than not, tend *not* to see themselves as "second best" wives. They may, however, feel that their situations place them in a "second best" set of circumstances. We have seen the advantages and disadvantages as experienced by the wives themselves and, though they may not always be thrilled to come second, most would do it again for the same man. Second thoughts, perhaps, are indeed best, and second marriages are the real thing.

12 *Second Wives Association of North America (SWAN)*

"From family to nation, every human group is a society of island universes.   *Aldous Huxley*

IT IS AN AMAZING characteristic of the human state that no matter how bad things may seem at times we are always able to entertain the hope that they will get better, or that something good may come of the situation. The same is true of the second wives who participated in this study. While in some cases their experiences had been very painful for them, most still retained the hope that things would improve or, failing all else, that someone would benefit from their experiences.

For this reason I decided in the second draft of the questionnaire to include one last question, so that after the respondents had answered all the other questions relating to ex-wives, children, finances, etc., they would have a chance to sum up their feelings or add comments of their own which were not part of the body of the research. Question 110 was: "How did you feel about filling out this questionnaire and what were your reasons for doing so?"

Aside from giving the wives a chance to add their own thoughts, I was curious as to why they had decided to fill out and return the questionnaires. Needless to say, I mailed out many more questionnaires than were returned, although the response was very good, comparatively speaking. Some women, no doubt, thought the questions too personal, or perhaps they saw the task as too time consuming, but so many did sit down and take the time and thought to fill out what is generally considered to be a rather long form for mailed responses. Many of these women bared feelings that they had never before discussed with anybody or perhaps even admitted to themselves. All were ruthlessly truthful, making no attempt to hide facts or whitewash their true situations. I wanted to know what motivated them to open up to me, a complete stranger. Evidently the subject of being a second wife was something of great import in their lives and to which they had given considerable thought before I came along with the questionnaire.

In the following pages you can read what some of the women had to say about why they participated in the research. For some, it was a cathartic experience, a way of finally getting things off their chest. For others it was a way of communicating their deepest feelings and hurts safely and anonymously. Almost all of the women who answered this last question said they felt that the experience of participating in the research for *Second Wife, Second Best?* had been a beneficial one for them and indicated that they hoped their efforts would help other second wives to cope with their problems. Whatever their reasons, their efforts will give hope to millions of other women like them or at least assure them that they are not "the only ones."

I felt good about filling out the questionnaire but I was mainly motivated by curiosity. I wanted to see how I would react to the questions. I am very pleased with the results. My husband and I went over it together for the hell of it and I have now filled it out on my own and have not changed any of my answers.

It takes a lot of hard work to make a marriage work. Especially a second marriage. You have to give more than you take. You know where you made mistakes the first time and I do my darndest not to repeat them. Both of our marriages ended as a result of the other person having an affair. Something like that shatters your whole world when you think you have been a good wife and mother. But it does take two to break a marriage. It is so much better the second time around and I just wanted everyone to know.

My reasons for filling out the questionnaire were mostly based on curiosity. To the best of my knowledge, no one has ever wondered about the second wife. Any literature I've read on divorce deals mainly with the poor ex, alone dealing with kids, when it's probably harder for the poor father who has to leave his kids in most cases. I wanted to let people know what the other side is like.

I listened to you on a radio programme but I didn't call in case my voice was recognized. It helped to know that I am not the only person with a problem, although I keep most of my emotions inside usually. But so many people come to me with their problems not knowing that I have ones of my own that I cannot handle. I feel that I have been totally honest in filling out the questionnaire although I am sure I could write a manuscript to answer some of the questions. I hope the results of the questionnaire will be beneficial to someone.

I hoped that my comments will help with the research on the subject and will somehow help someone else in the same situation. My own particular marriage did not work out.

I am glad to help anyone I can when it comes to dealing with the problems of a second marriage. People are afraid to honestly discuss their problems, I think mainly because they don't want others to know they are "experiencing marital problems" again and then have them think that there is something wrong with you because you are having trouble with another spouse. I believe that in second marriages there is a whole new set of problems you don't experience in first marriages especially because of the children. Perhaps as time passes, people of second or even third marriages will form self-help groups to discuss their mutual problems openly and honestly and offer support and advice to each other.

I listened to you on a talk show and found what you had to say to be very interesting and really, very applicable to my situation. Sometimes I feel like we never should have got married but when I am away from him I can't stand it. Being a second wife has a lot of downfalls but I would say that I am pretty lucky that he never compares me, our sex life, my cooking or cleaning to his first wife. We have a lot of problems but most of them I am sure we can work out. If there is love and understanding from both parties things will always work out. I enjoyed the questionnaire very much.

I am sure my reason for doing the questionnaire is the same as all the other women doing it and that is to try to give some insight into those contemplating being a second wife. To even go so far as to change one person's mind about marrying someone who has been married before and has children would be worth it. I emphasize children because I feel that the problems that apply to a man with children do not necessarily apply to one without. I feel that marriage to a man who was previously married but has children has just as much of a chance to succeed as marrying a man with no significant past. Thanks for letting me do the questionnaire, I thoroughly enjoyed it!

I filled this out because if I could save even one woman from going through the hell I have been through it would be worth it. This marriage has almost killed me and my son.

I feel at times I should be writing a book about my experiences. We have gone through so many crisis situations and finally I have my life in control. We are together because we want to be and all six children do get along, they accept me, and we do try to treat them equally. This is very difficult to do because blood is thicker than water and until you have gone through some of these experiences you cannot possibly understand how you will feel. The reason I wrote for this questionnaire was not simply to let you know about my personal life but to help others know they are not alone with their feelings. I'd really like to meet other second wives in my area and keep in touch.

I know that we are older than most of your respondents who by statistics will be in their 20s and 30s but I thought a little input from a more mature age group would be beneficial (this respondent is 58, her husband is 59). I think there is a decided difference between marrying a person who has been divorced as opposed to widowed. There aren't any bittersweet regrets from my first marriage because my husband died. I would like to say that the social climate today is rough on marriages but I think young people should work harder to preserve their marriages and not just throw in the towel when something goes wrong.

This questionnaire helped me recognize how I feel and share these thoughts with people that may feel the same way. From the program I saw and what you said about children being a common problem, I don't feel so bad for having the feelings I do. I would also like to see some sort of reference for people in second wife situations so that common problems can be tackled even before the wedding. I am more than happy to contribute anything I can. My husband and I are both interested in seeing the results of your research.

As I was filling out the questionnaire I felt that I might not mail it back because the questions brought a lot of my past feelings to the surface, especially those in the first two to three years of my marriage. If I had known when I first got married what I was in for emotionally I might have sought psychiatric help. If your book can help to prepare women for the emotional strain of coping with their feelings about his kids, family, his ex, etc., then my time spent answering this survey has been worth it.

I enjoyed filling out the questionnaire very much as I had to think about my answers. Also, I feel there is currently very little support for a second wife. I feel that I made the decision to marry so I must make the best of it and I don't talk about my problems to anyone. Pride may prevent me. I have looked for research to help me but have found little of any value. There remains a great need for more information in literature to help fill the void for the second wife. I hope my answers will be useful to you and helpful to other second wives.

I am a second wife and he is my second husband. You said that the troubled times usually occurred between 18 and 24 months. We have been married 19 months and I sure hope that things don't get any rougher than they have been. I answered your questionnaire as best I could and I will certainly be interested in your findings, because there are not many books to read on the subject of second wives, and ways to get some hope and advice.

I listened to you on the radio and was very interested in filling out your questionnaire. My husband and I have been married for three months but we have lived together for two years. During that time I was confronted with many situations which at times made me question our relationship. At first I thought it was just me and that I was young and naive and too sensitive (I am 16 years younger than my husband). But after hearing you speak I no longer feel that it is just me. Thank you for this insight and it has been a pleasure to assist you in the research.

It was tremendously encouraging to receive this kind of support for the research in addition to discovering that so many second wives were concerned about helping not only themselves but others. It became apparent that there was a need for second wives to communicate their feelings to someone in order to alleviate many of the pressures they were feeling. Women who had participated by filling out the questionnaire began to phone or write to see if there was a group or association dedicated to the subject of second wives—something like Parents Without Partners or the Step-Family Association—where they could obtain information or through which they could locate other second wives in their area and arrange for get-togethers.

It was not surprising to find that no such organization existed. No one, it seemed, had credited the needs of second wives with enough significance to set up an association for their very special status. Other self-interest groups that base their existence on particular family problems get almost daily mention in newspapers and magazines. This piece appeared in the "Letters to the Editor" section of the *New York Times Magazine* in response to an earlier article entitled "The Plight of the Gray Divorcée."

> *My 33-year marriage broke up when I was 55 and "Plight of the Gray Divorcée" tells it like it is. I wish that six years ago when I began my unilateral journey that I had been able to find a group like Ann Arbor's Divorce After 60.... What easier way for a man to hold onto that sense of irretrieveably lost youth than to forget about the aging woman at his side and seek a younger one.*

The article "Plight of the Gray Divorcée" received a lot of this kind of reader support. Group's like Ann Arbor's Divorce After 60 are not uncommon. Similarly, in the United States, there are federally funded groups in every state for dealing with the problems of "displaced homemakers." LADIES (Life After Divorce Is Eventually Sane) is another recently formed, self-help organization formed by and comprising the former wives of stars who feel that since their divorces they have become "figures of public ridicule, pity, and contempt." (LADIES has had the good fortune to get considerable nationwide coverage by the media.) It seemed a logical progression for me to begin the Second Wives Association of North America—SWAN—because no such forums existed for second wives.

As an association SWAN is still in its fledgling stage. We have approximately four hundred members as of this writing, but we are growing across Canada and the United States. SWAN acts as a voice to bring forward the issues which are particularly relevant to second wives (for instance, many of the recent and upcoming proposed changes in family law are extremely relevant to, second wives because anything that affects their husbands in relation to previous families and their rights is bound to affect the second wives, too). Second wives often write to the association asking for information about their particular area of difficulty, or sometimes they suggest areas that they feel are unjust and should be looked into. It is apparent from these letters that second wives are only now really beginning to think of themselves as a group with a point of view and no longer as isolated women who should bear their injustices silently.

Response to SWAN has been good. Second wives are beginning to realize that their individual problems extend far beyond the boundaries of their own marriages. The first step toward change is always the realization that the situation exists on a wide-ranging basis. Now that second wives as a group are beginning to appreciate that their rights and needs as women as well as wives need not be ignored or superseded by the rights and needs of others, the changes may begin to take place in our society that will rectify the current situation, and, once and for all, remove the second wife from the status of a second-class citizen.

There will be many people who will disagree with much of what is in this book. Indeed, many will continue to advance the cause of the first wife and children exclusive of all others, even to the extent of feeling morally justified in sacrificing the husband and his second wife. I do not feel that "sacrificing" is too strong a word because, as we have seen, there are second wives who simply cannot or will not accept the injustices they face, and, as a result, they are forced to walk away from their marriages—marriages that otherwise may have lasted. The point of this book has not been to deny the rights of first wives and children of first marriages, but to put forth for considera-tion the fact that people do get remarried, and second wives should have the same rights and privileges as first wives. It is really just that simple.

We all have our own idea of what marriage is, but when you break it down to its most basic components, it is a union between two people who care about each other enough to want to make a life together, to form their own individual family unit, and to develop a bond from which to derive strength and find comfort. In order to achieve this state, both parties are granted, by our laws and our conventions, a right of priority and a certain degree of exclusivity regarding one another, whether it be emotional, physical, or financial. A husband and his wife enjoy unique rights and responsibilities for each other that exist in no other union in our culture. Yet, for many second wives, the landscape of their marriages appears as a battleground populated by strangers who wield an incredible influence over every facet of their lives. Second wives often do not enjoy the exclusivity of their husbands or priority in their lives although their burden of responsibilities can be considerably greater. Most come to realize that the situation is not something which will necessarily pass in five years or ten years, but in many cases may go on for the rest of their lives. This is why the marriages of second wives are different. Most second wives accept their situations because they want to stay in the marriages. Some, however, cannot.

What it is that second wives really want is not more money, or fewer children, or a more secure future, it is the right to be the first priority of our husbands, the right to build lives together with them just like any other wives. We hope that this book will bring to light some of the inequities that second wives face and bring on the process of change, so that second wives in the future can expect to enjoy the same rights and degree of satisfaction from their marriages that first wives take for granted. The time is long overdue for us to recognize that all wives *are* equal and should be treated accordingly.

Appendix
Selected Questionnaires

SECOND WIFE?!
QUESTIONNAIRE

OCCUPATION OF RESPONDENT: _____*Recreational Therapist and Child Care Worker*_____ AGE: ___29___

HUSBAND'S OCCUPATION: _____*Manufacturer (self-employed)*_____ AGE: ___30___

Please answer the following questions. Remember, the purpose of this questionnaire is to ascertain your feelings about being a second wife, as well as to obtain the facts. Be as subjective as you like with your answers and give as much detail as you çan. Try to avoid simple yes or no responses where possible. Not everyone will be able to answer every question. Your ability to answer specific questions depends entirely on your personal circumstances. Therefore, answer the questions which are directly applicable to your situation.

1) **How did you and your husband meet?** *We were first girlfriend and boyfriend from ages eleven to sixteen. We met again when he called me after his separation.*

2) **How long did you know your husband before you were married?** *We are not legally married as yet, however, my commitment is as if we were already married. We were together for seven months before I moved in as mommy and wife.*

3) **Why do you think your husband asked you to marry him?** *I have mixed feelings about this. First, I was very different from his ex-wife and therefore attractive in that way, second, he says "love" and shows it! And third, he needed someone to care for him and his children, of whom he has custody.*

4) Why did you decide to marry your husband? *I feel very much in love and that is the prime motivation. Also, his children needed special care and I felt I was able to help.*

5) What was your wedding like? (i.e. large, traditional, small, city hall) *We are not married yet. It will probably be small.*

6) Who was invited to your wedding? (i.e. your family and friends, his family and friends, children etc.) *Probably family, close friends, and the children (of course).*

7) Did you have a honeymoon? Where? *I do not know yet.*

8) What was your husband's first wedding like? *Very large and quite a party.*

9) Did he honeymoon with his first wife? Where? *Yes, a week at his family's cottage.*

10) Did you live together before you were married? *Yes.*

11) If so, where did you live? (i.e. his place, your place, somewhere new for the two of you?) *We purchased a house together.*

12) Where did you live after you were married? (i.e. apartment, house, condominium etc.) *When married we will continue to live in the same house (to provide stability for the children).*

13) Where did your husband and his first wife live when they first got married? *In an apartment in their home town.*

14) Have you ever lived in the place he shared with his first wife? *Yes.*

15) If so, how did you feel about this arrangement? *Terrible! So did he, so we sold it and bought the present home. I felt that the house was her home.*

16) How long have you and your husband been married? *Together, as a married couple, for five months.*

17) Do you generally use your husband's last name or did you keep your own name when you got married? Why? *I am hyphenating my (our) names and will probably continue to do so when we are married.*

18) How does your husband introduce you? (i.e. "This is Jane," "This is my wife, Jane," "This is my wife," etc.) *"This is my wife."*

19) Have you ever been married before? How long? *No, but I lived with a man for four years, so it is possible that we were legally married.*

20) Is your husband divorced or widowed from his first wife? *Separated legally and will be divorced when necessary.*

21) Did your husband leave his first wife for you or did he meet you later? *She left him and the children. He called me a month later.*

22) Was your husband married more than once before he married you? *No.*

23) How many brothers and sisters do you have? *One brother.*

24) Does your husband have any children from his previous marriage? *Yes, two boys.*

25) What were their ages when he married you? *Four and seven.*

26) Did his children live with you when you first got married? Now? *Yes to both.*

27) If his children do not live with you does he see them frequently? *(not answered)*

28) Do you have any contact with his children? If so, what are the circumstances? (i.e. business, social etc.) *I am functioning as stepmother.*

29) Do you feel that his children have directly or indirectly been responsible for any problems in your relationship with your husband? Explain. *Directly responsible. The older boy has problems primarily due to his first mom. He has an extreme behavioral problem and also doesn't accept me or the fact that his mommy is not coming back.*

30) Do you and your husband have any children of your own? *No.*

31) If not, do you want to have children? *I do!*

32) Does your husband want to have children with you? *I am not sure! The older boy is enough of a problem that he is not sure that he wants to cope with more.*

33) If you wanted to have children and your husband did not, what do you think you would do? *I have not sorted this issue out as yet! It does worry me!*

34) How did you feel about your husband's children when you first got married? (i.e. like, dislike, indifferent etc.) *I liked them and was optimistic about the prognosis for the older boy.*

35) How do you think they felt about you? *The older boy was resentful, the younger boy was fine—accepting and not resentful.*

36) Has your relationship with his children changed since you have been married? *The older boy likes me and sometimes loves me, but still says that "if he can make me leave, mommy will come back." The younger is in love with me and is going to marry me—all is well there.*

37) If you and your husband had children of your own, how do you think his children would react? *The older boy would be threatened and angry, I think. The younger would be jealous, but there would be no serious problem.*

38) If you do have children with your husband, how do you think he feels about them compared to the children of his first marriage? (i.e. loves them the same, more than, less than) *(not answered)*

39) Did you work before you got married? *Yes.*

40) Do you work now? *No.*

41) How would you say that your marriage has affected your career? *It finished it. In my career areas you have to be active in order to be qualified. I would have to start from scratch again.*

42) Did your husband's first wife work before or during their marriage? *Yes. Not at first, but later in their marriage.*

43) Do you and your husband share living expenses or does he support you? *He supports me.*

44) Do you contribute to the support of his children from a previous marriage? *Yes, we have custody.*

45) Does your husband's contribution (if any) to the support of his previous family affect the standard of living which the two of you enjoy? *Yes, we live as a family of four.*

46) If so, do you feel any resentment? *No.*

47) If your husband were to make out a will, would he leave everything to you (and any children from your marriage) or would he divide his assets between you and members of his previous family? *To me and the children, as in other natural families.*

48) If you were to make out a will, would you leave everything to your husband, knowing that if he died after you, it might go to members of his previous family? *No, I would state clearly where my assets would go—first to my husband and then to the children in trust.*

49) Did your husband put assets acquired during their marriage in his first wife's name? *No.*

50) Has your husband put any assets acquired during your marriage in your name? *No. (But this will change as assets are acquired, we have discussed it.)*

51) How long did your husband's previous marriage last? *Ten years.*

52) Is his first wife still living? *Yes.*

53) If so, does your husband still maintain contact with her? Explain. *Yes, but not by choice. She has visiting rights with the children.*

54) **Why did your husband and his first wife get divorced?** *She didn't make a good wife or mother. She did not want to be either, and so she left. She chose to be a single working woman.*

55) **Have you ever felt responsible for breaking up your husband's first marriage? Explain.** *No.*

56) **If his first wife is deceased, does she still seem to figure prominently in his thoughts? (i.e. does he talk of her often to you or others, remember their anniversaries etc.)** *(not answered)*

57) **If so, how do you feel about this?** *(not answered)*

58) **Do you have any contact with his first wife? Explain.** *Yes. With my husband, through her visits with the children.*

59) **Is his first wife anything like you in appearance, personality, background etc.?** *No, I don't really think so at all.*

60) **Does your husband's first wife still expect him to do some of the things he did while they were married? (i.e. take care of her finances, fix things around the house, etc.)** *No.*

61) **How do you feel about this?** *It is fine with me.*

62) **Does he ever confuse you with his first wife? (i.e. calling you by her name, remembering things he did with her as though he had done them with you)** *No, he never has.*

63) **With what you know about his first wife, what do you think about her as a person?** *Not very much. She was my best friend in high school and they met through me. I know her personality and do not respect her.*

64) **Have you ever felt sympathetic to his first wife?** *Only slightly at times.*

65) **Would you say that your sex life is satisfying?** *Yes, very much so.*

66) **Do you think that previously married men generally make better lovers?** *I'm not sure, but in this case, experience is very useful.*

67) **Does your husband try to please you sexually?** *He is very caring and he does try to please me. My only complaint would be that we could have intercourse more often.*

68) **Do you think that your husband's first marriage contributed significantly to the shaping of his sexual habits?** *Yes. Their problems led to his being more aware of how to please and care.*

69) **Does your husband ever refer to his sex life with his first wife? Explain.** *Yes, but seldom and only in the negative. They did not have a good sex life.*

70) **To your knowledge was your husband sexually satisfied in his first marriage?** *No, definitely not.*

71) Do you think that your husband enjoys sex more with you than with his first wife? Why? *Yes, for many reasons—maturity, knowledge, care, and much love.*

72) To your knowledge has your husband ever had sex with his first wife since he has been with you? *No, definitely not. It is upsetting to him even to speak with her.*

73) Do you ever find yourself feeling jealous of the intimate moments he shared with his first wife? *Yes, but this is my insecurity.*

74) Since your marriage have you ever considered having an affair? Why? *No, and that surprises me, because that is what destroyed my first relationship. I am very satisfied here.*

75) To the best of your knowledge, has your husband ever had or considered having an affair since he has been married to you? *I do not think so. It's possible he has thought about it, but I am quite sure he has not.*

76) To the best of your knowledge was your husband faithful to his first wife? *Yes, I am quite sure, but she was not faithful to him.*

77) Do you ever feel that your husband is comparing you to his first wife? *Yes, mostly through comparing me positively. There is pressure not to be like her, and I am afraid to make any mistakes for fear of being seen to be like her.*

78) Has he ever tried to change you in any way to make you more or less like his first wife? *No.*

79) If so, have you complied with his wishes? *If he did, I would not comply.*

80) Have you ever felt that in some way your husband still feels married to his first wife? *I'm not sure—I don't really think so.*

81) Have you ever considered divorcing your husband? Why? *No, but I have felt like running away sometimes, because of problems with the older child.*

82) If you did decide to divorce your husband, do you think that the divorce settlement would be comparable to that of his first wife? Explain. *No. I would be much easier to deal with and I would be fairer in my requests.*

83) Which of you tries harder to make your marriage work? *I think we both try very hard, but as a woman I may be more sensitive to problems that arise.*

84) Are you basically happy in your marriage? *Yes.*

85) Are there any things about your marriage you would really like to change? *I would like to have the older child be more adjusted and I would like my husband to resolve some of the guilt and anger toward his first wife and his first marriage.*

86) Do you think these changes are possible? *Only in time, not immediately.*

87) When you and your husband argue, what would you say you argue about most often? (i.e. sex, money, children etc.) Why? *Pressures and changes—who is giving more support and who needs more support. The children, also.*

88) On vacations, has your husband ever taken you to places he went with his first wife? *Yes, but only because it's the family cottage. He wouldn't take me to their favorite "spot" because there wasn't one.*

89) How did you feel about this? *(not answered)*

90) Do you have any contact with friends your husband shared with his first wife? Explain. *Yes, including her brothers. This is mostly due to the children.*

91) Are you comfortable with these people? *Yes, they are very nice people.*

92) Do you feel comfortable with your husband's family (other than his children)? *Yes, they are very supportive.*

93) Does your husband still associate with his first wife's family? Explain. *Yes, but only slightly. Because of the children and because he still cares for them.*

94) How do you feel about this? *A little jealous.*

95) How did your family feel about you becoming a second wife? *Fine. There are no problems, but I do get warnings to go slow and be sure.*

96) How would you say your husband's friends from his previous marriage feel about you? *They seem to feel good about things.*

97) Do you ever feel that your husband loves you more or less than his first wife? *More. It's the energy he wastes on anger and guilt towards her that bothers me.*

98) Would you say that your husband is more satisfied generally with his second marriage than his first? *Yes, I think so.*

99) What would you say were the basic problems that a second wife should be prepared to face? *First, emotional involvement with the first wife, and second, the anger, guilt, and feelings of failure that are experienced by your husband. He may not trust you as a second wife.*

100) Were you prepared to face these problems or did they come as something of a surprise? *Not as prepared as I thought I was.*

101) What would you say are the advantages of being a second wife? *Experience—we've learned from previous mistakes.*

102) Do you ever wish you had been your husband's first wife or that he had not been married before he met you? *Yes, I feel that the first marriage did more damage than it was worth.*

103) Have you ever felt second best or in second place because you were your husband's second wife? *I still feel like an outsider and not a part of things, especially with the children refering to "mommy" all the time.*

104) Do you feel that there is anything you have missed in your relationship with your husband because you are his second wife? *Optimism, the innocent trust and optimism of a new start together.*

105) With what you know about being a second wife, would you marry a man who had been married before if you had the chance to do it over again? *I can't answer this. If I were to feel the same again, the situation wouldn't matter.*

106) If you have been both a first wife and a second wife, what would you say were the differences between the two situations? *There is less trust, there is more pressure to live up to what was or was not like the first wife. Children are a very large complication.*

107) Do you think that your husband ever feels guilty about leaving his first wife? *She left him and it was for the better. I don't think guilt is a prime emotion.*

108) Have you ever had any guilt feelings that relate to your being a second wife? Explain. *No.*

109) Would you say that in some ways your husband still feels possessive about his first wife? Explain. *He has stated that deep down he may still love her and does still care for her.*

110) How did you feel about filling out this questionnaire and what were your reasons for doing so? *As I am new at being a second wife and it is the most important move of my life to date, I felt that the questionnaire would help the marriage to grow and strengthen. I also feel that this is a relatively unexplored area and think that research would be valuable, and I enjoyed filling out the questionnaire.*

When I completed this questionnaire, I gave it to my husband to read. At the end, he stated that there was nothing really to talk about because all these issues (generally) had been dealt with. Our conclusion was that we are communicating well. I hadn't been aware of this until the completion of this questionnaire.

SECOND WIFE?!
QUESTIONNAIRE

OCCUPATION OF RESPONDENT: ___Teacher___ AGE: ___40___

HUSBAND'S OCCUPATION: ___Sales Engineer___ AGE: ___51___

Please answer the following questions. Remember, the purpose of this questionnaire is to ascertain your feelings about being a second wife, as well as to obtain the facts. Be as subjective as you like with your answers and give as much detail as you can. Try to avoid simple yes or no responses where possible. Not everyone will be able to answer every question. Your ability to answer specific questions depends entirely on your personal circumstances. Therefore, answer the questions which are directly applicable to your situation.

1) **How did you and your husband meet?** *On a blind date. Neither of us was "interested," but it completed a foursome.*

2) **How long did you know your husband before you were married?** *Four years.*

3) **Why do you think your husband asked you to marry him?** *I honestly knew he loved me very much—enough to give up his children and all personal securities.*

4) **Why did you decide to marry your husband?** *I "wanted" him more than I "needed" him. He's a gentleman, interesting conversationalist, has a sense of curiosity. I thought he'd be a good companion.*

5) **What was your wedding like? (i.e. large, traditional, small, city hall)** *Very small—fifteen guests. At our church. Reception at "our" apartment.*

6) **Who was invited to your wedding? (i.e. your family and friends, his family and friends, children etc.)** *My family and my (originally) friends.*

7) **Did you have a honeymoon? Where?** *Yes. To Stratford, Ontario for the weekend.*

8) **What was your husband's first wedding like?** *I don't know.*

9) **Did he honeymoon with his first wife? Where?** *I don't know.*

10) **Did you live together before you were married?** *Sort of ... although he had his own apartment nearby.*

11) **If so, where did you live? (i.e. his place, your place, somewhere new for the two of you?)** *My place.*

12) **Where did you live after you were married? (i.e. apartment, house, condominium etc.)** *He officially moved into my apartment.*

13) Where did your husband and his first wife live when they first got married? *They rented a house.*

14) Have you ever lived in the place he shared with his first wife? *No.*

15) If so, how did you feel about this arrangement? *(not answered)*

16) How long have you and your husband been married? *Six years.*

17) Do you generally use your husband's last name or did you keep your own name when you got married? Why? *I use my husband's last name. I feel it's a sign of respect to your husband to carry his name.*

18) How does your husband introduce you? (i.e. "This is Jane," "This is my wife, Jane," "This is my wife," etc.) *"I'd like you to meet my wife, _____." Always as if it is a pleasure.*

19) Have you ever been married before? How long? *Yes, for four years, then I was separated for three years before my divorce.*

20) Is your husband divorced or widowed from his first wife? *Divorced.*

21) Did your husband leave his first wife for you or did he meet you later? *My husband left his first wife for me because I was an alternative. They had considered separating a few years earlier.*

22) Was your husband married more than once before he married you? *No, just once.*

23) How many brothers and sisters do you have? *Two sisters.*

24) Does your husband have any children from his previous marriage? *Yes, two.*

25) What were their ages when he married you? *Twelve and nineteen.*

26) Did his children live with you when you first got married? Now? *No, they lived with their mother.*

27) If his children do not live with you does he see them frequently? *The daughter now lives nearby, so we see her once or twice a month. The son lives (300) miles away, so we see him two or three times a year.*

28) Do you have any contact with his children? If so, what are the circumstances? (i.e. business, social etc.) *As little as possible. I play hostess when they are here and try to be sociable, but I carry a great deal of resentment because of their demands.*

29) Do you feel that his children have directly or indirectly been responsible for any problems in your relationship with your husband? Explain. *Definitely. I must admit that I feel jealous (which makes me feel like a teenager—and that bugs me too) of his atten-*

tions. I used to be afraid that they would take him away. They fantasize about "yesteryear" and I think they should be realistic. They've been a financial drain.

30) **Do you and your husband have any children of your own?** *No.*

31) **If not, do you want to have children?** *I wanted to, but we could not afford to exist on one pay check when he had to support his other family.*

32) **Does your husband want to have children with you?** *He knew it wasn't economically possible, so he had a vasectomy.*

33) **If you wanted to have children and your husband did not, what do you think you would do?** *I accepted the fact that we wouldn't and have doted on my niece and nephew instead.*

34) **How did you feel about your husband's children when you first got married? (i.e. like, dislike, indifferent etc.)** *I liked them before we were married, because when they visited I was free to do my thing (visit girlfriends or family). After marriage, I had to stay home and act as hostess. Because I don't approve of the way he never says "no," I have come to dislike them.*

35) **How do you think they felt about you?** *They accepted me as someone who made their father happy. I'm grateful for that.*

36) **Has your relationship with his children changed since you have been married?** *They're no warmer or closer, but his daughter and I talk openly and pretend we're friendly.*

37) **If you and your husband had children of your own, how do you think his children would react?** *They'd be pleased because they both like small children.*

38) **If you do have children with your husband, how do you think he feels about them compared to the children of his first marriage? (i.e. loves them the same, more than, less than)** *(not answered)*

39) **Did you work before you got married?** *Yes.*

40) **Do you work now?** *Yes. I have to!*

41) **How would you say that your marriage has affected your career?** *It has cramped my career because if I were single, I'd sign up to teach overseas. He believes a wife should be at home, so I try to curb extra-curricular activities and rush home before he's due to arrive from work.*

42) **Did your husband's first wife work before or during their marriage?** *No, she was always home to keep chores done and be free to go whenever they wanted to.*

43) **Do you and your husband share living expenses or does he**

support you? *We share expenses, but I carry the larger share—and at times I feel that I'm just a convenience. I look after myself and the house while he looks after himself and his family mainly.*

44) **Do you contribute to the support of his children from a previous marriage?** *You might say so. Although I have not consulted him, next month I am paying off a $4,000.00 loan for his daughter's summer wedding. I hate debts!*

45) **Does your husband's contribution (if any) to the support of his previous family affect the standard of living which the two of you enjoy?** *Definitely. We usually go camping on our vacation while they fly to California and overseas regularly.*

46) **If so, do you feel any resentment?** *Definitely. Why should I be the only one who suffers?*

47) **If your husband were to make out a will, would he leave everything to you (and any children from your marriage) or would he divide his assets between you and members of his previous family?** *He would divide his assets between me and members of his previous family.*

48) **If you were to make out a will, would you leave everything to your husband, knowing that if he died after you, it might go to members of his previous family?** *No. I've already made out my will leaving the most to my sisters and parents.*

49) **Did your husband put assets acquired during their marriage in his first wife's name?** *He left everything with her—house, car, and bank account.*

50) **Has your husband put any assets acquired during your marriage in your name?** *He's been unable to acquire assets.*

51) **How long did your husband's previous marriage last?** *Twenty-three years.*

52) **Is his first wife still living?** *Yes, and still unattached.*

53) **If so, does your husband still maintain contact with her? Explain.** *Briefly. There have been contacts through and because of their children. Because of a guilt complex, he still gives her a Christmas present!!! (It's "better" for the children.)*

54) **Why did your husband and his first wife get divorced?** *Incompatability. Besides, I was on the scene.*

55) **Have you ever felt responsible for breaking up your husband's first marriage? Explain.** *No. He paid lip-service to his marriage and admits that now the only thing they have in common are the children.*

56) **If his first wife is deceased, does she still seem to figure prominently in his thoughts? (i.e. does he talk of her often to you or others, remember their anniversaries etc.)** *(not answered)*

57) **If so, how do you feel about this?** *(not answered)*

58) **Do you have any contact with his first wife? Explain.** *When my husband was in the hospital last spring, she phoned me to get a medical report. I don't even wish to talk to her, let alone meet her. She keeps informed through the children usually.*

59) **Is his first wife anything like you in appearance, personality, background etc.?** *To her, life is a series of parties and outings. I prefer nature, handwork, small gatherings.*

60) **Does your husband's first wife still expect him to do some of the things he did while they were married (i.e. take care of her finances, fix things around the house, etc.)** *She's gotten over that.*

61) **How do you feel about this?** *I'm glad she's done so.*

62) **Does he ever confuse you with his first wife? (i.e. calling you by her name, remembering things he did with her as though he had done them with you)** *Only twice did he call me by her name, but that was before we were married. He has too good a memory to make slips regularly.*

63) **With what you know about his first wife, what do you think about her as a person?** *She's not my kind of person, although she seems to make friends easily and has many close associations.*

64) **Have you ever felt sympathetic to his first wife?** *Only recently, when a friend of mine "lost" her husband to another woman. I now understand how hurt she must have felt from witnessing my friend's experience.*

65) **Would you say that your sex life is satisfying?** *No, but being a teacher I suffer from "burn-out." July and August are much more "sex-ful" than January or April!*

66) **Do you think that previously married men generally make better lovers?** *Yes. They know a woman's body and moods better.*

67) **Does your husband try to please you sexually?** *He tries to please me, but I feel that sex is for his pleasure more than mine, so I try to accommodate him.*

68) **Do you think that your husband's first marriage contributed significantly to the shaping of his sexual habits?** *Yes, because he desired loving and knowing he was loved. He was ready to give and to receive.*

69) Does your husband ever refer to his sex life with his first wife? Explain. *No way.*

70) To your knowledge was your husband sexually satisfied in his first marriage? *No.*

71) Do you think that your husband enjoys sex more with you than with his first wife? Why? *Yes, because when I'm relaxed I can be aroused and that makes him feel better. I seem to arouse him easily.*

72) To your knowledge has your husband ever had sex with his first wife since he has been with you? *No, I know that he hasn't.*

73) Do you ever find yourself feeling jealous of the intimate moments he shared with his first wife? *Yes. I think they shared that unique joy of bringing children into the world. That must be special to them.*

74) Since your marriage have you ever considered having an affair? Why? *No. I don't need another man to complicate my life!*

75) To the best of your knowledge, has your husband ever had or considered having an affair since he has been married to you? *No.*

76) To the best of your knowledge was your husband faithful to his first wife? *Yes, until he met me.*

77) Do you ever feel that your husband is comparing you to his first wife? *Yes, but favourably so.*

78) Has he ever tried to change you in any way to make you more or less like his first wife? *No, but probably he would like me to be more relaxed about entertaining. I'm too much of a perfectionist, but he prefers organization and neatness anyway.*

79) If so, have you complied with his wishes? *Yes, I go out of my way to be more organized so that I can relax and enjoy company. Or, I plan easier meals.*

80) Have you ever felt that in some way your husband still feels married to his first wife? *No.*

81) Have you ever considered divorcing your husband? Why? *No, it would break his heart. Besides, I'm not a quitter unless I can honestly see there's no hope—as I did at the conclusion of my first marriage.*

82) If you did decide to divorce your husband, do you think that the divorce settlement would be comparable to that of his first wife? Explain. *No way. He can barely keep his nose (let alone his head) above the surface as it is.*

83) Which of you tries harder to make your marriage work? *I think my husband does. Sometimes I say "why me?" He says he has changed a great deal and has become more domesticated.*

84) **Are you basically happy in your marriage?** *Content maybe, but certainly not ecstatically happy.*

85) **Are there any things about your marriage you would really like to change?** *I wish he'd take on more responsibilities around the house, as I tire of home and school duties too. I wish he didn't have to pay so much alimony.*

86) **Do you think these changes are possible?** *Not too likely. He's satisfied with the way things are and is committed to his family. His first wife has the best of both worlds. She gets his money, but not his dirty laundry.*

87) **When you and your husband argue, what would you say you argue about most often? (i.e. sex, money, children etc.) Why?** *The money he spends on his children after he's paid his alimony each month. Often our arguments are based on misinterpretations of household problems.*

88) **On vacations, has your husband ever taken you to places he went with his first wife?** *Yes, but he was from England and wanted me to enjoy the beauty of places where he had lived.*

89) **How did you feel about this?** *I felt most uncomfortable, being in "their" territory.*

90) **Do you have any contact with friends your husband shared with his first wife? Explain.** *A few, but only rare visits when they're in the city. I've always found that they received me very warmly and seem to understand why he divorced and remarried.*

91) **Are you comfortable with these people?** *Yes, once I've met them, although I always worry beforehand. We don't overdo visits as it puts a pressure on anyone with regard to "taking sides."*

92) **Do you feel comfortable with your husband's family (other than his children)?** *Yes, but I'm not bosom pals with any of them—as his former wife and sister are.*

93) **Does your husband still associate with his first wife's family? Explain.** *No. They are deceased. Any fringe family still lives in England.*

94) **How do you feel about this?** *(not answered)*

95) **How did your family feel about you becoming a second wife?** *They worried that he would not be able to support me and that I'd likely have to spend my hard-earned money to support him while he financed his family. They were right, but love is blind.*

96) **How would you say your husband's friends from his previous marriage feel about you?** *OK.*

97) Do you ever feel that your husband loves you more or less than his first wife? *I think he loves me more.*

98) Would you say that your husband is more satisfied generally with his second marriage than his first? *Yes, generally, but then he's one who keeps a great deal to himself.*

99) What would you say were the basic problems that a second wife should be prepared to face? *Realize that you do not just marry the man, but also take on his past family and all their problems. You do not start with a clean slate as with a first marriage.*

100) Were you prepared to face these problems or did they come as something of a surprise? *No, I was not prepared, and yes, they came as a surprise.*

101) What would you say are the advantages of being a second wife? *None. It is to his advantage to be my second husband, because I know he's a better person than my first husband—considerate, attentive, and sober.*

102) Do you ever wish you had been your husband's first wife or that he had not been married before he met you? *Yes, and I wish his other wife would remarry so that we could change our lifestyle.*

103) Have you ever felt second best or in second place because you were your husband's second wife? *Definitely. Always.*

104) Do you feel that there is anything you have missed in your relationship with your husband because you are his second wife? *Yes, financial worries have killed the romance that was present before marriage. I was then independent and unaware of his financial drain.*

105) With what you know about being a second wife, would you marry a man who had been married before if you had the chance to do it over again? *Not if he were paying alimony or had children who were dependants. There's something to be said for just living together; you're still free.*

106) If you have been both a first wife and a second wife, what would you say were the differences between the two situations? *There is little difference in my case because I am not free again to say what's on my mind. But because my husband is an "ostrich," we have fewer confrontations than I did in my first marriage.*

107) Do you think that your husband ever feels guilty about leaving his first wife? *No, but he feels guilty about the effect it has had on his younger child.*

108) Have you ever had any guilt feelings that relate to your being a second wife? Explain. *Yes, because sometimes I long to spread my wings and do my own thing again without having to ask permission.*

109) **Would you say that in some ways your husband still feels possessive about his first wife? Explain.** *No. He resents the fact that her hand is so often out for extra cash.*

110) **How did you feel about filling out this questionnaire and what were your reasons for doing so?** *I've enjoyed getting a great many matters off my chest, matters which I usually only discuss with my closest friend who is also a second wife. I can't complain to my family, of course! Thank you for giving me this opportunity.*

Anyone "in love" probably won't heed any words of advice if they're considering becoming a second wife, but I think it's important that they know it's a whole different ballgame once they say "I do." To have a dependable friend and companion is just as good as having a husband. Only when introducing him does it raise eyebrows, but society is accepting close relationships without marriage.

I'm glad I happened to catch your request for volunteers, and I am looking forward to reading your book.

P.S. *As I reread this, I'm aware of the impact money (or lack of it) has on our marriage. I was brought up with the understanding that if you wanted something, you saved up for it—or did without.*

In my husband's case, whatever he wanted went "went on the tab," and he had little contact with cash. During his first marriage, he had a very "good" paying job, but he had to quit for medical reasons and take an "average", paying job. His family still continued to live the "good" life—they preferred that! Because of guilt and pride, my husband can never say "no" to: the big wedding, hockey skates, membership to a racquet club, airplane tickets, etc., etc., etc. when his ex-wife or children want anything, they receive a check. When he wants (or needs) something, he puts it on his credit card (He's thousands of dollars in debt!), and when I want something (even a house), I save until I can buy it. When we were courting, I thought he could cope with bills.

SECOND WIFE?!

QUESTIONNAIRE

OCCUPATION OF RESPONDENT: ___*Homemaker*___ AGE: ___27___

HUSBAND'S OCCUPATION: ___*Airline Pilot*___ AGE: ___31___

Please answer the following questions. Remember, the purpose of this questionnaire is to ascertain your feelings about being a second wife, as well as to obtain the facts. Be as subjective as you like with your answers and give as much detail as you can. Try to avoid simple yes or no responses where possible. Not everyone will be able to answer every question. Your ability to answer specific questions depends entirely on your personal circumstances. Therefore, answer the questions which are directly applicable to your situation.

1) How did you and your husband meet? *I worked with his sister and met him one day when he came to visit her.*

2) How long did you know your husband before you were married? *I knew him for two months before we moved in together. We will have lived together for four years when we marry.*

3) Why do you think your husband asked you to marry him? *I think he loves me very much. I am the type of woman he has always wanted but never met. We share ideas, thoughts, and values, all of which are important.*

4) Why did you decide to marry your husband? *I love him very much. We have a good, solid relationship which, I think, is hard to find. We are very close and share everything.*

5) What was your wedding like? (i.e. large, traditional, small, city hall) *Our plans are for a small but traditional wedding with a reception (dinner and dance).*

6) Who was invited to your wedding? (i.e. your family and friends, his family and friends, children etc.) *We have invited both our families and joint friends. No children.*

7) Did you have a honeymoon? Where? *We are chartering a boat (we both sail) either in the Virgin Islands or Greece, depending on which is cheaper.*

8) What was your husband's first wedding like? *Small and semi-traditional in that it was in a church, but the bride wore blue and he wore an old suit. It was a quickie—she was pregnant.*

9) Did he honeymoon with his first wife? Where? *No. They had a five-day vacation about six months later at a family cottage.*

10) Did you live together before you were married? *Yes.*

11) If so, where did you live? (i.e. his place, your place, somewhere new for the two of you?) *At his place for five months, then we rented a house for three years. We now live in our own home.*

12) Where did you live after you were married? (i.e. apartment, house, condominium etc.) *In the house we both own.*

13) Where did your husband and his first wife live when they first got married? *A low-rise apartment.*

14) Have you ever lived in the place he shared with his first wife? *Yes, for the first five months we were together.*

15) If so, how did you feel about this arrangement? *Extremely uncomfortable. She felt it was still her home and would barge in, or enter while we were out.*

16) How long have you and your husband been married? *We have been living together for four years and will be married in the near future.*

17) Do you generally use your husband's last name or did you keep your own name when you got married? Why? *Legally I use my own, but sometimes for convenience I use a hyphenated name.*

18) How does your husband introduce you? (i.e. "This is Jane," "This is my wife, Jane," "This is my wife," etc.) *"This is my lady, _____."*

19) Have you ever been married before? How long? *No, never, although I lived with someone else for two years.*

20) Is your husband divorced or widowed from his first wife? *Divorced—she left him.*

21) Did your husband leave his first wife for you or did he meet you later? *He met me later.*

22) Was your husband married more than once before he married you? *No, only once.*

23) How many brothers and sisters do you have? *Two sisters and three brothers.*

24) Does your husband have any children from his previous marriage? *Yes, one daughter.*

25) What were their ages when he married you? *She was five when we moved in together; she is nine now.*

26) Did his children live with you when you first got married? Now? *She never has in the past, does not now, and will not in the foreseeable future.*

27) If his children do not live with you does he see them frequently? *Never. He did initially, but it became awkward for all concerned and he was used as a pawn.*

28) **Do you have any contact with his children? If so, what are the circumstances? (i.e. business, social etc.)** *None. I did initially, but the child liked me. The first wife felt threatened and went to her lawyer.*

29) **Do you feel that his children have directly or indirectly been responsible for any problems in your relationship with your husband? Explain.** *Yes. I feel that many of the problems in this situation are heightened when a child is involved.*

30) **Do you and your husband have any children of your own?** *No, not at present.*

31) **If not, do you want to have children?** *Yes, I do. It is very important to me.*

32) **Does your husband want to have children with you?** *Yes, very much. We both have our hesitations, but these are because of our reservations about the way society is today, rather than because of any bad personal experiences from the past.*

33) **If you wanted to have children and your husband did not, what do you think you would do?** *Since a family is extremely important to me, I would probably leave. It would be obvious we didn't want the same things.*

34) **How did you feel about your husband's children when you first got married? (i.e. like, dislike, indifferent etc.)** *I felt a little threatened by his daughter and found her a bit of a bother. I liked her well enough, but she behaved in ways I felt I wouldn't allow my child to behave.*

35) **How do you think they felt about you?** *She really liked me, unfortunately, too much. She would call and just speak to me. This made her mother feel threatened.*

36) **Has your relationship with his children changed since you have been married?** *We have no relationship now, and can foresee none in the future.*

37) **If you and your husband had children of your own, how do you think his children would react?** *She would probably be more curious than anything else.*

38) **If you do have children with your husband, how do you think he feels about them compared to the children of his first marriage? (i.e. loves them the same, more than, less than)** *Not applicable. I would be interested to find out.*

39) **Did you work before you got married?** *Yes, and all the furniture we have was mine because all of his disappeared in the separation agreement.*

40) **Do you work now?** *No. Because of his job, we felt it better that I stay home. He has quite a bit of time off.*

41) **How would you say that your marriage has affected your career?** *Very much. I no longer have one. I found that my relationship was more important to me and it took precedence.*

42) **Did your husband's first wife work before or during their marriage?** *No, never. She quit school, got pregnant, got married.*

43) **Do you and your husband share living expenses or does he support you?** *When I worked we split everything fifty-fifty, despite the discrepancy in our wages.*

44) **Do you contribute to the support of his children from a previous marriage?** *At one point much of my salary was needed to cover costs, the largest of which was maintenance.*

45) **Does your husband's contribution (if any) to the support of his previous family affect the standard of living which the two of you enjoy?** *Yes, very much. They are well supported.*

46) **If so, do you feel any resentment?** *Yes, very much. The sum seems steep for one child. Since we have to scrimp the way we do, I can't help but feel this way.*

47) **If your husband were to make out a will, would he leave everything to you (and any children from your marriage) or would he divide his assets between you and members of his previous family?** *He would leave it to me with the understanding I would give a percentage to his daughter.*

48) **If you were to make out a will, would you leave everything to your husband, knowing that if he died after you, it might go to members of his previous family?** *No, we've discussed this. As most of our possessions were mine initially, what I would leave of a personal nature would go to my friends and family.*

49) **Did your husband put assets acquired during their marriage in his first wife's name?** *Yes. They had a plane in joint ownership. He sold his share, but had to continue paying for her share after they split up.*

50) **Has your husband put any assets acquired during your marriage in your name?** *We have a sailboat in joint ownership, and we have a house. We had a car, which was in my name, but we sold it.*

51) **How long did your husband's previous marriage last?** *They were together for six years with a three-year waiting period for the divorce.*

52) **Is his first wife still living?** *Yes, unfortunately. She has made things very difficult. That sounds cruel, but at times it would be easier if she weren't.*

53) **If so, does your husband still maintain contact with her? Explain.** *None at all. It was too difficult. There was no fairness in the situation. The checks are simply mailed.*

54) **Why did your husband and his first wife get divorced?** *They had to marry to begin with, which isn't really a good reason to marry. They are such different people, and it was really only a matter of time.*

55) **Have you ever felt responsible for breaking up your husband's first marriage? Explain.** *Not at all, although his parents do blame me because they had hoped there would be a reconciliation. They are very religious and do not accept divorce.*

56) **If his first wife is deceased, does she still seem to figure prominently in his thoughts? (i.e. does he talk of her often to you or others, remember their anniversaries etc.)** *(not answered)*

57) **If so, how do you feel about this?** *(not answered)*

58) **Do you have any contact with his first wife? Explain.** *I did initially. When she wanted anything she would call and speak to me. Because we lived in the same area, we would bump into each other. Then we moved.*

59) **Is his first wife anything like you in appearance, personality, background etc.?** *We both have long dark hair, but figure, face, background, personality, and interests are extremely different.*

60) **Does your husband's first wife still expect him to do some of the things he did while they were married (i.e. take care of her finances, fix things around the house, etc.)** *Initially, yes, (for the first few months), but only in regard to the child. Her attitude was one of still "owning" him regardless of circumstances.*

61) **How do you feel about this?** *Very annoyed. It was the old "I don't want him but no one else can have him" thinking. She would call him up, expect him to ask her out, tell him what to do, etc.*

62) **Does he ever confuse you with his first wife? (i.e. calling you by her name, remembering things he did with her as though he had done them with you)** *In a few instances at the beginning of our relationship. Now, only in the sense that it feels to him as if we've always been together. He doesn't even think of her.*

63) **With what you know about his first wife, what do you think about her as a person?** *I don't think much of her. I feel I tried to be fair, but she wouldn't. She wanted to have her cake and eat it too, and she tried to put me down as if she were better, more important, more right.*

64) **Have you ever felt sympathetic to his first wife?** *Not really. At one point I let my guard down only to be stepped on. It didn't happen again. She has problems.*

65) Would you say that your sex life is satisfying? *Yes, very.*

66) Do you think that previously married men generally make better lovers? *Not necessarily. When one is married young, often experience does not grow in the marriage—boredom does.*

67) Does your husband try to please you sexually? *He makes every effort to please me.*

68) Do you think that your husband's first marriage contributed significantly to the shaping of his sexual habits? *Only in that it makes him appreciate a sexual person—she wasn't much of one.*

69) Does your husband ever refer to his sex life with his first wife? **Explain.** *They didn't have much of a sex life. They were both very inexperienced.*

70) To your knowledge was your husband sexually satisfied in his first marriage? *Initially he was because he wasn't at all experienced and it was all he knew. Compared to ours—no.*

71) Do you think that your husband enjoys sex more with you than with his first wife? Why? *Yes. Physically I'm more attractive and I would say a little more liberated sexually.*

72) To your knowledge has your husband ever had sex with his first wife since he has been with you? *No. Absolutely not.*

73) Do you ever find yourself feeling jealous of the intimate moments he shared with his first wife? *Yes, at first, when I was extremely insecure of myself. I think for a period of time one is extremely paranoid.*

74) Since your marriage have you ever considered having an affair? Why? *At times I have felt like finding someone else and starting again. It would be so nice. I don't think I could do it, though.*

75) To the best of your knowledge, has your husband ever had or considered having an affair since he has been married to you? *No, never.*

76) To the best of your knowledge was your husband faithful to his first wife? *Yes. He was very straight. That's just the way you do it. If things are rough you just stay together and make the best of it.*

77) Do you ever feel that your husband is comparing you to his first wife? *(not answered)*

78) Has he ever tried to change you in any way to make you more or less like his first wife? *(not answered)*

79) If so, have you complied with his wishes? *(not answered)*

80) Have you ever felt that in some way your husband still feels married to his first wife? *No, not at all.*

81) Have you ever considered divorcing your husband? Why? *No, we've been through a lot and it has only made us closer. We have our downs, but basically I feel I'm very lucky. We have a good relationship.*

82) If you did decide to divorce your husband, do you think that the divorce settlement would be comparable to that of his first wife? Explain. *Yes, in regard to any children. Aside from that, I am sure we could come to some agreement on possessions. Quite a lot is mine (and was mine before our marriage).*

83) Which of you tries harder to make your marriage work? *(not answered)*

84) Are you basically happy in your marriage? *Yes, very.*

85) Are there any things about your marriage you would really like to change? *I wish it could be his first.*

86) Do you think these changes are possible? *Not at all.*

87) When you and your husband argue, what would you say you argue about most often? (i.e. sex, money, children etc.) Why? *Initially, during the first four years, we would always argue about his past. After that, we just had normal misunderstandings.*

88) On vacations, has your husband ever taken you to places he went with his first wife? *He has on occasion—but not to anywhere special or exotic—just to local places.*

89) How did you feel about this? *I did not like it at all. Somehow I felt cheated.*

90) Do you have any contact with friends your husband shared with his first wife? Explain. *Yes, with some of them.*

91) Are you comfortable with these people? *With some of them.*

92) Do you feel comfortable with your husband's family (other than his children)? *I only feel comfortable with one sister who has been through it all herself. The rest of the family do not accept me.*

93) Does your husband still associate with his first wife's family? Explain. *Not at all. He did initially when we first met, because at one time they had lived with them, but that didn't last.*

94) How do you feel about this? *It bothered me when it happened. His mother-in-law would pick up his mail, babysit, etc., but luckily it didn't last.*

95) How did your family feel about you becoming a second wife? *They do not know. They just wouldn't understand and would react very negatively.*

96) **How would you say your husband's friends from his previous marriage feel about you?** *Close friends are happy we met because he is so happy. I get along with them, but they are mainly male.*

97) **Do you ever feel that your husband loves you more or less than his first wife?** *He loves me more—a much more mature and deeper love than he was able to feel before.*

98) **Would you say that your husband is more satisfied generally with his second marriage than his first?** *Extremely satisfied or we wouldn't be together, and he wouldn't get married again.*

99) **What would you say were the basic problems that a second wife should be prepared to face?** *His past and all that it entails, reactions from both families and friends on both sides, and the attitudes of people. You have no idea how others will react to you, him, the situation. One thing is certain, you learn who your true friends are: people who will stand by you, regardless of their personal values, because they respect you and what you feel is right. A lot of things such as rights and relationships, which you take for granted, can disappear without any real reasoning behind it. Emotionally it can be very trying and hurtful. You learn quite a bit about people and often it isn't pleasant.*

100) **Were you prepared to face these problems or did they come as something of a surprise?** *They were a complete surprise. I didn't realize how callous and narrow many people are.*

101) **What would you say are the advantages of being a second wife?** *I suppose if you can stay together through all of the trials and tribulations, you will have a pretty solid relationship.*

102) **Do you ever wish you had been your husband's first wife or that he had not been married before he met you?** *Yes, always. I know he wouldn't be the same person had he not gone through this experience, and I concede that he wouldn't be quite the same man I fell in love with. Still, I wish he had only lived with her or something, so that there would have been less legal hassle and responsibility, and hopefully no children. It would have made it so much easier.*

103) **Have you ever felt second best or in second place because you were your husband's second wife?** *Yes, always, unfortunately more because of the reactions of family and friends than because of him.*

104) **Do you feel that there is anything you have missed in your relationship with your husband because you are his second wife?** *Yes. The first of everything. He has done it all before and I haven't. Everything is so special to me, but he has done it all—marriage, children, etc. My feeling of being special is somewhat diminished.*

105) **With what you know about being a second wife, would you marry a man who had been married before if you had the chance to do**

it over again? *No. I didn't realize what I was getting into until I was too involved to turn back. It was worth it, but to start all over ... I couldn't— knowing what I know. It takes too much out of you having to accept so many things that are very difficult to swallow. I don't think I'd take this road again, knowing what I know. It would be much easier to get involved with someone who isn't so involved! Marriage itself is something that needs work and tending on its own, without the added complications of there having been a previous one.*

106) **If you have been both a first wife and a second wife, what would you say were the differences between the two situations?** *(not answered)*

107) **Do you think that your husband ever feels guilty about leaving his first wife?** *No, not at all. His feelings are that if it weren't for the child, the whole relationship was a farce.*

108) **Have you ever had any guilt feelings that relate to your being a second wife? Explain.** *Yes.*

109) **Would you say that in some ways your husband still feels possessive about his first wife? Explain.** *Not at all. He feels more resentful at the responsibility she represents.*

110) **How did you feel about filling out this questionnaire and what were your reasons for doing so?** *It feels really good. After four years there are still a lot of feelings of resentment, confusion, hurt, etc. It feels good to get some of the causes down on paper and having my side, our side, opened up, instead of hearing again about the poor abandoned wife trying to support a family. I know these people exist, but the fact is that quite a few ex-wives deserve to be ex-wives and only try to make their ex-husbands miserable. We all know both parties have a lot of emotions involved, but so do second wives and we are a part of it, whether we like it or not, simply by being with the man we love. I wanted to fill out the questionnaire because quite often I have felt so alone with my feelings to the point I almost hated myself. I know that a lot of women are going through the same thing and must be feeling similar feelings. It's time our side was heard and our thoughts shared. Maybe we can help others as well as ourselves.*

SECOND WIFE?!
QUESTIONNAIRE

OCCUPATION OF RESPONDENT: *Registered Nursing Assistant* AGE: __25__

HUSBAND'S OCCUPATION: *Sales Manager* AGE: __30__

Please answer the following questions. Remember, the purpose of this questionnaire is to ascertain your feelings about being a second wife, as well as to obtain the facts. Be as subjective as you like with your answers and give as much detail as you can. Try to avoid simple yes or no responses where possible. Not everyone will be able to answer every question. Your ability to answer specific questions depends entirely on your personal circumstances. Therefore, answer the questions which are directly applicable to your situation.

1) How did you and your husband meet? *I was at a bar with a group of girlfriends for a celebration. There were nine of us. One of the girls spotted my husband and a friend at a far table. She took an interest in them and asked the waiter to move them to our table. My best friend and I weren't interested at the time, however, we are both now married—me to my husband and her to the friend he was with that night.*

2) How long did you know your husband before you were married? *One and a half years.*

3) Why do you think your husband asked you to marry him? *Because he loves me.*

4) Why did you decide to marry your husband? *Because I love him.*

5) What was your wedding like? (i.e. large, traditional, small, city hall) *Large, with family and friends, dinner and a dance.*

6) Who was invited to your wedding? (i.e. your family and friends, his family and friends, children etc.) *Both his and my family and friends.*

7) Did you have a honeymoon? Where? *No, we were both working at the time we were married. It was in the fall, and we decided we would rather take our holidays during the summer. I had to take a week before the wedding to go home and help with arrangements, but we did stay in a motel overnight.*

8) What was your husband's first wedding like? *Just the two of them at city hall. His first wife dislikes both her family and his. She has only one friend and dislikes all of his.*

9) Did he honeymoon with his first wife? Where? *Not really. They stayed at a friend's farm for a few days.*

10) Did you live together before you were married? *Yes, for almost a year.*

11) If so, where did you live? (i.e. his place, your place, somewhere new for the two of you?) *Somewhere new for both of us.*

12) Where did you live after you were married? (i.e. apartment, house, condominium etc.) *In the same apartment we lived together in. It was the first place I had had on my own and I loved it.*

13) Where did your husband and his first wife live when they first got married? *In a commune. They caught the tail end of the hippie movement, when he was nineteen and she twenty-one.*

14) Have you ever lived in the place he shared with his first wife? *No.*

15) If so, how did you feel about this arrangement? *(not answered)*

16) How long have you and your husband been married? *Five years.*

17) Do you generally use your husband's last name or did you keep your own name when you got married? Why? *I use my husband's last name. I just never though of using my own and I was happy to take his, even though I liked my own.*

18) How does your husband introduce you? (i.e. "This is Jane," "This is my wife, Jane," "This is my wife," etc.) *If it's to someone we don't know, he introduces me with "This is ____, my wife." If it's to someone I've met before, he says "You remember _____."*

19) Have you ever been married before? How long? *No.*

20) Is your husband divorced or widowed from his first wife? *Divorced.*

21) Did your husband leave his first wife for you or did he meet you later? *He met me later.*

22) Was your husband married more than once before he married you? *No, only once before.*

23) How many brothers and sisters do you have? *Two sisters and one brother.*

24) Does your husband have any children from his previous marriage? *Yes, one boy.*

25) What were their ages when he married you? *Almost four years old.*

26) Did his children live with you when you first got married? Now? *No, and no.*

27) If his children do not live with you does he see them frequently? *For the first three years every second Sunday, and now, one or two times a month.*

28) **Do you have any contact with his children? If so, what are the circumstances? (i.e. business, social etc.)** *Yes, when my husband sees him I am around. They go off together, maybe to the zoo, but when they get back, I am there.*

29) **Do you feel that his children have directly or indirectly been responsible for any problems in your relationship with your husband? Explain.** *Only in that my husband can't completely cut his ex-wife out of our lives because of the child.*

30) **Do you and your husband have any children of your own?** *Yes, we have a three-year-old boy and a six-month-old girl.*

31) **If not, do you want to have children?** *(not answered)*

32) **Does your husband want to have children with you?** *(not answered)*

33) **If you wanted to have children and your husband did not, what do you think you would do?** *(not answered)*

34) **How did you feel about your husband's children when you first got married? (i.e. like, dislike, indifferent etc.)** *I liked and disliked him. He has a lot of behavioral problems and it's not always easy to like him.*

35) **How do you think they felt about you?** *He was indifferent when his dad was present and not too bad if left alone.*

36) **Has your relationship with his children changed since you have been married?** *Not really since we've been married, however, it changes as the child grows older.*

37) **If you and your husband had children of your own, how do you think his children would react?** *(not answered)*

38) **If you do have children with your husband, how do you think he feels about them compared to the children of his first marriage? (i.e. loves them the same, more than, less than)** *I believe he loves them the same, though maybe he likes the second set more because he knows them better. They are more open and loving with him because they know him better.*

39) **Did you work before you got married?** *Yes, I was an RNA.*

40) **Do you work now?** *Now, because I have just had a baby, I am not working. I really enjoy being with my children, but I will probably go back when they are in school.*

41) **How would you say that your marriage has affected your career?** *Not at all, except I try not to do so much shift changing and working weekends, which is agreeable to both of us.*

42) **Did your husband's first wife work before or during their marriage?** *Yes, she worked before and during their marriage.*

43) **Do you and your husband share living expenses or does he support you?** *He used to support us while I saved and bought "luxuries" (furniture, car, clothes, etc.). Right now I'm bringing in no income, so he supports us.*

44) **Do you contribute to the support of his children from a previous marriage?** *We pay child maintenance, yes.*

45) **Does your husband's contribution (if any) to the support of his previous family affect the standard of living which the two of you enjoy?** *When I first quit work to have my first child it did quite a bit, but now it's not too bad, although she drags him to court every now and then to try and get more.*

46) **If so, do you feel any resentment?** *Yes, I did. When my first son was born we had very little money and we were going into debt just to feed ourselves. My son was born with problems, and he being my first, I felt I was the only one capable of seeing he got all his medication on time. I still feel this way. But my husband's ex was always wanting more money for private schools, summer camps, ten-speed bikes, etc., when we couldn't even afford what we were already giving her.*

47) **If your husband were to make out a will, would he leave everything to you (and any children from your marriage) or would he divide his assets between you and members of his previous family?** *He has left everything to me.*

48) **If you were to make out a will, would you leave everything to your husband, knowing that if he died after you, it might go to members of his previous family?** *No, I wouldn't, but he would never do that anyway.*

49) **Did your husband put assets acquired during their marriage in his first wife's name?** *They acquired nothing except life insurance, which is now in my name. Before he met me it was in his son's name, and before his son was born it was in his ex-wife's name.*

50) **Has your husband put any assets acquired during your marriage in your name?** *Everything we have is in both our names.*

51) **How long did your husband's previous marriage last?** *Three and a half years.*

52) **Is his first wife still living?** *Yes.*

53) **If so, does your husband still maintain contact with her? Explain.** *Only when necessary, that is, regarding the child, or the money he gives for his support.*

54) **Why did your husband and his first wife get divorced?** *They didn't get along. She has a lot of psychological problems. She doesn't feel she can cope unless she has someone else to be responsible for. When she married him she took sole responsibility for his life. She sent him to university, made doctor and dental appointments, etc. Being an independent person he hated this. When they had a son, she took over with him and asked her husband to leave because she had someone else to look after. He wouldn't have left on his own because of his son.*

55) **Have you ever felt responsible for breaking up your husband's first marriage? Explain.** *Never.*

56) **If his first wife is deceased, does she still seem to figure prominently in his thoughts? (i.e. does he talk of her often to you or others, remember their anniversaries etc.)** *(not answered)*

57) **If so, how do you feel about this?** *(not answered)*

58) **Do you have any contact with his first wife? Explain.** *Yes, she's on the phone harassing me all the time. When we first married, it was to tell me the intimacies of her marriage to him. Needless to say, I got a private line. Now the line is open again so that his son can contact his father, and she phones to complain all the time, but I have learned to hang up or unplug the phone.*

59) **Is his first wife anything like you in appearance, personality, background etc.?** *Truthfully the only thing we have in common is the color of our hair (except this is not true any longer because she dyes hers).*

60) **Does your husband's first wife still expect him to do some of the things he did while they were married (i.e. take care of her finances, fix things around the house, etc.)** *At first she did, but he made it quite clear (it took three years to get the point across) that he was not available at her beck and call.*

61) **How do you feel about this?** *I don't see any reason for it. I can and do take care of repairs around the house. As for finances, I would be mortified to admit that I couldn't support myself and one child. I know that I could quite nicely.*

62) **Does he ever confuse you with his first wife? (i.e. calling you by her name, remembering things he did with her as though he had done them with you)** *Never.*

63) **With what you know about his first wife, what do you think about her as a person?** *I think she is very unstable, selfish, unfriendly, persecutive. She dresses like she doesn't have a penny to her name (she clears $20,000 plus overtime a year). I don't believe I'd like her*

under any circumstances. She is one of those people who tries to commit suicide in a room full of people, knowing the pills she took aren't enough to do anything. She treats all people as if she hates them.

64) **Have you ever felt sympathetic to his first wife?** *There was time when I did and would try to help with money and babysitting, but it didn't take long after I got to know her for all of my feelings to turn negative.*

65) **Would you say that your sex life is satisfying?** *Yes.*

66) **Do you think that previously married men generally make better lovers?** *Being a small-town girl of nineteen when I met him and never having had sexual relationships before, I wouldn't know. I found him more mature than boys I had dated and more sure of what he wanted, but then he was older, and I had only dated boys my own age.*

67) **Does your husband try to please you sexually?** *Sometimes he tries to please me, sometimes I try to please him.*

68) **Do you think that your husband's first marriage contributed significantly to the shaping of his sexual habits?** *Not in the least.*

69) **Does your husband ever refer to his sex life with his first wife? Explain.** *He never does, but his ex likes to tell all, so he sometimes feels he has to explain his side.*

70) **To your knowledge was your husband sexually satisfied in his first marriage?** *From what both he and she have said, he tried hard to avoid it except for about the first six months.*

71) **Do you think that your husband enjoys sex more with you than with his first wife? Why?** *Yes, I do, because there is never a time when he doesn't want it and never a time when he doesn't say it was good for him.*

72) **To your knowledge has your husband ever had sex with his first wife since he has been with you?** *Only once, before we were serious. He tried it, but he found he couldn't go through with it. I was informed of this by both of them.*

73) **Do you ever find yourself feeling jealous of the intimate moments he shared with his first wife?** *Not really jealous, but funny, because it's all a first for me, but not for him, even though I know that our intimate moments mean more to him than theirs.*

74) **Since your marriage have you ever considered having an affair? Why?** *No, I am quite happy.*

75) **To the best of your knowledge, has your husband ever had or considered having an affair since he has been married to you?** *I know he has never had an affair because he can always be*

accounted for. Also, it's just not his style. He didn't even have one in his first marriage. As for considering it, I doubt it, but who knows?

76) To the best of your knowledge was your husband faithful to his first wife? *Yes, he was.*

77) Do you ever feel that your husband is comparing you to his first wife? *If he does it would have to be with regard to how opposite we are. Truthfully we are not the same in any way, either in looks or personality.*

78) Has he ever tried to change you in any way to make you more or less like his first wife? *No, I think he choses to believe his first wife never existed.*

79) If so, have you complied with his wishes? *(not answered)*

80) Have you ever felt that in some way your husband still feels married to his first wife? *No.*

81) Have you ever considered divorcing your husband? Why? *No.*

82) If you did decide to divorce your husband, do you think that the divorce settlement would be comparable to that of his first wife? Explain. *No. I would not file for money because I don't feel that these days anyone can afford to give up part of their salary. He would have equal say in matters relating to his children as well the right to visit them whenever he and they wanted (provided it did not interfere with something important like school, doctors, or plans made by myself).*

83) Which of you tries harder to make your marriage work? *I think we each work equally hard at it.*

84) Are you basically happy in your marriage? *I'm very happy.*

85) Are there any things about your marriage you would really like to change? *Only the fact that we have to remain to some extent involved with his ex. It's not knowing she's there that bothers me, it's having to have contact with her. We avoid it as much as possible. All contact with her is hostile and creates tension.*

86) Do you think these changes are possible? *Not unless I ask him to have no contact with his son, which really isn't fair either.*

87) When you and your husband argue, what would you say you argue about most often? (i.e. sex, money, children etc.) Why? *Most often we argue about money, never about our children.*

88) On vacations, has your husband ever taken you to places he went with his first wife? *No, we generally go places in the vicinity of my hometown so I can see my family.*

89) How did you feel about this? *(not answered)*

90) Do you have any contact with friends your husband shared with his first wife? Explain. *Yes, because most of their friends were originally his (except one that I have no contact with) and have remained his. There isn't one of them who likes her or keeps in touch with her.*

91) Are you comfortable with these people? *Yes, very. They are around frequently and I like them all. The only time they refer to my husband's first wife is to ask if we've had any trouble from her.*

92) Do you feel comfortable with your husband's family (other than his children)? *Yes, I feel very comfortable. My mother-in-law always wanted a daughter and treats me like one. My young brother-in-law and I are very close. He also hates my husband's ex-wife with a passion as do the rest of them.*

93) Does your husband still associate with his first wife's family? Explain. *He's never met them.*

94) How do you feel about this? *(not answered)*

95) How did your family feel about you becoming a second wife? *At first they figured I should stay away from a married man because they were afraid that we might be just as quickly divorced. But after the first time they met him they fell in love with him. He's very sensitive and friendly and anyone can look at him and read that in his eyes.*

96) How would you say your husband's friends from his previous marriage feel about you? *I am very close to all of them. I know they like me because they have told me so. They stop off for visits frequently. Most of them only saw my husband a handful of times during his first marriage and one only visited once.*

97) Do you ever feel that your husband loves you more or less than his first wife? *I feel he loves me more.*

98) Would you say that your husband is more satisfied generally with his second marriage than his first? *I'm sure of it.*

99) What would you say were the basic problems that a second wife should be prepared to face? *Outside interference, (mainly from the ex-wife). An ex-wife who isn't ready to let go. If it's your first marriage, then just knowing that what you are experiencing is secondhand for him and because it's not for you, you can't know exactly how he separates it.*

100) Were you prepared to face these problems or did they come as something of a surprise? *I was prepared to face them although they seem to get worse as we go along instead of better. I thought that by now she'd want to get on with her own life.*

101) What would you say are the advantages of being a second wife? *Only that having been in a bad scene before he made sure he really loved me and that it would work this time.*

102) Do you ever wish you had been your husband's first wife or that he had not been married before he met you? *Yes, I do. We wouldn't have any problems then.*

103) Have you ever felt second best or in second place because you were your husband's second wife? *Only when my first child was born it was so thrilling for me, but he had already been through it. And she gave him a big healthy boy and mine was so small and sick, but he was the most beautiful baby in the world to me. When I told my husband what was wrong, he cried and I knew that our baby meant the world to him.*

104) Do you feel that there is anything you have missed in your relationship with your husband because you are his second wife? *No.*

105) With what you know about being a second wife, would you marry a man who had been married before if you had the chance to do it over again? *It would depend on how much I loved the man, but I would try to avoid one with children or payments because this forces them to maintain a relationship of some sort.*

106) If you have been both a first wife and a second wife, what would you say were the differences between the two situations? *(not answered)*

107) Do you think that your husband ever feels guilty about leaving his first wife? *No.*

108) Have you ever had any guilt feelings that relate to your being a second wife? Explain. *No, because my being here or not wouldn't make any difference to the relationship he has with his first wife.*

109) Would you say that in some ways your husband still feels possessive about his first wife? Explain. *No, he never defends her even if someone says the worst about her.*

110) How did you feel about filling out this questionnaire and what were your reasons for doing so? *It made me realize that I'd rather put up with all the problems his ex-wife gives me than to have to sit around wondering if my husband still cares for her. I think it would be worse to be insecure about your relationship with your husband. At least this way I know his feelings for her are negative, although knowing this makes me wish she would disappear.*

   My reason for doing this was mostly curiosity. Also, no one, to the best of my knowledge, has ever wondered about the second wife. Any literature, I've read deals mainly with the poor ex-wife alone, dealing with the kids, when it's probably harder for the poor father who has to leave his kids in some cases.

Bibliography

Bardwick, Judith M. *Psychology of Women: A Study of Bio-Cultural Conflicts.* New York: Harper & Row, 1971.

Bernstein, Claire, D. *Legal-ease.* Toronto: Fleet Books, 1982.

Centre of Alcohol Studies, Rutgers University, New Jersey. *Journal of Studies on Alcohol* 39 (February 1978).

Cronback, Lee, J. *Essentials of Psychological Testing.* 3rd ed. New York: Harper & Row, 1970.

Dowsling, Janet, and MacLennan, Anne, eds. *The Chemically Dependent Woman: Recognition, Referral, Rehabilitation.* Toronto: Addition Research Foundation, 1978.

Faber, Bernard. *Family Organization and Interaction.* Novato, Ca.: Chandler & Sharp, 1964.

Forward, Susan, and Buck, Craig. *Betrayal of Innocence: Incest and its Devastation.* New York: Penguin, 1979.

Herman, Judith Lewis. *Father-Daughter Incest.* Cambridge, Mass.: Harvard University Press, 1982.

Hite, Shere. *The Hite Report.* New York: Dell, 1976.

271

Horney, Karen, M.D. *Feminine Psychology*. New York: W.W. Norton & Co., 1967.

Irving, Dr. Howard H. *Divorce Mediation: The Rational Alternative*. Toronto: Personal Library, 1980.

Kincaid, Lucy. *Time for a Tale*. Cambridge, England: Brimax Books, 1983.

King, Lyn. *Marriage, Separation and Divorce*. Toronto: James Lorimer and Co., 1980.

Kronby, Malcolm C. *Canadian Family Law*. Toronto: General Publishing, 1981.

Lazarus, Richard S., ed. *Personality*. London: Penguin, 1967.

MacLennan, Anne, ed. *Women: Their Uses of Alcohol and Other Drugs*. Toronto: Addiction Research Foundation, 1976.

Maslow, Abraham H. *Motivation and Personality*. 2nd ed. New York: Harper & Row, 1970.

Masters, William, and Johnson, Virginia. *The Pleasure Bond*. New York: Bantam, 1980.

Mead, Margaret. *Male and Female: A Study of the Sexes in a Changing World*. New York: Marrow Quill, 1949.

My Own Book of Fairy Tales. London: Ramboro Books, 1983.

Pietropinto, Anthony, M.D., and Simenauer, Jacqueline. *Beyond the Male Myth*. New York: Signet, 1977.

Renvoize, Jean. *Incest: A Family Pattern.* London: Routledge & Kegan Paul, 1982.

Rush, Florence. *The Best Kept Secret: Sexual Abuse of Children.* New York: McGraw-Hill, 1980.

Shultz, Clayton. *Matrimonial Settlements: The Tax and Accounting Implications.* Vancouver: Butterworth and Co., 1980.

_____.*Supplement to Matrimonial Settlements: The Tax and Accounting Implications.* Vancouver: Butterworth and Co., 1982.

Silverman, Hirsch Lazar. *Marital Therapy: Moral, Sociological and Psychological Factors.* Springfield, Ill.: Charles C. Thomas, 1972.

Sonenblick, Jerry. *The Legality of Love.* New York: Jove Books, 1981.

Statistics Canada. *Divorce Law and the Family.* Ottawa: 1983.

Vaillant, George E. *Adaptation to Life.* Boston: Little Brown, 1977.

Vivelo, Frank Robert. *Cultural Anthropology Handbook.* New York: McGraw-Hill, 1978.

Wakil, S. Parvez, ed. *Marriage, Family and Society.* Toronto: Butterworth and Co., 1975.

Wolfe, Linda. *Women and Sex in the 80s — The Cosmo Report.* New York: Bantam, 1982.

Glynnis Walker is now doing research into the special case of women who marry men older than they are by at least twelve years. If you are in such a situation and would like to participate in a survey similar to the one on which **Second Wife, Second Best?** *is based, contact Ms. Walker at Box 978, Station F, Toronto, Ontario M4Y 2N9.*